"Dean Oliver is the OG of analytics. He broke down the numbers to clarify and improve my game, from shooting and getting to the foul line to rebounding and contesting shots. He knows how to identify the meaningful numbers for players."

—**Kristaps Porziņģis,** NBA All-Star player

"Changing the game, Dean Oliver gives insights as a veteran of basketball analytics. He explores the shift in mindset where instincts and old-school wisdom meet the numbers, redefining how players navigate today's analytical landscape."

—**Corey Gaines,** former NBA player and coach

"It's rare to get such detailed insights from someone who has thoroughly studied and conceptualized how analytics can enhance the way we understand basketball, as well as physically sat in the rooms of basketball decision-makers at the highest level. A true pioneer, Dean Oliver continues to help evolve the game by sharing his one-of-a-kind experiences and takeaways."

—**Brittni Donaldson,** assistant coach for the Atlanta Hawks

"In *Basketball on Paper* Dean Oliver set a foundation for basketball analytics that so many of us have benefited from. I was thrilled to see that in *Basketball beyond Paper*, he builds on that foundation with the experience and insight of the last twenty years of his work in basketball."

—**Ben Falk,** creator of Cleaning the Glass website

"Dean Oliver is one of the most well-rounded professionals in the world of sport analytics. He is a thought leader who excels at combining the numbers behind the game with the personal and group qualities that lead to high performance. Oliver's experience collaborating with staff members across disciplines in the industry is unmatched, and he brings a perspective that can make any team, player, or organization stronger. His work has impacted countless athletes, and the lessons he shares translate to all forms of performance, no matter if you work between the lines or off the court."

—**Jeremy Rahn,** mental performance coach for the Washington Wizards and Philadelphia Flyers

"What I loved most about working with Dean Oliver was that he wasn't just some guy talking numbers that he sees on a computer screen. He actually got involved and wanted to find reasons for the numbers he saw. Oliver was heavily involved in practice, meetings, and film sessions so that he could identify the cause and effect of the numbers. He was able to speak actionable results to analytics as a result of being involved with what the staff taught and emphasized."

—**Jarell Christian,** general manager and director of the Maine Celtics basketball and player development

"I've always appreciated Dean Oliver's desire to keep learning. This book highlights his unquenchable thirst for finding solutions, as it explores the balance between analytics and the human side of basketball. Oliver has been informative and inspirational to us for decades, and by sharing sideline-view basketball insights with the world, he gives us even more to ponder."

—**Oliver Eslinger,** men's head basketball coach for the California Institute of Technology

"In *Basketball on Paper* Dean Oliver laid out the groundwork for the coming analytics revolution in basketball as an outsider. Two decades later, he's taken what he learned working for multiple NBA organizations in the front office and on coaching staffs to offer a more complete perspective on how statistics can help us understand basketball—and their limitations—in this enjoyable read."

—**Kevin Pelton,** NBA writer for ESPN

"Analytics in basketball are tools for understanding the game at a deeper level. As a player, I relied on instinct and skill, but as a coach, I've learned that blending these instincts with analytics helps sharpen our game plan and decision-making. Analytics help me turn complex data into simple, clear advice for our players."

—**Pablo Prigioni,** assistant coach for the Minnesota Timberwolves and former NBA and international player

"Analytics is an equalizer for teams . . . and clarifies what is important on both ends of the court, leading to a more efficient, confident team. Analytics played a big role for the Japan women's national basketball team's first silver medal, and for the success of our men's team at the 2023 World Cup. Dean, thank you for paving the way."

—**Tom Hovasse,** Japan men's national basketball team head coach

"With experience working in NBA front offices, as a coach, and in the media over the past twenty years, no one is better placed than Dean Oliver to tell the story of the evolution of modern basketball statistics."

—**Mike Zarren,** vice president of operations and team counsel for the Boston Celtics

Praise for *Basketball on Paper*

"Excellent writing. There are a lot of math guys who just rush from the numbers to the conclusion. . . . Dean is more than that; he's really struggling to understand the actual problem, rather than the statistical after-image of it. I learn a lot by reading him."

—**Bill James,** author of *The Bill James Historical Baseball Abstract*

"At the risk of succumbing to hyperbole, *Basketball on Paper* is a revolutionary strike for statistical analysis of the game of basketball. . . . There has never been a basketball book quite like [it]."

—**Hoopsworld.com**

"Oliver's book provides an insightful framework for basketball. . . . This book is a unique and surprisingly practical addition to a coach's library."

—**Dean Smith,** former University of North Carolina coach

"Often humorous in tone, the book is undoubtedly geared to a serious and knowledgeable basketball audience, and by all accounts can already be found on the bedside tables of many an NBA GM, coach, and scout."

—**NBA Blog**

Basketball beyond Paper

BASKETBALL BEYOND PAPER

Insights into the Game's Analytics Revolution

DEAN OLIVER

University of Nebraska Press · Lincoln

The University of Nebraska Press is part of a land-grant institution with campuses and programs on the past, present, and future homelands of the Pawnee, Ponca, Otoe-Missouria, Omaha, Dakota, Lakota, Kaw, Cheyenne, and Arapaho Peoples, as well as those of the relocated Ho-Chunk, Sac and Fox, and Iowa Peoples.

Library of Congress Cataloging-in-Publication Data
Names: Oliver, Dean, 1969- author.
Title: Basketball beyond paper: insights into the game's analytics revolution / Dean Oliver.
Description: Lincoln: University of Nebraska Press, [2024] | Includes bibliographical references and index.
Identifiers: LCCN 2024006191
ISBN 9781496240491 (paperback)
ISBN 9781496241986 (epub)
ISBN 9781496241993 (pdf)
Subjects: LCSH: Basketball—United States—Statistical methods. | BISAC: SPORTS & RECREATION / Basketball | SPORTS & RECREATION / Reference
Classification: LCC GV885.55 .O54 2024 | DDC 796.323072/7—dc23/eng/20240403
LC record available at https://lccn.loc.gov/2024006191

Designed and set in Lyon Text by L. Welch.

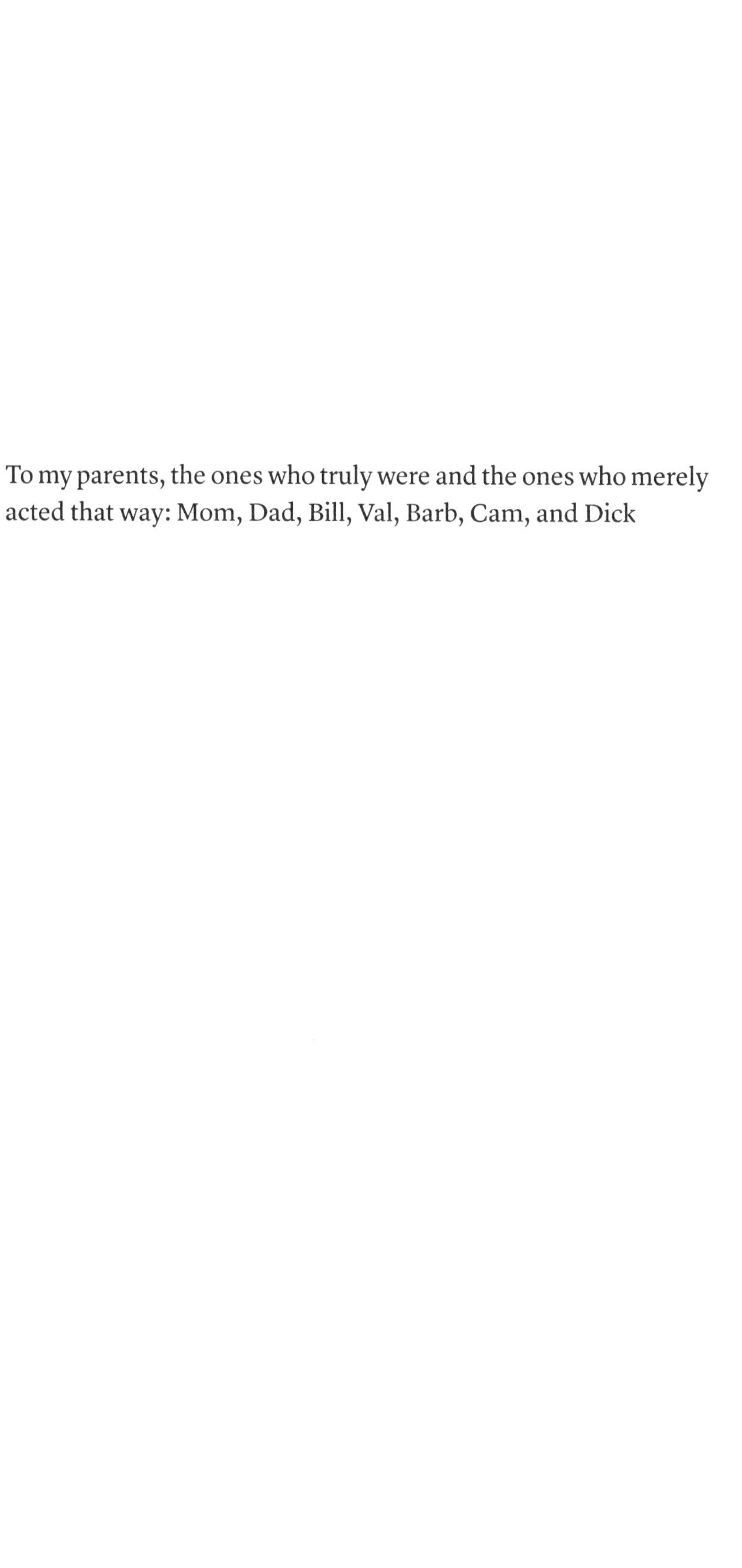

To my parents, the ones who truly were and the ones who merely acted that way: Mom, Dad, Bill, Val, Barb, Cam, and Dick

Contents

Illustrations

Tables

Acknowledgments

Opportunity is the greatest gift you can ever give or receive. Because I was given it by various people over the past twenty years, I have the experience to write this book.

Pete Palmer got me my first publisher. Wally Walker gave me my first NBA job after Yvan Kelly got me the introduction. Mark Warkentien gave me my first opportunity to do a lot in a front office. Tommy Sheppard and Scott Brooks gave me my first opportunity to work as a coach. Steve Hellmuth, Charlie Rohlf, and Ken DeGennaro gave me the opportunity to work with incredible NBA data. The NBA's general policy of making data relatively available has been a tremendous boon to the sport, so whoever decided on that—I thank you. Basketball-Reference.com and Second Spectrum made things easy, too. Doug Steele made it easy before those came along.

I had so many incredibly useful conversations over my years in the NBA with coworkers. Some of those people are Rick Sund, Rich Cho, Dwane Casey, Dean Demopoulos, Herb Livsey, George Karl, John Welch, Chad Iske, John Carideo, Tim Grgurich, Mike Dunlap, Jamahl Mosely, Bret Bearup, Pete D'Alessandro, Rishabh Desai, Anthony McClish, Rahsaan Gethers, Greg St. Jean, Elvis Valcarcel, Landon Tatum, Corey Gaines, Jarell Christian, Kam Sufi, Alex McLean, Mike Batiste, Joe Ajike, Daniel Villarreal, Ryan Lumpkin, Zach Guthrie, Joseph Blair ("JB"), Eric Sebastian, Ryan Richman, Mike Miller, Jeremy Rahn, Mike Terpstra, Carlos Bustamante, Anthony Iannarino, Mike Ashton, Mark Simpson, Wes Unseld Jr., John Thompson III, Brett Greenberg, Joe Sill, Kathy Evans, Jacob Goldstein, Andrew Lawlor, Zain Jafri, Ben Eidelberg, Kristaps Porzingis, Daniel Gafford, Aaron Holiday, Anthony

Gill, Delon Wright, Kyle Kuzma, Kentavious Caldwell-Pope, Ish Smith, and Corey Kispert.

Other people in the NBA that I didn't work with also generated great thoughts: Jordan Cohn, Brittni Donaldson, Ben Falk, Gabe Farkas, Sachin Gupta, Sam Hinkie, Somak Sarkar, and Mike Zarren.

John Thorn, Rob Taylor, and Taylor Martin were helpful in the acquisition and publication process.

I worked on some hard analytics problems with people at ESPN who made me think about the work more broadly: Jeff Bennett, Alok Pattani, Albert Larcada, Matt Morris, Ben Alamar, Hank Gargiulo, Kevin Pelton, Krishna Narsu, and Royce Webb.

My coworkers at TruMedia Networks always pushed me to think about the value of data and how it was presented, particularly Jeff Stern, Rafe Anderson, T.J. Creath, and Albert Larcada.

Doc Eslinger and I talked about sports psychology and basketball a lot of hours. Ray LeBov and I talked about basketball for hours.

Mike Fienen, Michael Alvarez, Colin Camerer, and David Berri love science and care about sports, making our conversations and collaborations productive.

Bill James has inspired me to write and to look for truth since the 1984 *Baseball Abstract*. He also pushed me to write after a lot of years when I was not writing.

Bill and Solveig Bertka put me to work as an advance scout in the early 1990s, an experience that really forced me to integrate my math skills with basketball.

Dan Rosenbaum and Roland Beech were early companions on the journey to the NBA.

Alok Pattani and Somak Sarkar particularly gave me feedback on chapters as I worked through them.

My wife, Marcia Fournier, is a CEO, a mother, a brilliant woman, and truly an inspiration to many. To me, she is the girl I am always trying to impress, including with my writing.

Abbreviations

ASTr Assist rate. Assists per teammate field goals made.

BLKr Block rate. Blocks per opponent field goal attempt.

DARKO *D*aily *A*djusted and *R*egressed *K*alman *O*ptimized metric. Individual player metric from Kostya Medvedovsky, mostly predictive.

DR% Defensive rebounding percentage. Defensive rebounds as a percentage of available defensive rebounds.

DRTG Defensive rating. Points allowed per one hundred possessions. For individuals, this is points allowed by the individual using division of credit per hundred possessions that they were credited for. The NBA has defined this differently for players.

eFG% Effective field goal percentage. Field goal percentage with extra credit given to three-point shots.

EPM Estimated Plus-Minus. Individual player metric from Taylor Snarr, dunksandthrees.com, partly predictive.

FG2% Two-point field goal percentage. Field goal percentage on two-point shots.

FG3% Three-point field goal percentage. Field goal percentage on three-point shots.

FG3r Three-point field goal rate. Percentage of total field goal attempts taken as three-pointers.

FG use Field goal usage. Percentage of team field goals attempted; percentage of team field goals taken by individual.

fit Smoothed fit. An approximate estimate of the points-per-forty-eight-minutes value of a combination of players, or the average across lineups for an individual.

FTr Free throw rate. Free throws made per field goals attempted.

G Games played.

LEBRON *L*uck-Adjusted Player *E*stimate Using a *B*ox Prior *R*egularized *On*-Off. Individual player metric from Krishna Narsu and the Bball Index, mostly predictive.

MPG Minutes played per game.

NetPts Net Points. Individual player metric used primarily in this book.

Net Rtg Net rating. Difference between offensive rating (ORTG) and defensive rating (DRTG).

OR% Offensive rebounding percentage. Offensive rebounds as a percentage of available offensive rebounds.

ORTG Offensive rating. Points produced per hundred possessions. For individuals, this is points produced by the individual using division of credit per hundred possessions that they used. The NBA has defined this differently for players.

PF/48 min. Foul rate. Fouls per forty-eight minutes.

PPR Pure Point Ratio. Developed by John Hollinger, it is a more stable version of assist-to-turnover ratio.

RAPTOR *R*obust *A*lgorithm Using *P*layer *T*racking and *O*n/Off *R*atings. Individual player metric from FiveThirtyEight.com, mostly explanatory.

RPM Real Plus-Minus. ESPN's individual metric (second version).

STLr Steal rate. Steals per opponent possession.

TO% Turnover percentage. Percentage of possessions on which there is a turnover.

TR% Total rebounding percentage. Total rebounds as a percentage of available rebounds.

Usg Usage. Percentage of a team's possessions that a player used. Can also be defined as percentage of team's FGA (field goal attempts) + 0.44*FTA (free throw attempts) + TO (turnovers). These are often similar.

WAR *W*ins *a*bove *r*eplacement. Wins added by an individual player to his team above what a replacement-level player would add.

Basketball beyond Paper

1

Beyond Paper

Herb Livsey is an eighty-plus-year-old scout for the Denver Nuggets. He watches complete games of college players, looking for what they do well on offense and defense, taking notes by hand and remembering fine elements of how players moved on the court. He talks to a player's coaches and parents and friends and "anyone who knew the player" for information about the kid. He famously followed Morehead State's Kenneth Faried around campus for two days to see who he was as a college kid—how prompt he was, whether he was friendly and respectful—in hopes that it would tell him something about whether Faried could survive in the NBA.

Herb is all about the *game* of basketball. He is not in it for the *show*—the lifestyle, the lights, or the celebrities, or to be famous himself. He is most often found in a gym, watching five-on-five, listening to players talk to each other, studying player tendencies in the context of what their coach is telling them.

He is a natural teacher who for decades ran the Snow Valley Basketball Camp, a high-end program that had NBA players and top coaching talents working it. Herb's former campers recall sessions of getting up too early to do far too much up on a hill near Santa Barbara. Camp days started early with drills but ended near midnight with games. This camp was not one for sleeping, nor was it an Amateur Athletic Union–type showcase. Each day started with disciplined drills and ended with competitive scrimmages.

Herb is old-school basketball. He believes what his eyes tell him, and he relies on his gut. He is supposed to be the kind of person who hates numbers.

But that is not Herb Livsey.

Herb and I worked in the Nuggets organization together under general manager Mark Warkentien, who was named executive of the year in the 2008–09 season when we made it to the Western Conference Finals and, frankly, when we collectively felt the terrible pain of having our season end before the NBA Finals.

Mark was called "Wark" or "Stein" by different people because he was the kind of person that others gave nicknames to. He was easy to talk to, had a lot of stories, and generally just knew how to get along with people.[1] Mark was also a natural in the profession of identifying and recruiting talent. In fact, that was his background before he ever joined the NBA.

Mark told the story of how he arrived on the campus of the University of Nevada Las Vegas (UNLV) in 1980 to be an assistant under legendary coach Jerry Tarkanian. He got there and saw Coach Tarkanian and the other assistant, Tim Grgurich ("Grg"), working closely with players, getting their full attention, and teaching them skills. "Those guys were real teachers. They were *the best* at it! I immediately knew that my contribution was not going to be that. I was going to be the one bringing in talent." So Mark went to high school gyms, he talked to coaches, he read reports, and he studied all the high school kids he could find. He listened to what Tark and Grg wanted—"get us some good players" was about as detailed as they needed to be—and he looked into a lot of players across the Southwest to find some that could play.

This was before UNLV became a nationally known program. At the time, UCLA was clearly the dominant college basketball program in that part of the country. For UNLV to sign talented players who hadn't already committed to UCLA or another top program, Mark had to find the kids that were good enough to make it without being so good that they had already been recruited. Mark watched a lot of bad basketball, learning how to discard players by eye pretty quickly. Most leads went nowhere, but some leads found him Talent with a capital *T*.

And Talent is what Mark told me was the key to winning basketball. Despite the great coaching of Tark and Grg at UNLV, Mark's list of the four key things in having a great team began with Talent. Next was getting players to Play Hard. Then it was getting them to Play Together. And fourth were the Xs and Os, the in-game tactics.

Mark told me about these key things early on in our time working together. I asked him then how much weight he would put on each of those, but he couldn't tell me. I have thought about them for more than a decade now, and I'm not sure I could put weights on them easily either, but I've never really disagreed on the order. Talent definitely was number one. Whether playing hard or playing together was number two was something I occasionally debated, but I couldn't come up with a way to know.

As with Herb Livsey, everything that Mark had done in his career could be considered traditional basketball practice, not the analytics and the numbers—the aspects that thrust me into the business. What got me the job working with Mark and Herb, though, was their undying desire to learn about the game and identify Talent. And each of them was more than willing to use numbers to do that, so we all got along very well.

Mark learned about the value of numbers from blackjack players that he met in Las Vegas when he was an assistant coach at UNLV. The gamblers simplified it for him—"You *can* hit on 17, get a 4, and believe that you were super smart because you got 21, but you were lucky. The casinos want you to win a hand that way so that you get drunk on being stupid. They want your money, and they know that you, playing against the odds, will give it to them."

Mark evolved in his career by applying their simple wisdom to identifying players: Learn what history says about players and then go with the odds. A lot of that history was statistics, relatively simple ones until he met me, but they worked pretty well, nonetheless.

For example, here is a typical question that Mark would ask of me: "How often does a guy fail if he is a first-round pick, takes less than three minutes to get a rebound, and takes less than fifteen minutes to get a blocked shot in college?"

If this were around 2008 and we threw out the first-round criteria, the list of players who met those statistical standards would include about forty players. There were some all-time greats like Tim Duncan, Shaquille O'Neal, Hakeem Olajuwon, David Robinson, and Dikembe

Mutombo. There were also long-time players like Antonio McDyess, Ervin Johnson (not Magic Johnson), Bill Cartwright, Tony Battie, Nazr Mohammed, Manute Bol, Dave Corzine, Shawn Marion, Greg Ostertag, and Kurt Thomas. There were a few guys who didn't last very long in the NBA. For instance, Walter Berry had trouble getting along with coaches in his three years in the NBA, so he played in Europe for many years. But especially when you consider only first-round players, those who didn't play very much in the NBA make up a short list: Berry, Curtis Borchardt, Yinka Dare, Earl Jones, John Turner, and Sharone Wright. Placing a bet on players who reach these standards is a better-than-even winner. If they don't work out, it doesn't mean that you made a dumb bet, at least.

In that 2008 draft, there was another prospect who met these criteria. He was mostly not considered a first-round draft pick, despite being a starter and a key part of a great Memphis team. That player was Joey Dorsey, who was selected early in the second round of the draft by Houston Rockets general manager Daryl Morey.

Morey is, in many ways, the face of the basketball analytics movement. He's a tall Northwestern graduate who likes pickup basketball, went to business school at MIT, and worked in sports statistics between classes. His start in the NBA came on the business side of the Boston Celtics, but his name spread quickly across the league. In 2006, when Houston Rockets owner Leslie Alexander went looking for a general manager to groom, he brought in Daryl Morey.

That was only a few months after I first talked to Daryl in a call between two of the few people in the NBA looking to apply numbers in basketball. We bonded over the work and how we could find ways for it to help. Whereas Daryl had been doing mostly business-side analytics, I had been doing more on-court relevant analytics at that point, working on the draft and some with the coaching staff. We talked about how someone from the analytical side had to get an opportunity to actually lead a team because that would be the best way to really test what works.

We were both ambitious, so I was not entirely happy when he was announced for that Rockets job that I had not even heard about. But I was also rooting for him, knowing that his success would open up doors for a lot of people.

And Daryl had success. At first, it didn't add a lot to the win total, but he got some high-profile publicity. Michael Lewis, the author of *Moneyball*, wrote an article about the Rockets titled "The No-Stats All-Star" for the *New York Times*. It was nominally about Shane Battier, a Rocket on Daryl's team whose impact was being measured using "new stats," like how well the team played with Battier on the floor versus off the floor. But it really highlighted for people the analytical approach that Daryl was bringing to the basketball operations group in Houston.

Daryl's success with the Rockets came around the time that the phrase "basketball analytics" was coined, thanks mainly to a conference put on by Daryl's old school, the MIT Sloan School of Business. In fact, that annual meeting was originally called the Sloan Sports Business Conference but quickly became the Sloan Sports Analytics Conference when organizers realized how popular analytics were becoming.

A decade after his hiring, Daryl's success had gone far beyond popularizing the practice of analytics. He won the Executive of the Year award in 2017–18 for bringing in the talent that led to the league's best record. His move in 2013 to trade for eventual MVP James Harden, giving away just role players, was key to winning the award. There were people around the NBA who had resented Daryl's high profile in the media "without winning anything," but that resentment had to have diminished quite a bit for so many peers to vote him the award.

But in the case of Joey Dorsey, the selection of this older, undersized center was not a highlight for Daryl. We know this not only from the outside perspective but also because Michael Lewis told some of the inside story in his book *The Undoing Project*.

Daryl had had luck the previous year following a mathematical model of college players that seemed to work, yielding legitimate NBA players in Carl Landry and Aaron Brooks with picks after number twenty. That same model also projected Dorsey to be good.

That "model" could well have been something along the lines of what Mark had laid out in his question to me—something capturing the rebounding and block rates of Dorsey. Morey's model wasn't that simple, but it used those statistics. When we in Denver talked about Dorsey that year, Mark instantly said, "But he's old. He's twenty-five or something, isn't he?" Mark knew to take Dorsey off the list because he was an older prospect, "a man playing against boys." Yes, drafting Dorsey *could* work—as it worked for Dikembe Mutombo when he was drafted at nearly the same age—but that would be like hitting on seventeen in blackjack.

So Daryl added age to his model, per the Lewis story. Beyond that, we don't know the details of what else he did. We know that he generally learned actively from both his mistakes and his successes. That is a hallmark of the analytical process.

Daryl has served as an important ambassador of analytical approaches to basketball. Probably the biggest thing he pushed was a more analytical form of shot selection. Many simple studies have suggested that three-pointers and layups are the best shots to take, and Daryl pushed that internally more strongly than even the most forward-thinking coaches did. The Rockets moved every year toward taking more of these shots and ditching the midrange game, a scheme that earned the nickname "Moreyball." Moreyball was tested to a greater extreme in the NBA's minor league, the NBDL, now called the G-League. The Rockets' minor league franchise, the Rio Grande Vipers, set scoring records and won championships, playing an extreme form of this style, taking almost exclusively layups and threes, taking threes from farther out, and pushing the pace.

That was Daryl, experimenting and studying the results with the goal of bringing what he learned to the NBA. He tried simply finding good players and asking them to play the Moreyball way, but that wasn't as easy as identifying players who already tended to play that way, then asking them to do it more. By 2018 the Moreyball Rockets had reduced their midrange shots to a league low 20 percent of their total shots. The players on the roster had almost all been acquired through trade or free agency and came with some of the pedigree to take only those shots.

Daryl also experimented with technology. He was one of the first to acquire a player-tracking data technology, which involved installing special computer-linked cameras in arenas to identify players as they moved around the court. Initially called SportVu, this technology existed in only a few arenas at first and produced many errors. But Daryl (and a few others of us) recognized the potential of the technology for analyzing the game like never before.

The NBA and the company that owned the technology, STATS Inc. (whom Daryl used to work for), allowed some of that early data to go to researchers to see if they could do something with it. Those researchers, not coincidentally, ended up presenting their findings at the same MIT Sloan Sports Analytics Conference that Daryl was associated with.

And that was when SkyNet was turned on—without the lasers and launch codes of the *Terminator* movies.

Machine learning, as applied to basketball, gave computers the ability to do one part of what Herb Livsey did—watch the game in great detail. Computers could see where every player was at every fraction of a second. They could then mark a "pick-and-roll with the defender going under" and could do it at more than a hundred times the speed of Herb. They could do it with greater certainty, if with a little less nuance.

The rise of machine learning began with this kind of classification of play types, defenses, and player roles, but it has extended well beyond that. It has also been used in breaking down the steps that go into getting a rebound and measuring players' abilities to do those things. It has evaluated what is a good shot and what is a bad shot. Some work has gone into the value of spacing and the optimal configurations of players in different situations. The concept of an "Expected Point Value" during every microsecond of a possession was developed, suggesting how moving the ball increases or decreases the number of points that are likely to be scored.

This was a huge step up from simply counting dribbles or adding up how far players went, which were the earliest things done with the data. Coach Stan Van Gundy notably once told a story about how someone told him that Paul George went 3.2 miles in a game. Stan said what a lot of us would think: *What the hell do I do with that? What does that mean? How does that help me?*

Machine learning started getting at questions more relevant to Stan, Daryl, Mark, Herb . . . and me, the analyst.

My previous book is called *Basketball on Paper*, and I wrote it in 2002. It helped create the current basketball analytics industry by presenting a framework of how to use numbers to evaluate teams better, to evaluate players better, and to understand various situations in basketball. I myself began working in the NBA not long after the book's publication, my job being to apply numbers to many of the decisions that had previously been made by gut feel.

I did a lot of analysis and believed what the numbers said. I was supposed to be the kind of person who fought with the old-schoolers like Mark and Herb. But because of who they were and who I was, that's not what happened. The title of that book, *Basketball on Paper*, was itself meant to be self-deprecating, an acknowledgement that the framework for studying basketball was good "on paper," yet prone to mistakes made by relying too much on numbers.

So I listened to Mark, Herb, coaches, trainers, and psychologists, who spoke their basketball wisdom. I learned to find the things in what they said that could be quantified, which indirectly helped me understand the things that couldn't. For example, even when new data came along to show the *mechanics* of how to improve shooting, the words of coaches, trainers, and psychologists said why players could or could not achieve those mechanics, whether it was their form, their flexibility, or their frame of mind. I could see how the new data and the supposed old-schoolers combined to make players better.

That's what I wanted to put in this book: how the analytics framework is enhanced by both better data and old-school wisdom. How good are players now that better data can go into metrics? What are the mechanical factors that make players better or worse, like movement at the shot, dribbling ability, defensive positioning, and so forth? But then what can the numbers suggest about the importance of emotional and psychological factors, things that we can only occasionally measure? Yes, we can sometimes measure those factors, as you'll see.

Even though the amount of data and information has exploded, the decisions being made now are the same as they were twenty or even fifty years ago. You still just want to identify the best players and maximize what they can do for you through development and the right roles. We won't ever solve the human mystery that remains happily part of the game, but a good framework and ever improving data mean that we can go well Beyond Paper.

Just as I couldn't explain to Herb and Mark all the details of what I do, I can't explain all details of the work in this book. The mathematics of machine learning and of basketball analytics are enough to fill a textbook. I want to explain the concepts and give enough details for readers to implement a lot, but I don't want the publishers to have to print Greek letters and matrix algebra.

It is also difficult to cover in this book every analytics question that has been raised. I hope to add some new insight, for sure, but understand that there are online resources that have been working on basketball analytics problems for a while. These include CleaningTheGlass.com, KenPom.com, the Nylon Calculus, the NBA's own stat site, and a few others that aren't necessarily consolidated. One of my major goals for this book is that it will inspire more people to do the kind of high-quality work that has built this industry.

2

The Journey, Part 1

Before I ever knew Herb or Mark or Daryl, I was a person who did what he was supposed to do. I went to college, got a stable job, and rejected offers from a couple of companies that were starting up. I didn't take a lot of chances with my career. I was raised with some fear instilled in me that I could end up living on the street if I didn't follow the familiar career path.

College and grad school were both about following the conservative path but also about exploring what I loved, which was basketball. I played basketball my first two years at Division III Caltech,[1] then stopped in order to focus on a mountain of engineering classwork. But I couldn't stay away and talked to the head coach about staying on as an assistant coach, which I did in my junior and senior years.

My grades were good, so I applied to a lot of good graduate schools—Stanford, Harvard, MIT, Johns Hopkins. I got in to all of them, but I turned them all down to go to the University of North Carolina because it had, in addition to a good engineering program, a great basketball program. It was the school of Michael Jordan, legendary coach Dean Smith, and decades of both success and fans passionate about the game. At the University of North Carolina, I was studying statistical applications in science, so it was natural for me to also think about statistical applications in basketball. In fact, in grad school I worked for Bill Bertka, an assistant coach for the Lakers, doing advance scouting of college teams. The early form of basketball analytics was becoming concrete in my head.

I wasn't sacrificing the conservative career path, I felt. I was having some fun adding on to it through basketball. When I finished grad school, I could have joined the NBA as a scout, but I stuck to engineering. Fortunately, the internet was in its early stages, and I figured out quickly to write about my basketball ideas there. So I continued working on the conservative path but dabbling in basketball.

After three years with an engineering firm, the big promotions came and my responsibilities increased. With that, I mostly stopped writing about basketball so that I could focus on chasing an engineering career. I was involved in some high-end litigation cases, which also satisfied some of my need for competition. But I couldn't stay away from basketball. I watched games, I took notes, I tracked games manually. I sacrificed going out with friends who weren't as interested in basketball so that I could watch basketball, often alone or in a bar filled with people I didn't know but who also loved the game.

I wrote a few articles but primarily let ideas churn in my brain. It was the beginning of the tech bubble of the early 2000s, and a few friends were recruiting me for new ventures. I stayed with my company, however, doing the job but thinking about basketball in my free time. I was also saving money so that I could take time to write a book, and that would be easier if I stayed with my standard job. But the friends who recruited me to new ventures, even if they didn't succeed, introduced to me an excitement around chasing their dreams.

In early September 2001 I sent an email to Bill James, the author of some of the most famous books on baseball analytics, about potentially helping me to find a publisher. He asked me to send him some of my writing and I did. A few days later, September 11 happened, and I didn't hear back from James for one month, then two months, then three months. The world was a different place with different priorities, so I understood and kept plugging away at my job, including being one of about ten people (out of seventy normally in the office) who actually went to work on September 11.

In January 2002 I wrote back to James about what he thought of my writing. He wrote back the scariest email I ever received: he said that he was going to write his own basketball book.

I had to beat Bill James.

Why the Journey?

Despite the overall success of the basketball analytics movement, the ride from the beginning to now has not been an easy one. Herb Livsey and Mark Warkentien may have been good to me, but there were people who hated me, argued with me, or just dismissed me. There were people who told me that I was useless and should be replaced. On plenty of occasions it became clear that my voice wasn't wanted. Some of that dysfunction was out of my control, but I still think about what more I could have done to control it. Telling some of the stories of my journey is about helping others to navigate their journeys better than I did.

Part of pushing analytics further into basketball and doing it right is to acknowledge that basketball is a people business, first and foremost. People are subject to the irrational biases that Michael Lewis documented in both *Moneyball* and *The Undoing Project*. We supposedly play this game to win a championship, but only a handful of teams every year have a realistic chance of doing so. As long-time NBA coach George Karl once told me, a lot of teams are just playing for entertainment, not to win.

There are strong reasons for teams to want to win. Winning maximizes revenue, not only immediately but also in the long term, because a championship banner brings extra revenue to a team for years afterward. For all the weakness in the human ego, winning boosts that ego enormously, making for much happier players, coaches, management, ticket sellers, and ticket buyers (as well as their spouses).

When the goal is simply to win, teams should care about valuing players the right way, teams should want every piece of information that can help their decisions, decision-makers should want to know how best to use all that information. When other goals rise to the top of the priority list, all the rational reasons and ways to chase winning start getting relegated. An owner can just hire a big name for a coach or general manager because that will at least draw interest from the media and fans, regardless of whether they help the team win. A general manager will find it easy to do a favor for a player agent by signing his mediocre player, even if an analytical approach can find a clearly better player.

So don't be blind—winning is *not* everything in basketball. Winning is the ambitious goal, the concept behind why so many people play sports as children, the thing that is easier to accomplish during childhood, before all the talent gets concentrated at the very top.

But basketball is a lot about the *people* in it, because it is fundamentally a *team* sport. If you are a straight-A data science student thinking that you can change the game with your technical skills in basketball analytics, you can't do that without knowing how to convince the people on a team that you're useful. They have to learn to trust you. They probably need to like you. They definitely need to feel that you're on their side, that you're not there to make them feel like they aren't helping the team. If you think you have all the answers, then what do *they* have?

As a result, part of this book is about the human side of bringing numbers and analysis to a team setting. If you're trying to work in basketball analytics, you're the math person among people who didn't want much to do with math. You need them and they need you.

I will convey parts of the human journey I took while working in the NBA. Part of that was overcoming the cautious, stable lifestyle that I was brought up to hold on to.

Back in 2002

When James told me about his plan to write a book on my subject, I was in my office at work. I got up from my chair and took two steps out of the office toward where my boss worked, then paused, and returned to my office. I closed the door and paced in the tiny room. I wanted to quit my job right then and there and start writing and finding an agent or a publisher or whatever else I desperately needed to do. I cursed James a couple times, but I mostly just wanted to beat him.

I slept on my thoughts for a night and decided the next day to tell my boss about this hidden side of my life, the life in basketball. I called her to ask for a meeting that afternoon, and when she asked what it was about, I said, "Writing." It was vague enough to be relevant for my office job but also about the bigger truth.

"You should probably know that, over the last several years, I've been working on the science of basketball," I started the meeting off with. She was always very pleasant, not one who got flustered, so she calmly smiled through everything I told her, which was about developing statistics for basketball, writing a book, and getting the email from James. At the end, I said what I planned: "So I either need to quit or need to take time off to write this book."

I was finally putting my career on the line to chase a dream. I didn't know what she'd say.

There really was no negotiation. My boss saw what I was willing to do, and the company valued me. She gave me the time off.

I wrote *Basketball on Paper* during the spring and summer of 2002, aiming constantly to beat Bill James. I didn't know or care what he was going to write about, but I knew he had the name to get a publisher. On my end, I was sending query letters to publishers and agents every week in the early months of 2002. Most never got back to me, and the couple that did were bluntly not interested.

The book chapters were going well, but finding someone else who cared about it was hard. In April 2002, after a couple months of rejections, I got an email from someone out of the blue who asked, "How can I help?—Pete." That "Pete" was Pete Palmer, a rival to Bill James and the author of his own share of books on using statistics in sports. He would end up finding me a publisher, but why did he reach out to me at all?

It turned out that Pete had emailed me to ask about helping with a project I started months before to chart defense in the WNBA. In an online advertisement aimed at sports fans who liked numbers, I was offering to get people into games if they just tracked various simple aspects of defense. The details of the project don't particularly matter anymore, but just doing that project got my name out to the person who would be key to my getting a publisher for my book.

With the security that I would have a publisher, I was able to finish writing the book by September 2002. I returned to my safe and secure office job as an engineer that same month. I worked with the publisher on edits and the index over the next few months, well into 2003. On a spring afternoon in Oakland, California, when I was mostly done with editing, a friend called me and told me to turn on the radio. There was an interview with "some guy who is doing what you do but in baseball for the Oakland A's." I turned on the radio and heard Michael Lewis talking about his new book, *Moneyball.* As I listened to his stories about how the A's—my home team—used statistics to guide their baseball decisions, to win games that people didn't think they could win, to sign good players that no one else believed in, I immediately knew that my book could change my career from an engineer in an office to working for an NBA team.

Basketball on Paper hit the shelves of Barnes and Noble in October 2003, about six months after *Moneyball* came out. There was no fanfare and no advertising for my book. I tried to push the manager of my local bookstore to highlight it *somehow*, but she had no reason to believe that my book would amount to much.

Despite the muted debut of the book, I notified my engineering employer about a month later that my last day with them would be January 2, 2004. I was going to chase the dream of getting to the NBA. I had enough money saved, I thought, to last about a year and a half while I tried to turn the book into a job with the NBA, especially if I could sleep on friends' couches and at cheap hotels while on the road. The money would have to cover the costs of food, a lot of driving, some flying, car insurance, health insurance, admission to summer league games, and storage for household items that I wanted to keep.

In the weeks leading up to my departure from the company, I had to do what a lot of people have to do—transfer projects to other people, tell my clients that I'd be leaving, and fill out forms. The company told me that I had to be physically in the office on my last day. My plan was to do that, then drive up to Seattle on January 3 so that I could meet with the Seattle SuperSonics, the first team I had set up a conversation with.

The New Year's holiday came right before my last day of work, so I went to Tahoe to celebrate with friends. On December 31 a big snowstorm barreled through Tahoe, dumping several feet of snow. On January 1, the day I had expected to drive back to the San Francisco Bay area so I could be at work on January 2, the roads were all shut down. All news sources were saying that I couldn't get out of there. Fate was slapping me in the face; a friend joked, "You're not really leaving engineering." I prepared to deal with the problem of missing my last day of work and then being unable to get to Seattle in time to meet with one of the owners and their assistant general manager. Fortunately, destiny came back to my side, the people in charge of the roads opened them for a couple of hours, and I got into that window before they were shut down again. The drive down the mountain through near whiteout conditions was the risk I had to take to stick to my plan. I saw multiple cars spin out, and I drove no faster than twenty-five miles per hour for a couple of hours before I got far enough down the hill to encounter lighter snow and safer driving conditions.

The next day, January 2—my last day as an engineer—was like the last day at school as a kid when you know you passed all your classes and you're just saying goodbye to friends. I left a little early that day, around 4 p.m., and walked around the office, took in the view of the Golden Gate Bridge, and waved goodbye to the physical structure as I left the office. I honestly didn't know then whether I'd have to come crawling back eventually. It was a major gamble, but I felt good walking out the door, knowing that I was doing what I had to do.

I drove to a friend's house with the few things that I was going to be taking with me—a suitcase with casual and dress clothes, some basketball shoes, a box of my books, and a backpack that had the necessities—a Dell laptop, phone charger for my flip phone (no smartphones then), money and ID, a notebook to write on, and an ethernet cable (public Wi-Fi being harder to find than ethernet ports).

On January 3, 2004, I headed north in my eight-year-old Acura Integra on Interstate 5 toward Seattle. During the thirteen-hour drive, I listened to the radio and a CD player, since streaming music didn't yet exist. I was thinking about how to pitch what I could do for the Sonics. Analytics were so simple back then—basic team ratings to say how good offenses and defenses were, the Four-Factor statistical breakdown of why they were good (see below), some player projections, and RoboScout, which was a tool I used for identifying the key actions in stopping an opposing team. But in that audience of NBA people, no one really knew anything about basketball analytics, so I was an expert. Explaining why points *per possession* mattered more than points *per game* took five to ten minutes. Explaining the Four Factors of shooting, turnovers, rebounding, and free throws—that was another five to ten minutes. Explaining that I had spent years doing advance scouting, college scouting, and thinking about the math to help it—that was the rest of the time. I didn't need a lot of content because everything needed time to explain.

When I walked into the office of Sonics president Wally Walker on January 5, it was my first time meeting the higher-ups of an NBA organization. Walker was 6 feet 7 inches tall and had been a college and NBA player, but he also studied finance, so he was comfortable with numbers. Rich Cho was the assistant GM and had been an engineer in college himself. Though neither of them knew much about what I was doing, they were comfortable with the concept that numbers could provide a framework for making better decisions in the game. We talked through what I had planned, and the meeting went very well. I ended by saying, "I hope we can find a way to work together." There was no offer at that time, but it was only less than a week into my journey.

Over the next few months, I got to talk to a handful of teams but not at particularly high levels in the organizations—someone in public relations, a couple of scouts, a few from lower-level basketball operations, and one assistant general manager. For perspective—I am not the most vocal person, I don't enjoy tooting my horn, and I had never before had to make cold calls or send cold emails. I could definitely talk about my work and why it was useful, but the small talk that helps get you to a job interview was not my specialty, especially when the person on the other end was somewhat famous and skeptical of anyone who walks up to them.

Fortunately, I was joined in my hunt for an NBA analytics job by two other people: Roland Beech and Dan Rosenbaum. We all were on the outside and trying to get inside. Instead of competing against each other, we coordinated our schedules, shared notes on our conversations, and, to some degree, gave each other contacts.

Roland was the founder of a website called 82games.com, which aggregated play-by-play data off the web and summarized it for users. It was a big step in the early 2000s toward using more than box-score data for understanding the game. He lived in Northern California, not too far from me, so we could get together at times.

Dan was a young professor of economics at the University of North Carolina in Greensboro and the developer of one of the first forms of adjusted plus-minus, a method of valuing basketball players by using play-by-play data.

The three of us traveled to Chicago in early June to attempt to get into the NBA Combine,[2] where team personnel gather to get good looks at the players in the upcoming draft. Dan got in by obtaining a media credential from a newspaper in his Indiana hometown, and I got in through a contact in the NBA league office. Roland didn't find his way in, and I felt bad that I didn't ask for a second credential for him. But I knew that I was lucky to get in any door, so I didn't want to knock too hard on that one for fear of someone locking it shut.

I remember walking into the gym to pick up my credential for the Combine, having some paranoid fear that my name wouldn't be on the list. As I walked into the gym, there was Larry Bird and Mitch Richmond and Danny Ainge and Bill Cartwright and a host of other former players who were working for teams. I had been in gyms with NBA players before then but only as a kid looking to play ball and not having dreams of actually working in the league. This camp in Chicago was my big opportunity and I knew it.

A friend told me before the Combine that I needed a twenty-five-word pitch on how I could help all these famous people in basketball. Also called the "elevator pitch," mine was this: "Hi, my name is Dean Oliver. Did you read *Moneyball* on how to use statistics to win in baseball? This is how you do it in basketball." It was a couple words longer than twenty-five, and it relied on the concept that people I met had read *Moneyball*—so it wasn't the greatest, but it was what I had.

It worked for about twelve, maybe fifteen, people in that room, but it was enough to identify an audience. I gave away books, I got contact information, and I had good conversations about how I could help. At the same time, some of the people at the camp were talking about the NBA Finals between the Los Angeles Lakers and the underdog Detroit Pistons. I had done some work that suggested the Pistons matched up particularly well against the Lakers, so I was picking the Pistons in various friendly conversations. Although the Lakers won the game that was played during the Combine, the Pistons later ended up winning the title and I felt validated, knowing that people would remember me. As Dan, Roland, and I flew back from Chicago, I felt I had made a big stride toward getting a job in the league.

The next stop was at the Utah summer league, then the Long Beach summer league. These weren't heavily attended by the public, and it was actually pretty easy to get access to NBA personnel who were there. In both places, I was able to sit next to general managers and coaches in the stands or even along the sideline, watching the 2004 draft picks get their first taste of NBA action. Sonics president Wally Walker asked me during summer league whether I thought the numbers in summer league meant much. I had only a couple years of numbers then, but my initial sense was that playing badly in summer league was a bad sign, probably meaning a longer development time in the regular season. I told him that was just my preliminary sense. Walker liked that answer, and I could feel my chances of getting a job improve. I also sat next to Suns assistant general manager David Griffin, who asked me whether his team paid too much to sign Steve Nash. I said that the numbers loved Nash, which was something he wanted to hear. It sparked a good conversation, and I thought that I opened up a real possibility for a job there. I talked to him again by phone a few weeks later. He was interested in bringing me in, but when he said, "I wish you good luck," I knew it wasn't going to happen right then.

Despite all my new contacts, when the summer leagues ended, team personnel went on vacation and my phone went silent. As with the Sonics and the Suns, I developed good relationships but nothing even close to a real prospect. After mid-July, I could only work on getting better at what I was promising teams that I could do and hope that someone would both remember what I said and believe that it could help.

Dan and Roland were in similar positions, except that Dan had a professor's job and Roland was making money from websites that he ran. I, on the other hand, was living off savings and paying a friend minimal rent to sleep and work in her place. I had always planned for a year and a half of not making money, but I was wondering what my next move would be.

Life was under my own control. I was going to have to find my next opportunity to talk to people so that I didn't end up living under a bridge.

In the meantime, for my technical challenge, I found myself working on how to divide credit and blame among players.

3

Who Blamed J.R.?

In the last 4.5 seconds of Game 1 of the 2018 NBA Finals, George Hill missed the second of two free throws that would have put the Cavaliers up by 1. His teammate J.R. Smith leaped in to get the offensive rebound, then raced out toward half-court to avoid getting fouled and to run out the clock. But the game was tied! *The game was tied!* By running away from the basket, he ruined the Cavaliers' chances of winning at that moment and ultimately gave the Warriors the game!

That was the narrative that blamed J.R. Smith for the subsequent overtime loss suffered by the Cavaliers in that game. J.R. was the goat, the one guy to pin all this on.

Not Hill, who missed the second of two free throws that would have "nearly sealed the game." His excuse was normal—you're allowed to miss a free throw when you make about 75 percent from the line. But J.R.'s mental error of not knowing the score, something that 99 percent of all players know—that was inexcusable.

That's how to blame people for a collective failure. The whole group of Cavaliers lost, but to simplify who was responsible provides value. That process of laying blame is, essentially, how to figure out how a group of teammates interact.

If you can step back and ignore the terrible error that Smith made, you can see that Hill's free throw miss was costly and was at least partially to blame.

If you step back farther, you look at how the Warriors got their lead prior to the free throws on a drive by Stephen Curry with an and-one due to a Kevin Love foul. Maybe you blame Kevin Love, but you honestly don't remember.

If you go back a little farther, to 36 seconds left, when LeBron James drew a charge on Kevin Durant that was somehow changed in video replay to a block, you can blame the refs! Everyone loves blaming the refs.

But it was mostly J.R.

Blame is given when something went wrong, and people are looking for an explanation for their misery. Often, though, the misery gets in the way of a good explanation.

This book is about explanation and not misery (at least I hope you're not feeling misery just a couple chapters in) and that is the part that is useful in basketball. Having a good explanation for what happened in the past can help prevent similar problems in the future. In this case, maybe Cavs coach Tyronn Lue should have told J.R. before the free throw what the score was and what to do if he got an offensive rebound (or if he doesn't get a rebound). Maybe he should have simply recognized that J.R., as physically talented as he was, needed a little extra advice in critical situations. But that's jumping ahead.

How do you explain the dynamics of the team here? What rules can we establish to lay blame on J.R. or George Hill or LeBron or whomever for this fiasco? That is the analytical challenge here.

There are a few important concepts to accept up front.

1. *First, what is "this fiasco" that we're blaming players for?* Is it the whole game? Is it the missed free throw plus the offensive rebound plus the running out the clock? Or is it just the running out the clock? The breadth of the event you're trying to lay blame for changes how you do it and probably how well you do it. It's seemingly easy to blame J.R. for just the part about running out the clock, but once you put the missed free throw into it, it gets murkier.
2. *Keep blame within the team.* This was a Cavs failure, so "blaming" the Warriors, their opponent, for the team failure doesn't make a lot of sense. The Warriors wanted the Cavs to screw up. The Warriors may have their own "who's to credit" situation, but that is separate from blaming individual Cavaliers for the team

failure. Beyond this, we're not going to blame the fan noise or astrological signs or slippery floors. And we're not going to blame the refs. Sorry.

3. *Don't create massive hypotheticals.* Assign blame for what did actually happen, not what could have happened. The players did what they did. J.R. ran away from the basket and that's what matters. The possibilities for what he could have done if he hadn't run away from the basket are vast. He could have taken the shot. He could have passed it to LeBron. He could have thrown it out of bounds. He could have called timeout. He could have decided to go say hello to someone in the stands because he thought there was a timeout (it's J.R.—he's done it before). A tornado could have hit the arena and caused the refs to stop play (I was in a situation like this). For this purpose, he ran away from the basket and everything else gets lumped into "that didn't happen."
4. *The blame has to add up.* The blame for everyone on the Cavs should add up to the total "fiasco" that is defined in point 1.

The first concept is important because the answer to "What is the overall impact of what just happened here?" defines a lot. It defines the scale by which we're looking at things. A lot of times, when we blame people for what happened, the scope of what we're looking at changes, causing disagreement. Each step along a timeline changes the odds of some result, in this case, the Cavaliers' loss. If you lay blame for each step, you are blaming those players for the change in odds, not the entire loss. Table 1 shows the events in this game step by step, beginning with the foul that Klay Thompson committed on George Hill with 4.5 seconds left.

This sequence of plays took the Cavaliers from a 35 percent chance of winning to a 47 percent chance,[1] so their odds actually went up, albeit in a very roller-coaster-like way. If you just want to ask who's to blame for this sequence, you're actually "blaming" Cavaliers for things that were an *overall positive*.

But that's not what people did. People focused on that last 4.5 seconds and blamed all of that on J.R. "All of that" was 16 percent of winning

Table 1. Sequence of events in the last 4.7 seconds of the 2016 NBA Finals Game 1

		Cavs' chance to win		Score difference	
Time	What happened	Start of event	End of event	Start of event	End of event
4.7 sec.	LeBron passed to Hill under the basket, Thompson fouled Hill	35%	57%	−1	−1
4.7 sec.	Hill made first of two free throws	57%	64%	−1	0
4.7 sec.	Hill missed second of two free throws	64%	38%	0	0
4.5 sec.	Smith got offensive rebound	38%	63%	0	0
4.5 sec. to 0 sec.	Smith ran around like Cavs were going to win the gamc	63%	47%	0	0

Note: Some media outlets report different win probabilities, but these represent a common pattern.

percentage, a possible 1 or 2 points. It felt like blaming him for the *entire* game, but it wasn't. The Cavs still had to lose the rest of that 47 percent in overtime, where LeBron missed all four shots he took and J.R. actually was responsible for three of the five total points that the Cavs scored.

In general, it is easier to divide credit on smaller events, but the smaller the events, the more of them that there are to divide credit on. In basketball, where events are recorded at 1⁄25th of a second,[2] you could conceivably divide credit on every frame. That is an effort left to future generations. The effort left for this chapter is to divide the blame on the events above.

That's where the other three concepts become important.

Keeping the blame within the team means that whatever we're dividing—the 16 percent of win percentage or the one potential point lost—is going to the players on the floor for the Cavaliers—J.R., LeBron, Hill, Tristan Thompson, and Jeff Green. Don't blame the coach, don't blame the teammates holding towels over their faces. Their influence is indirect, perhaps causing the players on the floor to play better (or perhaps not). For now, leave them off the floor and off the accounting.

This also means that you don't blame the opponents for your loss. They're trying to beat you. Dividing blame is about identifying who on your own team didn't do what they needed to do and dividing it in such a way that it is helpful, not purely emotional.

Next, divide the blame based on what the players actually did and the chance that they did what they did. This gets at why J.R.'s mistake was so egregious—the chance that a regular NBA player would do that is very small, so pinning nearly all the blame for the last 4.5 seconds on him makes sense. Giving him credit for a difficult offensive rebound—you could give him all the credit for that, but it's likely that any player in that position would accomplish that. He gets less "credit" for that positive contribution than blame for the negative contribution. Behind all of this lurks mathematics that would scare most people, but hopefully the concept is clear and not scary.[3]

Lastly, whatever blame J.R. gets, things have to add up across his teammates on the floor. If we give J.R. 99 percent of the blame for running out the clock, give 1 percent to his teammates for not calling timeout in time. If we give J.R. 80 percent for the offensive rebound, the other 20 percent should go to his teammates for blocking out, or if it was lucky, his teammates get credit for being lucky along with J.R.

Those are the concepts behind dividing blame and credit. Those concepts, whether you like or dislike the details of them, are useful. You can't just blame the entire game on J.R. and then look at the box score to see Jordan Clarkson was an awful 2 for 9 from the field, then blame him for the entire game. Blame part of different events on each of them when they're in the game, then add it all up over the course of the game.

That gives you the useful explanation for what happened in the game that comes out of asking, "Who's to blame?"

J.R. Smith took a good part of 16 percent, but there was plenty of blame to go around.

Reality Box

We blame people all the time in real life. We blame the boss for our not getting a promotion. We blame the kids for our not sleeping at night. We blame the politicians for the economy. If you turned on a news channel in the last decade or so, you saw someone blaming a politician for something.

In popular culture, blame is an emotional thing that doesn't necessarily resolve a situation. This book is not meant for the self-help section, I assure you, so I'm trying to assign blame on small events in basketball that help understand who could have done what better. And I think that this process of looking at why an event happened should go beyond sports. Ideally, that process does break things down into a series of steps so that we know what happened and who was involved. Not that life is sports or that sports is life, but sports does give us harmless analogies for life that can be helpful.

A lot of life's situations to assign blame are not harmless. One of those was the *Challenger* space shuttle explosion of 1986, when a crew of seven died about a minute after launch. At first, no one knew what happened or why. It took months of investigation to unpack the details of the engineering and the decision-making process, specifically the steps that failed. It's not that any single one of those failures was the entire cause, but each one increased the odds that something bad would happen, from engineering the O-rings that could not do their job in the cold to a decision to launch despite the cold weather to various communication failures that didn't clarify how serious the danger was.[4]

In most situations, unpacking the details is more difficult than assigning blame. Understanding why a government shutdown happens when negotiations occur over weeks or months behind a lot of closed doors—that's not easy. Blame for a single drug overdose often gets laid on the drug user, but blame for an overdose epidemic going to a corporation or to doctors implies that every individual case has a bigger complex process at work.

It may be foolish, but I have some hope that basketball can provide a harmless laboratory for better dividing blame (and credit).

4

Data, Data Everywhere, but Not the Time to Think

In 2010 the company STATS Inc. was talking to NBA teams about purchasing the player tracking data known as SportVu. It was in its infancy, and like all infants, it had a lot more potential than actual use. And like all infants, that investment of time early on would pay off down the road.

It's not that the early data is of any use now. That early data was, uh, cute with all of its errors and its limited coverage across the league—one player would sometimes morph into another in the middle of a play, for example. The most valuable thing about early data was that someone in those early-adopting organizations had to think hard about how to use it. Getting a head start of several years of just *thinking* about the data helped build it into something far more valuable—at least when it finally became reliable.

At the time STATS Inc. was shopping the data, I wrote up a justification for the early $35,000-per-year investment. Just going through that exercise—without actually *seeing* the data—was hugely beneficial, because it made me think about what questions the data would help me answer. These were some of those ideas from back then.

On-ball defense. Who was guarding who? How close were they to the shooter at shot time?

Speed and quickness. How fast was a player with his dribble? How quickly could players rotate to open shooters?

Shooting contested versus uncontested shots. What guys really need a lot of room to get their jump shot off? What players shot well only when uncontested?

Ball handling and passing. How much did players dribble? Who liked to shoot off the dribble? Where did passes start and end? Did they draw a double-team before a pass? So many coaches preached more passes, but did that actually help an offense?

Paint touches. Did getting the ball into the paint improve the chance of scoring in a possession? Did it matter how deep into the paint?

Play types. What teams and players were good running off screens? Who ran pick-and-roll to set up the roller versus themselves versus other shooters? What teams were running a lot of handoffs, and how often did they fake it?

Fatigue. Did some players get tired after playing a few minutes? How much did transition defense wear players out?

After I wrote up my thoughts, I wrote the following statement:

> I see this as a very important part of the future of basketball analysis, a potential way to get ahead and, with good people, to stay ahead. It can give unprecedented data that requires good analysis. If we as a team are investing in good analysis, we can use this to stay ahead.

Data was the early financial investment, but the *mental* investment was the part that paid off for the early adopters. It took some time to create the actual statistics (and not all of them have been built even today), but knowing what to do with those metrics in advance allowed for a much quicker route to application.

What the Tracking Data Actually Does

When the player tracking data finally went league-wide in 2013, a lot of metrics were created from it. Some of them are in the list above, but there were so many more that teams can now use. Here are some of the key ones that I have used and will refer to at points in the book.

Shot Quality

Shooting from the field is far and away the most important factor that drives offense and defense in basketball. But what drives shooting?

That is one of the most important questions in the game, and player tracking helped answer it. Player tracking could look at whether a player was shooting off the catch or off the dribble, whether they were moving and how fast, how far a defender was from them at different times, and (to some degree) whether the defender's hand was up, on top of how far the shot was, for which we actually had data before. All of those factors went into two metrics of "shot quality."[1] The two versions of shot quality were different only in that one was independent of who was shooting, and the other one included that information. This meant that a contested jump shot by Stephen Curry or Russell Westbrook twenty-five feet from the rim would have the same "QSQ" (the *q*uantified *s*hot *q*uality that was independent of shooter) but different values of "QSP" (the *q*uality of the *s*hot *p*ersonalized for Curry being a much better shooter than Westbrook).[2] QSP is the more accurate one, but QSQ captures what the defense did, independent of who the shooter was, allowing you to understand generally how important being close to a shooter is, for instance. From a defensive perspective, you can't control who the shooters are for the other team, but you can control your defense.

I can tell you firsthand that these metrics don't correspond perfectly to what NBA people see as a "good shot" or a "bad shot." Shot quality numbers on three-point shots are usually no higher than about 60 percent,[3] which means only a 40 percent chance that the shot is actually going to go in. And that means that those people thinking "good shot" are going to be disappointed a lot. But as the data gets more widespread, I could see the gap between perception and the shot quality numbers shrink. I would say that these metrics are now routinely discussed in the NBA to understand the game and manage shot attempts throughout the year.

Note that shot quality metrics are evaluated *at the time of the shot*. This is the time that most people care about it, but there are reasons to care about shot quality at other times, like when a player catches the ball or when a player passes the ball to a potential shooter. A passer is often mentally making their own calculation that if they pass to a specific teammate, that is a "good shot." Models of shot quality at these different times are not widely used, but they would be useful in evaluating decision-making, which takes some time before a shot is actually attempted.

Rebounding Probability

Rebound totals have been pretty good statistics since before player tracking. Player tracking, though, added new information. Now we can know which players were good at improving their odds of a rebound from the time of the shot to the time the ball hits the rim, meaning that they're getting into better position.

For example, these are players that improved their chance at a defensive rebound consistently from the time of the shot to when the ball hit the rim:[4] Dejounte Murray, Cole Anthony, Will Barton, Deni Avdija, Josh Hart, Luka Dončić, Nickeil Alexander-Walker, Kyle Kuzma, Jayson Tatum, Jaylen Brown, Tobias Harris, John Konchar, R.J. Barrett, De'Anthony Melton, Donte DiVincenzo. These are almost all perimeter players who crashed the boards.

The players whose chance *declined* tend to be big men who would have been going away from the rim a good amount to help on shooters: Joel Embiid, Clint Capela, De'Andre Jordan, Robert Williams, Daniel Gafford, Mitchell Robinson, Dwight Powell, Ivica Zubac, Montrezl Harrell, Isaiah Hartenstein, Steven Adams, Jakob Poeltl, and Jock Landale.

This kind of data did not exist prior to tracking.

Some of these players offset each other—like Atlanta's Clint Capela and Dejounte Murray. Capela helps on a shooter, lowering his chance of a defensive rebound, but Murray comes in to help on the defensive glass. Boston's Robert Williams goes away from the rim to help, but his teammates Jayson Tatum and Jaylen Brown both help on the glass. There are at least seven pairs of teammates with representation on each list (depending on how you count guys who change teams), implying a complementarity in skills.

This simple insight, that perimeter players could really help big men on the glass, wasn't new in the world of coaching, but the data quantified how much it helped.

The overall team probability of a rebound at the time of a shot is also helpful for understanding how big a risk a shooter is taking. If there is a good chance of an offensive rebound, their risk is smaller, whereas a jump shot that doesn't move the defense probably has a low chance of having an offensive rebound.

Transition

The NBA has historically counted fast break points as occurring within a specific time after a team gets the ball, usually six seconds. Coaches have generally hated this cutoff point, as their definition tries to capture whether defenders were back and in position. The NBA's definition limited the number of transition points a lot more than coaches wanted it. Fortunately, machine learning was applied to the player tracking data to capture a version of transition that was more acceptable to coaches.

The analytical benefit of the coaching definition is that it more truly captures how the defense is doing its job. Half-court defense involves matching up, then helping and recovering. Transition defense means taking away the rim and the ball first, *before* matching up. If we're going to properly divide credit and blame on defense, knowing what really is transition helps a lot. It helps on offense, too, with an outlet passer being much more relevant in transition than in half-court, for example.

This use of tracking data helped overcome a lot of headaches I had while working with coaches.

Matchups

The tracking data gives information on which defender is matched up with which offensive player. We never had this information before tracking data, so you couldn't know if one particular defender was getting torched when Giannis Antetokounmpo scored 50 in a game. The matchups give you that now, and they usually show that defenses try different defenders on big scorers. The matchups also show that about 20–25 percent of points are scored when no one is matched up—like in transition or after a loose ball.[5]

Play Types

Knowing whether points got scored off pick-and-roll or a post-up or an isolation play is helpful in understanding which situations players are good at. Though some of this information existed before, the new data had much more depth to it.

With the old data, you could ask, How good is Luka Dončić when running a pick-and-roll? He generated more points out of it in 2023 than anyone, but Damian Lillard wasn't far behind.

With the new data, you could ask a lot more about what else happened on those pick-and-rolls: What was Dončić's assist-to-turnover ratio when running pick-and-roll and the defensive big man is playing in drop coverage? It was 2.9, above the league average, but not elite like Chris Paul and Tyrese Haliburton, who were over 4.0.

Those play types are incredibly helpful not only in managing offensive and defensive decisions but also in dividing credit and blame for players on the floor.

Passing Information

It turns out that more passes in a possession are not better, despite what coaches have wanted to say. In general, one to two passes in a possession have been associated with much higher efficiency than when there are three or more. Throwing more passes usually means the defense has been able to *force* another pass. It's the *quality* of the passes, not the quantity, that is most relevant.

One of the new metrics is potential assists, which, along with shot quality, can give you a pretty good idea of which players are making high-quality passes, but we'll save that for chapter 7, when Nikola Jokić's magic with the ball can be fully quantified by using data like this.

Even though these new metrics are important additions to basketball's data story, they are only filling in the details. The information they provide doesn't suddenly turn LeBron James from a great player into an average one. They can move the value of some players up or down by a reasonable amount, especially defenders, but they aren't going to turn our perception of the game on its head.

The Time to Think

In one of my early years in Denver—before the concept of even having player tracking came about—I was normally giving analytical advanced scouting indicators to one of the assistant coaches. It was short and succinct, usually one to two pages of text, not tables of numbers. In preparing for one game, that coach asked me a few questions about where the analysis came from, and I explained it. For some reason, I decided that, for the next game, I'd give him all of the support information I used to create the succinct report. That support information was about forty pages of charts and tables that normally formed the basis of my summary. Not long after emailing all the info, the coach came into my office, slammed the printout on the desk, and said, "Never give me that again."

He had no time to review all the data I gave him. Some of that data meant nothing to him without interpretation. The data was *my* tool to build insights that grew to be trusted, but it was not a tool that others could use. It was *my* job to translate from the numbers and charts into basketball language.

In the modern age, with so much more data available, it's easy to slip into the bad habit of just presenting the data, not putting it in terms that a coach or a scout or a personnel director can use. They may want more detail at some point, but starting with too much detail doesn't get you anywhere. This is especially true in a sport with so many games and so little time between them to prepare. The important part is thinking about the data. What is most important for beating this team? What can be communicated easily enough to make a difference?

Sometimes questions will come back that you can't answer. And sometimes you will want to say, "We need more data" or, "We need better data."

But the answer to everything is not always "more data." Analytics got its name because it's both data and analysis.[6] The analysis sometimes gets forgotten, but that is how to maximize the information that you can get from existing data. Too many people complain about not having enough data before thinking about whether analysis of existing data can get close to the answer. Before we had play-by-play data, I had to maximize what we could get out of box score data, which is mostly what *Basketball on Paper* was built on. Only a few years after having good play-by-play data, the player tracking data came into play; then another ten years later, a higher level of player tracking came about, introducing "pose tracking," which is the position of all players' bodies at every frame. If people don't think enough about how to use all of this data, the explosion of data can create a lot of shrapnel that actually obscures their decision-making.

The modern world is driven by data, but make sure for yourself that it's not just the machines that are learning from it.

Reality Box

Imagine that "They" could record every move you made, just like They record what NBA players do. Let's say They're recording not what you're doing at home but every move you make at work. It's already possible technically, if not economically. That would make you want to work from home, now wouldn't it?

But what would They even do with that data? It has taken us years to figure out what to do with movement data in the game of basketball, basketball being a job that is *all about movement*! Outside basketball, a lot of people have jobs that are only partly about movement, if about it at all. Assume, for example, that you're a barista and you have to take orders and bring the coffee from here to there, which could be tracked, but that tracking is often missing the important part of the job, which is capturing the accuracy of an order and giving the customers a pleasant experience. Are They going to record every word you say and then somehow analyze it for whether it's nice enough, friendly enough, selling the banana bread often enough? That's possible, too.

But that's not capturing what's in your head, right? Thinking is a big part of the job, you believe, and there's no way that They can get that! But Disney actually developed a technique for capturing people's true emotions about movies they're watching. The company films an audience and interprets the individual expressions in a way that captures people's responsiveness to their films clearly better than the survey taken after watching. So, yeah, They can read your mind.

Scary, isn't it?

Would you want that for yourself?

We already do it for basketball players. We just do it with our eyes every time we watch a game, analyzing every little thing they do on the floor. We study their shot technique, whether they block out, and how well they defend, as well as their body language, how much they yell and scream, and how much they congratulate or berate their teammates, and we listen to their words that aren't bleeped out. Basketball is just a big aquarium to watch and criticize everyone in it, because the players are totally exposed in an environment that is changing fast.

I'll use this opportunity to speak up for Russell Westbrook, who was with the Wizards for a year when I was there. There were road fans that showed a lot of disrespect toward him over the years, dumping popcorn on him, trash-talking him for what he did on the court, and criticizing him and his family, actions based almost exclusively on what he does on the court, where he is not a great shooter but still shoots frequently. But Russ—as he is known to those who spend time with him—is a tremendously good teammate. He was a leader to players on and off the court, getting them to focus on the game and getting better. He was strict with our guys, not wanting them to let down in those hours at the arena before the game. He took care of the Wizards staff more than any other player did, providing shoes and clothes. He did a number of things under the radar that got him no publicity but were simply acts of kindness. One kind thing that ended up getting unintended publicity was when he tipped the hotel cleaning staff over $1,000 per week during the bubble of 2020. A lot of players *can* do that. He actually did it, and he did it quietly.

Russ was a lot more than the intense competitor that people saw on the court, more than the moving dots in the data, more than what any of the eyes, ears, or numbers could observe during games. He was a thoughtful, classy leader for our team.

5

Beyond the Four Factors

You probably don't remember the 2016–17 Miami Heat team. LeBron James was long gone. Dwyane Wade was gone. They had no superstars, but they were special, nonetheless.

At the halfway point of the year, that Heat team was 11-30, the second worst team in the league. Over the rest of the year, they were 30-11, the second best team in the league. They didn't change coaches. They didn't make any big trades. The top five guys in minutes played through the first half of the season were the same top five guys in minutes during the second half of the season.

How did they do it? The Heat did what so many teams want to do— take what they already have and just make it better. Shedding even a little light on this change can be useful.

There is a structured analytical route to *begin* to answer this question, one that can focus the search later. The first step in that process is to ask whether it was an offensive or a defensive change. Offensive ratings, which are points *scored* per 100 possessions, and defensive ratings, which are points *allowed* per 100 possessions, answer this question quickly. The Heat's offensive rating went from 103 to 112, which meant going from twenty-seventh to seventh. Their defensive rating went from 108 to 105, which meant going from sixteenth to third. So there were pretty big improvements on both sides of the ball, but the offense took the bigger leap.

But *how* did the offense improve? And *how* did the defense improve?

Answering these questions gets to the next level of the analytical process. There are four factors that completely explain each of the offensive and defensive ratings, providing more detail about what happened.

Those Four Factors get capitalized because they are so useful, capturing shooting, turnovers, rebounding, and getting to the foul line using these corresponding statistics:

Shooting: effective field goal percentage (eFG%), which is just a regular field goal percentage with extra credit given to three-point shots. This is easily the most important factor.

Turnovers: turnover percentage (TO%), which is how many turnovers a team commits per possession used. This is the second most important factor in most leagues.

Rebounding: offensive rebounding percentage (OR%) and defensive rebounding percentage (DR%), which capture how many rebounds a team gets as a percentage of available ones. This is the third most important factor in most leagues, though often close to turnovers.

Foul line: free throw rate (FTr),[1] which is just free throws made per field goals attempted. It is the least important factor.

For Miami, tables 2 and 3 show the changes in the offensive and defensive Four Factors from the first half to the second half.[2]

What the first table says is that Miami shot the ball a lot better in the second half of the season, going from twenty-eighth to fifth in the league. They also did better on the offensive glass, but that is probably secondary to the shooting improvement (see chapter 7 for confirmation). They committed a few more turnovers, though their rank dropped more than the number itself. The second table says that their defense got a little better in limiting shooting and got a lot better forcing turnovers, though they also committed more fouls.

That's it—that's the by-the-book way to study any team's problem. Step 1 is to look for whether it's offense or defense; here it was more offense but also some defense. Step 2 is to break down which of the Four Factors is making the biggest differences. For big changes like Miami's, the shooting factor has to be part of the story.

But that's not The Answer, is it? Those are symptoms. The tables list them, and the narrative is like the doctor delivering them in his thirty seconds with the patient. But it's not *the cause*. To get at causes, you have to go deeper, you have to go beyond the Four Factors. You can

Table 2. Miami's offensive Four Factors in the first half and second half of the 2017 season

Factor	First half	Second half
Shooting, eFG%	48.9% (28)	53.6% (5)
Turnovers, TO%	13.7% (9)	14.2% (18)
Rebounding, OR%	23.5% (15)	25.0% (8)
Foul line, FTr	16.6% (29)	18.8% (26)
Offensive rating	102.7 (27)	112.1 (7)

Note: League rank is in parentheses.

Table 3. Miami's defensive Four Factors in the first half and second half of the 2017 season

Factor	First half	Second half
Shooting, eFG%	49.9% (7)	49.4% (3)
Turnovers, TO%	14.3% (20)	15.3% (12)
Rebounding, DR%	76.4% (16)	76.5% (16)
Foul line, FTr	20.8% (15)	23.2% (26)
Defensive rating	107.6 (16)	105.2 (3)

Note: League rank is in parentheses.

break each of the Factors down—you can look at the *process*—or you can look at the *players*, but likely both. There is no guaranteed answer to be found by doing this. The Four Factors automatically point you in a direction, but there is a lot of space to get lost.

I did indeed get a little lost while looking into this Miami Heat team. I looked deeper into the numbers behind the process and the players, finding some dead ends, but then I found my way back to a story. In doing so, I also got help from human eyes and ears. Not just outsider eyes and ears, either.

How Miami Turned It Around

First of all, let's be clear: the turnaround happened in part because Miami started *worse* than they should have been. They were expected to win thirty to thirty-five games, but the first half of the season implied a twenty-two-win season, well below projections. Some of that poor start was getting unlucky—even Coach Erik Spoelstra said so, highlighting that they lost a lot of close games (going 7-20 in games decided by under ten points). Never underestimate the element of luck in basketball. It is basically that part of what happened that you can't explain, the part that the coaches can't explain, and the part that the players can't explain. Sometimes the ball bounces the wrong way and sometimes it bounces the right way. You can't use the "bad luck" excuse too much during a season, but everyone in the league knows that it's relevant.

They got some bad luck, but there were things about that poor start that were predictable, too. **The team prepared all offseason for their star power forward Chris Bosh to be back**, but training camp opened with him failing the physical and being ruled out. Coaches plan for months in the summer how to build their team on the assumption that certain major players will be there, and Bosh would have been one of those.

That unexpected event affected veteran point guard Goran Dragić, as he then had to become the Man, the player who would lead the team on offense. He had never done so in his career, but the only other possible candidate on the roster was Dion Waiters, a former top-five pick in the draft who liked to shoot a lot but had already shot himself off two other teams in four years. In the first half of the season, Dragić shot 3 percent under his career average, and Waiters, who did continue to shoot a lot, shot 5 percent under his already poor career average.

On top of Bosh's absence, Miami was bringing a lot of new players together, some of whom got hurt at the start of the season, **delaying the time it took to learn each other's playing styles.** Waiters, Luke Babbitt, Rodney McGruder, and Wayne Ellington were all wings who were brand-new to the team, with both Waiters and Ellington missing a good amount of time early. James Johnson and Derrick Williams were additions at Bosh's power forward position, making six new players who would end up in the rotation, a rotation typically being about nine players.

Other guards or wings potentially in the rotation were Justise Winslow and Josh Richardson, both second-year players returning to the team with expectations of improvement, plus Tyler Johnson, who was a year ahead of them in experience. Hassan Whiteside was the other returning player, the team's twenty-seven-year-old starting center who had been Miami's reclamation project a couple years earlier, after he was out of the league for two years. Whether it was him or the staff there (it's always some of both), that reclamation project had turned into giving him a four-year $98 million contract prior to this crazy season.

From the outside you can't know, but these players were dogs, guys who wouldn't back down if threatened. They were hungry, so when the injuries hit, someone else was stepping in and was willing to work, and the player who was hurt wanted to be back out there.

All of these players, with the exception of Ellington and James Johnson, started off the 2017 season shooting worse than they had in their respective pasts. They had no chemistry and didn't play as a team. They were taking the wrong shots because they didn't know each other.

Coach Spoelstra, or "Coach Spo," as the players called him, had the credentials for players to listen to him, having won titles with LeBron, D-Wade, and Bosh. But it wasn't just the credentials that had players listening—he had the voice, the words spoken in his unique way to show that he genuinely cared about his guys. He would criticize the best players and the worst players for *doing* something wrong but not criticize their character by doing it. He would sometimes warn his players in advance of a group film session that he was going to call them out in that session, so that it was fair and the session could be a learning moment, not a surprise confrontation. By speaking the way he did, he gave the players security and confidence, even if he was calling them out for their actions. By doing that, all the role players felt that they could do a little more. They could be the dogs that they naturally were, wanting to step in and step up.

The clearest point at which they got better was the very middle of the season, after game 41, on January 13. They hit that midseason record of 11-30 on a four-game losing streak and as winners of just two of their last twelve. Beginning with game 42, they won thirteen straight. That period may have been when the *results* clearly changed, but the process changed a little before then, specifically in the rotation. For one thing, Winslow hurt his shoulder and stopped playing at the end of December. At that point, he had the second lowest effective field goal percentage in the entire league. Then, on January 8, their thirty-ninth game of that awful first half season, Williams played more than ten minutes in a game for the last time all year. At that point, he had the fourteenth lowest effective field goal percentage in the league. So two players were both playing poorly and suddenly out of the rotation—one due to injury, the second due to general discontent with his play.

There may have been a little bit of addition by subtraction in their cases, but the full story is not that simple, because it wasn't only they who were shooting badly. Both McGruder and Waiters were in the bottom thirty in shooting in the league, too. Those two kept playing and got substantially better afterward. Would that have happened to Winslow and Williams if they had lasted to the second half of the season? The answer to that question is probably not knowable. They didn't play.

Those who did play got better, with the exceptions of James Johnson, Tyler Johnson, and Whiteside's backup, Willie Reed, who didn't play a lot. Not only did everyone else get better, but most got better than they ever had been, especially shooting the ball, the most important of the Four Factors.

Dragić, Waiters, Babbitt, and Ellington easily exceeded their career averages in shooting from three, all shooting over 40 percent from there in the second half of the year. Shooting 40 percent is hard to do, let me be clear. Only thirty-four players with at least one hundred attempts did that over that second half of the season, and four of them were with the Heat. **There was a teamwide emphasis to shoot the three over the midrange, and that only built the players' confidence to shoot them. That confidence built on itself as they won games.** Only Tyler Johnson and Richardson didn't outshoot their career numbers in the second half of the year.

It's not as though players took shots that were more open, **but they felt more open.** The three-point shots that guys took were essentially the same quality as in the first half of the year, as measured by the tracking data. They just got better at making them. The confidence that they had built is not in the shot quality numbers from the tracking data.

But behind the scenes, they practiced smart, too. Prepractice was for the young guys and the players who weren't playing regularly, and they got both the normal experience of running through plays and the training in mental readiness for when they had to play meaningful

minutes. In practice, the staff taught players specific situations where they had to read the defense, not just run the play. They practiced pick-and-roll as 2-on-2, 3-on-3, and even 2-on-3 where the coaches would randomly change their defensive scheme. That training created realistic situations where the players had to read specific defenses.

One player, though, also taught *himself* something important. This was the year that Houston's James Harden made a mockery of the NBA's rules on fouling jump shooters, drawing an insane number of calls by taking a shot whenever there was any kind of contact. **In Miami, Dragić saw that and decided to do the same, particularly when he went over the screen in pick-and-roll. If there was a defender holding his jersey, he would just go up for a shot to draw a foul.** It worked beautifully. In the first half of the season, he drew one shooting foul on three-point shots, but in the second half, he drew twenty-three of them, second only to Harden. That number was worth probably two wins on its own. **When defenders started giving up all those free throws on threes, they had to stop grabbing Dragić, which opened up his overall pick-and-roll effectiveness. He could go where he wanted, make the passes, or take the shot depending on what the rest of the defense was giving him, because his man was left behind, not able to hang on.** His numbers running pick-and-roll in the second half of the season were among the best in the league. His midrange shot became an actual weapon, too, as he made 48 percent in the second half **by taking the ones that made sense, the ones that Coach Spo wanted him to take.** It probably also improved his three-point percentage, because some of those fouls would have been misses.

But even if you account for Dragić's newfound ability to draw fouls on three-point shots along with the team's emphasis on taking threes over midrange, strategy wasn't the biggest reason that Miami got better at shooting threes. It wasn't a redistribution of shots to good career shooters either. Babbitt and Ellington were good shooters historically, but it was Dragić and Waiters who took the majority of the team's shots, and they were two of the team's worst shooters from deep at the beginning of the year. No, their ability to *make* the three-point shot was the biggest factor. **And that came from the confidence and security that the coaching staff provided.**

Then there is Whiteside, their big man. One of his career-long flaws up to this point was that he was a bad free throw shooter. He shot 60 percent from the line for his career prior to the year and shot 55 percent in the first half of the year. There is no shot quality for free throws, because there is no defense for them, but his percentage shot up to 71 percent in the second half of the year! Whether that was confidence or practice or improving form or what—**it was confidence. Whiteside had always shot free throws well in practice, and the staff didn't try to change his shooting stroke. They just gave him confidence, trying to make him as comfortable in games as he was in practice.**[3]

Defensively, this team had a lot of different pick-and-roll coverages. With Whiteside, the team would be in "drop" coverage, where Whiteside would linger back in the paint, allowing him to protect the rim as was his natural instinct. When he was out, the coverage would change, but that kind of shifting of coverages took time for the players to get used to, maybe not the full first half of the season but definitely some of it. Ellington, in particular, was on his seventh team in eight years in the NBA and had seen a lot but had almost no continuity. He was injured to start the year and, so **when he jumped back into the rotation, he struggled on defense.** The team's defense was at its worst with him on the floor. But **as the staff gave him more reps and more confidence that they needed him**, the numbers got dramatically better. In the second half of the season, the team's defense was at its best with him on the floor. The three-point shots that were going in over him at 48 percent in the first half of the season—they went in only at 32 percent in the second half.

For a team that so dramatically improved, there are a lot of numerical *symptoms* of what they did right but only a couple of numerical *causes*—forgoing the midrange shot for threes and Dragić's ability to draw fouls on threes. **The other causes that are reflected in a different font in this summary** came from Dragić himself. Dragić emphasized Coach Spo's ability to infuse confidence in players by being genuine and communicating that each player was needed. Dragić said that the players were dogs who weren't going to back down from a fight. He also said that there was no chemistry among all of the new players at first and that they didn't know how best to work together then. Dragić told me about studying Harden and about what was emphasized in practice. It was his insider eyes and ears that filled in the gaps between the numbers.

That's what should happen. Combining eyes, ears, and numbers won't close all the gaps; there are still holes in this Miami story that could be filled. And there could be some bias in trying to attribute success in just one special case to things that other teams would say that they do, whether drills or the way of speaking to players. But Dragić's eyes and ears started going beyond the numbers to confidence, motivation, and better familiarity among team members. Those are things that the numbers couldn't capture.

But maybe they could. In my work, I couldn't measure what was in every player's head at all times, but there were specific times in my career when I knew that players weren't motivated. In those situations, how big was the effect on their play? I couldn't know the speed at which teammates got to know each other better, but I could do some things to evaluate how well different skill sets fit together. I couldn't know from the outside how player development was progressing, but I could affect player development from the inside on my own team.

I wanted to know those things better and deeper than the Four Factors could go. I had enough opportunity to try it in my years in the NBA. I didn't answer everything, but I did build up a deeper understanding of the psychological elements of the game. That knowledge is part of what will appear in some of the later chapters in this book.

I thank Goran Dragić for being the inside source on the Miami story. I have not usually tried to get the insight of a player or coach to contribute to the analytical stories that I work on. Part of it is an element of pride, being able to use my unique skills to extract information from the numbers that a lot of people can't see. Another part of it is an acknowledgement that most analytical work is from the outside. Even when you're an insider for one team, you're still an outsider for other teams if you're studying them, whether on film or in numbers. But this Miami Heat team was a special case, one where I wanted to make clear that, as much as analytics can tell a story, the players—who had to live through the speeches, the criticism, the film sessions, and more criticism—fill in the gaps, both here and on the court, to create the story we see and love in the game.

6

Everyone Hates Defense

A lot of people have tried to make defense glamorous. *Defense wins championships. Defense is toughness.*

But defense is not glamorous.

A lot of people just don't like defense. They like points. Low-scoring games bore them. The most fun that people have watching defense is when defenders are getting their ankles broken by an offensive player.

Defense just doesn't have a lot of heroes. Heroics are not its nature. In a world where people love heroes, defense has culprits. It succeeds when a lot of people incrementally do their job over the course of a shot clock. Only occasionally is there a singular event by a singular player that creates a defensive hero. And people usually overreact to that singular event, forgetting the other 99 percent of contributions, positive and negative.

Defense is often just forgotten. Some star scorers forget to play it. Some analysts forget to analyze it, especially when data about it is limited. Some media forget to cover it, even calling it bad offense in a game where teams are missing a lot of shots.

Some defense is in the spotlight, for example, when a defender is isolated on the ball. But a lot of defense is played in the shadows, doing its job far away from the ball. A light shines on it primarily when, out of nowhere, the player with the ball sees a defender in the shadows failing, then gets the ball to the man the defender was supposed to be watching. The job of an off-the-ball defender gets small credit and a lot of blame, yet it's what defenders are doing most of the time.

To defend is to protect against attackers trying to do damage. Preventing damage, preventing the bad guys from tallying up points is measuring nothingness over and over again. Measuring the lack of something is not as sexy as measuring the accumulation of something else.

Defense forces offense to change plans. Defense makes things inconvenient. Defense is what you're not supposed to play in the All-Star Game because you could hurt someone. Defense is consciously trying to make someone else miserable.

Everyone hates defense.

Okay, maybe not everyone hates defense. *Hate* is a strong word. But it got your attention.

What should get your attention is that the Golden State Warriors' defense won them as many games and titles as, if not more than, their offense, finishing in the top five as often as the offense did. Eighteen of the past twenty NBA champions have been in the top ten on defense; only fifteen of the past twenty have been in the top ten on offense. (*"A lot of people have tried to make defense glamorous"*—that's what I'm doing now.)

The Warriors were innovative with their defense. They switched a lot, something that most teams were hesitant to do before they did it. What that means for all the defensive haters is that when there was a screen set on a defender, which made it difficult for that defender to stay with their man, the defender on the screener would just switch onto that man.

The benefit of "switching" like this is that there isn't much time where an offensive player isn't being guarded. The switch happens quickly, and that time when a defender has to catch up to his man after being screened goes away. "Recovery" defense, where a player has to catch up to their responsibility, is a major disadvantage to the defense, allowing much higher rates of scoring. Without a lot of time in "recovery," it's easier for players to just stay in front of their respective man and cause the shot clock to tick away while the offense struggles to create an advantage. The Warriors' defense was regularly one of the best in forcing opposing offenses to go under eight seconds on the shot clock.

The downside of this switching defense is that it puts a lot of responsibility on players to guard their own man without a lot of help. But the Warriors had several good defenders who could do that (Klay

Thompson, Draymond Green, and Andre Iguodala, among others), and they continued to try to acquire the mobile defenders who could stay with even quick offensive players. For their players who were prone to mismatches—either due to quickness (like their big men) or size (like Steph Curry)—there would be help, but those players also drilled as individual defenders because help was not what the team wanted to do.

The Warriors have won four championships playing this way. That switching defense has been good not only in the regular season but in the playoffs, too.

The Milwaukee Bucks have won one championship since 2015, having one of the best defenses over that time, both in the regular season and in the playoffs. But they chose to play defense in an entirely different way. The Bucks didn't switch much, and they tried to always have a tall big man in the game (often Brook Lopez), whose main responsibility was to help at the rim. Whereas the Warriors chose to give less help, the Bucks chose to have their center "drop" back into the paint to provide *a lot of help* when offensive players drove in there to try to get layups.[1] Big men like Lopez allow a lot lower percentage at the rim than, say, the Warriors' more versatile but smaller defenders (see graph 1). But if Lopez's man drifted to the perimeter and got the ball out there, the recovery was long and they gave up good shots.

Because of their different styles, the Warriors allowed among the fewest three-point shots since 2015 whereas the Bucks allowed the most. But the Bucks made up for this disadvantage by allowing the absolute lowest field goal percentage at the rim. The Warriors didn't give the space for threes, but the Bucks did. The Warriors limited the number of shots at the rim because they always stayed matched up, but the Bucks severely limited how well offenses converted at the rim.

If you hate defense, you're probably wondering why the Warriors' style or the Bucks' style matters. Why should you care about details on the side of the ball you hate?

It matters because style of defense illustrates the balance between individuality and team. In the Warriors' defense, they emphasize the ability to defend *individually*. In the Bucks defense, they emphasize a specific kind of *team* defense. Different, but both require communication and coordination. Different, but both require some element of the

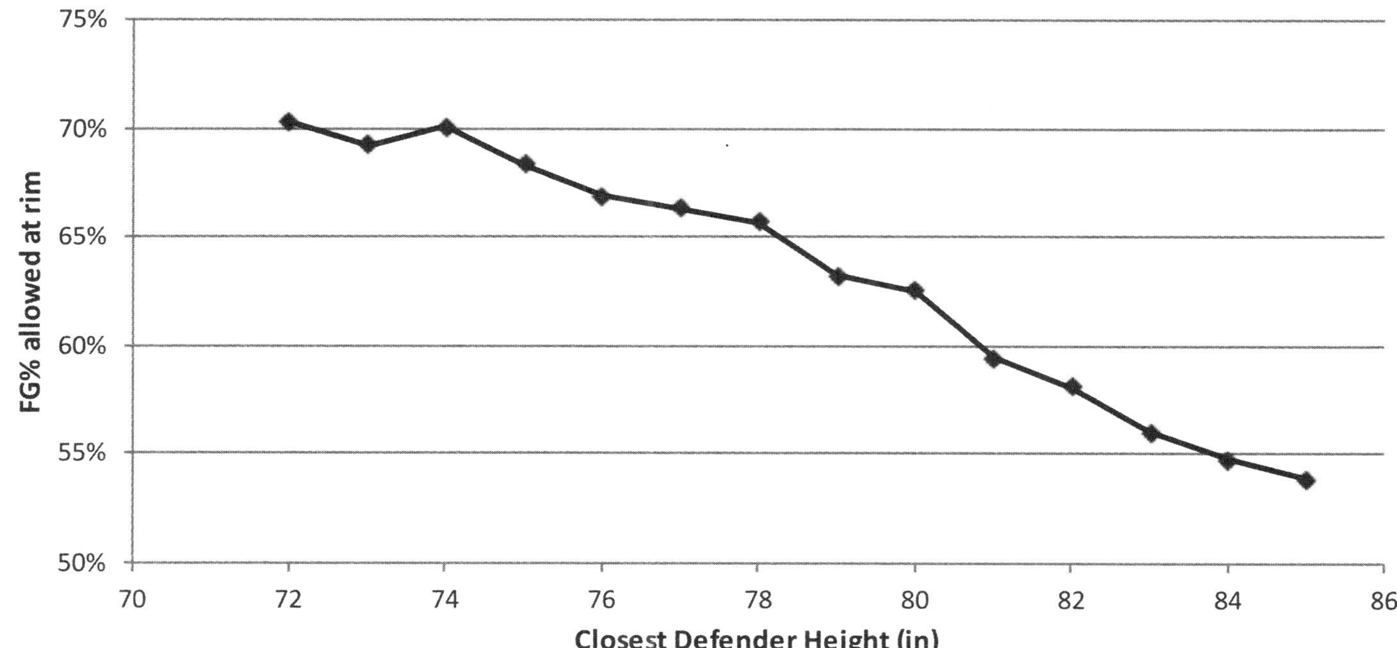

Graph 1. Field goal percentage (FG%) allowed at the rim based on the height of the closest defender.

other, Milwaukee still needing individual defense and Golden State still having to help and recover. It's just that the balance is different.

The style contrast between the two also matters, because different amounts of individualism and help change how credit and blame are divided.

Imagine this common pick-and-roll: Milwaukee's guard Jrue Holiday is screened and chases his man over that screen, following him into the paint where Lopez is waiting. If the offensive player makes a floater, that is on both Holiday and Lopez. If the player misses the floater, that is credit not only to both of them but also to the other teammates who didn't allow an easy pass to their open man. (*"A lot of defense is played in the shadows"*—those other teammates were the guys in the shadows.)

On the score, Holiday allowed *his* man to score and Lopez allowed *his* help responsibility to score. On the stop, neither Holiday nor Lopez nor *any other* Milwaukee Bucks defender allowed their man to score. On defense, it takes everyone to succeed.

Now imagine a similar situation but for Golden State: In a pick-and-roll, the Warriors' big man Draymond Green switches onto Steph Curry's man, and that offensive player then pauses before trying to drive to the rim. If he makes it, Green has a lot of responsibility because the Warriors don't provide a lot of help. If he misses it, Green still gets a lot of responsibility, even though his teammates share in it by not overhelping. The Warriors' general preference not to help focuses more of the blame and more of the credit on Green because it was more one-on-one.

Defense is complicated like that. Who gets credit and who gets blame for what happens depends on the way defenses are structured. I heard that a lot in the league. "How can you evaluate defense if you don't know the responsibilities?" But fundamentally, you can see structure in how much help they give, how much recovery they give up, and how they handle matchup advantages. Maybe defenders messed it up—they "overhelped" or they "didn't go where they were supposed to," but the data shows what the defenders actually did.

If you know from the inside what a defense was supposed to do, you can base credit and blame on that. If you don't know because you're an outsider—and every team is an outsider relative to every other team—

you have to base credit and blame on the help, the recovery, and the matchups that *actually* happened. That's defense—there is an insider version of how it happened and there's an outsider version.

There is a theoretical idea of how defense is *supposed* to work, and then there is reality. Defense is messy communication and coordination, because an offense is trying to confuse a defense. If you don't plan on the messiness, your defense will fail. By creating confusion and messiness along with mismatches and spacing, a half-court offense creates advantages (see BOX).

Confusion can cause a defender to be caught in between—not helping and not covering their man. Maybe they then give up a backdoor layup. Maybe the player they were supposed to help was just then made to look bad. (*"In a world where people love heroes, defense has culprits"*—who the culprit is can be hard to identify, but we see that *someone* screwed up.)

But that's actually *half-court* defense. Transition defense is a whole other thing.

If transition defenders get back and matched up, and the offense stops trying to push in transition, everyone forgets that they even played transition defense. (*"Defense is often just forgotten."*)

People notice transition defense mainly when it's bad. When several of the players get back, but the offense still finds its way to the rim, people notice. One person will say that it was this guy's fault for not protecting the rim, and another will say it's that guy's fault for not picking up the ball earlier. Another person will point out that the one defender who didn't get back at all was arguing with the ref over a missed call.

Because coaches mostly notice transition defense when it's bad, it's easy for them to think that their transition defense is generally bad. Even teams with good overall transition defense can *feel* that theirs is bad, because they—and the stat keepers themselves—don't even record when it's good.

Some transition defense is blatantly about culprits or heroes, and those tend to get noticed. When an offensive player throws a bad pass right into the hands of a defender who then proceeds down the court for a wide-open layup, that offensive player was "terrible" and "what was he thinking?" It was a one-on-none fast break, and the *defensive* culprit was the guy who made the *offensive* mistake. Yeah, that bad offensive play should get recorded as a bad defensive play, even though no attempt at defense was even made.[2]

But that situation also can create a hero. If that wide-open layup after the steal turns into a highlight chase-down blocked shot at the rim, there's your hero. Tayshaun Prince made a legendary one. LeBron James has done it over and over. Anthony Edwards is now doing it. The chase-down block turned a sure two points for the opponent into zero. (*"Only occasionally is there a singular event by a singular player that creates a defensive hero."*)

And that's what we count on defense. Giving credit on defense means adding up the zeroes, the stops, the empty possessions, and dividing each of those possessions based on what happened. Giving *blame* on defense means adding up the points and dividing each of them based on what happened.

That's how you add up the nothingness of defense into a player metric.

BOX: How Offense Creates Advantages

With the tracking technology that exists now, it is possible to estimate the number of points that a team will score in this possession based on where the ball is, where all offensive and defensive players are, as well as where they're going and the shot clock. This measure is called the expected possession value, or EPV for short.

The EPV is often pretty constant when a half-court offense is standing around. But there are three general ways that an offense can create a weakness in the defense, which means an increase in EPV.

1. Spacing or screening. In the former, the offensive players are spread apart, forcing the defenders to be far apart so that it's tougher to help and recover. In the latter, the offensive players get close to each other and screen defenders, keeping them from staying with their man, again making it more difficult to help and recover.
2. Establishing mismatches. Having a good offensive player against a bad defensive player usually requires help. Or it could be a size mismatch. A big offensive player typically has a significant

advantage on a small one near the basket. A small offensive player typically has a quickness advantage on a big one on the perimeter.

3. Creating confusion. Defenses drill against generic offensive situations over and over again. When they then see those situations in a game, they're usually pretty effective. But when they see something different or a twist in the generic situation, they have to communicate and coordinate at the last minute, which they're often not great at.

Offensive coaches talk about each of these in attacking a defense. They'll say, "We want good spacing. Get to your spots!" Or they'll say, "If we can get it to our best player, they'll have to double-team and get into rotation." And sometimes they'll say, "We want their defense to have to make a difficult decision."

There have probably been a million plays drawn up in the history of basketball, but what they try to do are these three things. Sometimes, a play will do just one of these. Sometimes, a play will have options for all three of them.

7

Cutting the Cake

The situation is this: You and your brother just got a small cake to divide between the two of you. How do you ensure that each person gets a fair share?

Those of you who had brothers—as well as parents who tried to keep you and your brother from beating each other up—have probably heard the solution: One person cuts, and the other person picks which piece they want. This gives the cutter incentive to cut it evenly so that the two pieces look essentially the same.

In the end, neither person can reasonably want what the other person got. Each person would be willing to either cut or decide. Even among competitive brothers who would evaluate the cut with a microscope, this truly limits battles over cake.

Let's change the situation a little now. One brother—let's say that is you—bought the eggs, the flour, the chocolate, and the milk, then did the mixing, baked it, and cooled it. Your brother played video games on his phone. Now how do you cut the cake?

The problem with this scenario is that "fair" is not what it was in the first case when we only knew it was two brothers. In that case, we wanted to treat the brothers equally. Now we know that you did a lot of work and that your brother has addictive tendencies. Why would you divide the cake evenly when one person clearly did more?

And that is the basketball problem.

"A win is a win."

"When the team wins, we all win."

"Winning solves all problems."

None of these clichés addresses the issue that players want not only to win but also to be the hero. The hero is the guy who gets the biggest part of that Win Cake.

How do we divide the cake for the hero versus the other guys? Despite there being a whole science to studying the normal cake-cutting problem, there isn't much work into how to cut the cake when you have people who do different amounts to make the cake. But there is one concept from the existing science that is useful—that cutting the cake means trying to keep everyone from being *envious*. A good solution for cake or basketball has no one wanting anything that the others have.

That is mostly a fantasy in basketball, where everyone is fighting for credit. To some degree, though, contract negotiations are often about comparing statistics that illustrate some level of work put in. But the ingredients of rebounds, points, assists, and so forth may be part of the Win Cake, yet don't make up the full recipe. Mixing the ingredients in the right parts and knowing what the missing ingredients are in the stats make a difference. That is what a lot of player value metrics in basketball attempt to do, using slightly different recipes and coming up with somewhat different-flavored cakes, if I can now stick a fork in that analogy.

There are *a lot* of different player metrics in basketball. Simple versions have been around since at least the 1960s. They have abbreviations like TENDEX, PER, PRATE, PC, LEBRON, RAPTOR, DARKO, BPM, APM, RPM, RAPM, and PIPM. By the way—the PM that is so common at the end of these abbreviations comes from the phrase "plus-minus," which, if it had been listed as "minus-plus," would have changed a few of those abbreviations into more pronounceable, though perhaps less acceptable, names.

With so many different player metrics, there are at least a few criteria that should be considered in evaluating them:

1. *They should add up to something real.* If it's a metric about wins, all the teammates should have win totals that add up close to the team total. If it's about points, all teammates should have point totals that add up close to the team's net point differential.

Ideally, if it's broken down into offense and defense, it adds to both the offensive and defensive points or net points. If a player metric doesn't have an actual meaning specifically relating to winning or points, or if it doesn't add up to close to the team level, it's not acceptable and should really be avoided.

2. *They should be relatively predictable.* A player metric that says a player is great one year but terrible the next is possible but should be rare for players who get a lot of minutes. Not that it should be the same every year; being the same every year is one version of predictable but not the best, because we know young players get better and old players get worse, for example. When you are looking to make a trade, you also want to be able to reasonably predict how a player will do in your system. That evaluation may start with some average level of performance but also ideally has elements that you can predict based on age and role.
3. *They should tell you why.* If you're sitting in a room with a coach or GM and you say that a player is good because a metric says so, you're going to lose that battle. You need to explain what that metric is seeing about the player—their offense or their defense, their passing or their shooting, their interior intimidation, and so forth—because the guys watching the game have their reasons. If you have a player metric that satisfies the first criterion but doesn't explain why, it has some use behind the scenes but less use in actually making decisions.
4. *Ideally, player value metrics are very granular*, meaning that you can calculate a metric not just over a season but also over a game, over a quarter, over all pick-and-roll plays, over each lineup within the last ten games, over all plays run with Chris Paul on the court, and so on—and it still meets the above three criteria. This consistency allows it to be used for diagnosing basketball problems. If you're having a problem stopping transition against teams with fast point guards, for example, the team metrics can tell you some of the story, but having a metric that tells you whether it is your point guard or your big men having the problem narrows things down. Further, if you have a

granular metric, you should be able to make predictions better, using all the context around the exact situation you're trying to predict.

5. *Ideally, player value metrics are able to expand with new data available.* New data about matchups, about screens, about play types, about spacing, about where their arms are, and so on is all available, and people talk about all of it. If Trae Young gets hidden to guard mainly the weakest offensive players and Marcus Smart guards the best players, that ends up a relevant talking point in comparing them, so it should ideally be in a player metric. If that data is not easily added to player metrics, the data is less valuable and the metric itself is less valuable.

Some existing player value metrics can be eliminated pretty quickly with the first criterion.[1] TENDEX, PER, PC (points created), and PRATE (a metric that already seems to have gone extinct) all generate numbers that don't add up to anything. They don't satisfy the first condition above, which is the one that must be satisfied. They don't add up to anything, and there is no way to really check their validity because the constraints of basketball that are built into points and wins are absent.

Most other current metrics of player performance are difficult to eliminate, but they can be criticized for inconsistently meeting various standards.

"Pure" adjusted plus-minus methods—APM, RAPM—look at lineups over the course of a season (or multiple seasons) and try to distinguish the value of individual players by measuring how lineup performance changes when players go in and out. For example, when a lineup with Russell Westbrook is worth +3 points per 48 minutes and that same lineup with Cameron Payne is worth −3 points per 48 minutes, it may be inferred that Westbrook is +6 points per 48 minutes better than Payne. These methods look for such differences across *all* lineups and help determine the best fit to the differences observed. These methods generally add up to team values, but because the values are unstable without a lot of data (which is why the methods often use three to five years of data), sometimes even this determination is only approximate. These methods also don't do much to explain *why* a player is good or bad. They say that the team played better with that player on the court and the improved performance seems to be associated with that player, but whether the improvement was due to shooting or rebounding or setting picks or going around picks—that isn't clear.[2] They are also not granular. You cannot apply them at even a game level.

The instability element of APM methods has led to various derivatives—Real Plus-Minus (RPM from ESPN), DARKO (from Kostya Medvedovsky), RAPTOR (from FiveThirtyEight.com), and Player Impact Plus-Minus (PIPM, from Jacob Goldstein), for instance. These "informed," or "stabilized," APM methods start by applying APM over a long period (usually many years) so that errors and instabilities are lessened. With those results and player statistics over that same period, methods like linear regression can be used to place average values on things like shooting percentages, rebound rates, assists, and so on. Those values can then be used with statistics over a shorter time span—like a season—and then balanced against a noisy APM result for that season to produce a more stable and predictable result. These methods are the most popular player metrics in use in the NBA as of the writing of this book. They are a little more explainable because they incorporate actual statistics. They are quite a bit more stable than straight APM approaches and can be used for longer-term predictions of performance. They are not, however, generally usable over time frames of less than a game (and sometimes not at that level). There is no informed APM that can be easily sliced for use in clutch situations or in the second quarter when down by fewer than ten points, for example.

If the adjusted plus-minus methods were stabilized by statistical weights to get to RPM or PIPM, there are extreme versions that use only the statistical weights, not balanced against an APM value. Box-score Plus-Minus (BPM) is one of those versions. Various other versions can be developed, but BPM was created as a standard that uses only typical box score stats. Other versions can include stats like blocks on layups and assists for layups, for instance, which are not in a typical box score. These methods are generally pretty good, but Westbrook "broke" a version of this metric in 2017 with his triple-doubles. The method exaggerated the impact of the combination of statistics, making him look so incredibly valuable that the sum of the individuals didn't add up to the total, being off by about 170 points over the season (about 2 points per game). That error was high, not a disqualifier on its own, but the method's supporters acknowledged that it exaggerated Westbrook's value. In particular, some of Westbrook's rebounds were less than valuable—he led the league in defensive rebounds on missed free throws. Some of his assists were due to his simply having handled the ball much of the time. If we ignore this case, this kind of method isn't bad but isn't very granular. Applying regression on a large time scale to get general values of statistics doesn't allow for accurate valuation on much smaller time scales.

A couple of other methods are, in some ways, similar to BPM. One is Win Shares, which is from Basketball-Reference.com and is based on methods in *Basketball on Paper*. Those methods used box score statistics and a couple of formulas on offense and defense. The defensive side of the ball particularly was limited, using just defensive rebounds, steals, blocks, and the team's defensive rating to arrive at an individual defensive efficiency. That method was not consistently predictable from year to year, though it got better when using, for instance, how well the team's defense played with that player in the game only, not how well the team defense played overall, which was the only thing available in 2002 when *Basketball on Paper* was written. As constructed on Basketball-Reference, Win Shares is not as representative of value as the informed adjusted plus-minus methods.

Wins Produced is another box-score-based player metric, based on work from David Berri, an economist. It uses regression approaches with *team* statistics to develop the value of various stats toward winning, then applies them to *individuals*. This is in slight contrast to what the stabilized APM methods do. Whereas stabilized APM methods apply regression methods to long-term player values, Wins Produced applies regression methods to team stats to create player values. It, unfortunately, doesn't generate a split between offensive and defensive Wins Produced, which limits its explainability. Wins Produced does not do much to evaluate individual defense with inputs from data, box score or otherwise. It has also been criticized for seemingly overvaluing rebounds (though the criticism is mostly based on instinct, not analysis, from what I can tell) and for effectively giving no value to shot creation, just shooting percentage. Wins Produced is also highly dependent on the position a player plays, with scaling factors by position that vary widely. The metric has some issues with predictability and adding up, but neither is awful. It is, like many others, not practical on a granular level.

Net Points

In this book, the player metric of choice is called Individual Net Points, or Net Points for short. It meets the above criteria—adding up to the team's total point differential, it is generally predictable from season to season, can be explained, is granular down to the play level, and is expandable with new data.

It follows the basic logic presented in chapter 3, dividing credit and blame for every action in the play-by-play. That division of credit is based on the available data and a concept of minimizing envy—players get what they deserve on a play level. It is looking backward only, explaining what happened. Methods to project it going forward, however, are also available.

This is not to say that Net Points is perfect. No metric is perfect, and no metric will ever be perfect. Every metric is still subject to the context in which it is measured. "Fit" matters—how the skills of teammates mesh. "Chemistry" matters—whether players generally respect each other and the coaching staff. Both of these variables will be brought to greater light in later chapters, but they fundamentally mean that player metrics only have so much portability from one situation to another.

This is also not to say that Net Points is the only metric used in this book. Looking at some of the others can give insight—both on what may be consensus and what are differences that decision-makers can take advantage of. Even if a decision-maker doesn't know which of these metrics is "right" or "best," understanding the range of their values and what other decision-makers seem to value can help in understanding other teams' thinking if not also facilitate deals.

In a lot of cases, the story with one metric is pretty similar to that of other metrics, and as a result, I will often use a "composite metric" in this book. That composite is a simple average of these metrics: DARKO, EPM, LEBRON, Net Points, RAPTOR, and RPM.

Metrics Comparisons

A summary of a broad range of player metrics is in table 4, highlighting where they stand in the factors mentioned above. The table itself is based on details in appendix 1. Here are a few notes to aid in reading the table:

Some of the metrics shown here are older but are included to capture some history. Most of the Linear Weights, for example, are not particularly useful because they don't add up to anything real. As a result, talking about the expandability of these (using tracking data, for example) is a bit inappropriate, since that implies that they're starting from a good place, which they're not.

I put BPM into the informed APM category, though its formula is effectively just adding and subtracting statistics, making it like a Linear Weights method.

There are different levels of acceptance of the various informed APM methods. DARKO, LEBRON, RAPTOR, and EPM are all public and generally respected. There is a reasonable correlation across the different informed APM methods (0.60 to 0.90 or so). DARKO and LEBRON are strongly correlated with each other.

Sometimes, predictability is built explicitly into the metrics. In particular, several of the informed APM methods are built to be predictive (DARKO and LEBRON, especially), trying at every point in a season to project the next game. Others (like Net Points and RAPTOR) are purely looking backward, but prediction methods may be adapted from them by using age, experience, growth curves, injury history, and so forth. As mentioned above, the simplest form of prediction is just assuming constant performance going forward for at least the next year, which is common among NBA decision-makers. This assumption usually fails early and late in players' careers, so explicit projection is better for those periods.

The informed APM methods are explainable to a point. They have a statistical base that gives explainability, but the component that effectively uses plus-minus isn't particularly explainable,

Table 4. Comparison of various player metric types

	Net Points	Pure APM
Add up	Yes	Reasonably
Predictable	Reasonably	So-so
Explainable	Yes	No
Granularity	Play level	Season level
Expandable	Yes	NA
Examples	Can include opponent adjustment or not.	RAPM, DANVAL
Notes	Method of choice for this book, usually with no opponent adjustment. If it includes opponent adjustment, it doesn't add up perfectly, but still better than others.	Requires a lot of data to be stabilized, over which time a player's value can change. Best used over multiple years for an average value.

Note: See appendix 1 for details on this table. NA = not applicable.

except as "the team played better with them on." Because some are focused on looking forward, it can be a little tricky to look backward to explain, for example, why the team lost five straight games. All metrics have some degree of challenge of explainability if you get into the details enough, but so does the human eye.

The first three metrics aim to add up to the total point differential of a team, at least roughly. Win Shares and Wins Produced aim to add up roughly to a win total. For the predictive metrics (much of informed APM), they aim to be predictive, and thus adding up to what happened in the past isn't quite what they're doing, but they should be at least somewhat close to the total point differential.

All of the metrics that at least roughly add up (in other words, *not* the Linear Weights metrics) can be presented in the form of a positive or a negative number per 48 minutes (or per 100 team possessions). In

Informed APM	Linear Weights	Win Shares	Wins Produced
Reasonably	Not to anything	Reasonably	Reasonably
Reasonably	Reasonably	So-so	Reasonably
Somewhat	Yes	Yes	Yes
Maybe game level	Maybe game level	Season level	Maybe game level
Yes	Yes	Not easily	NA
PIPM, BPM, EPM, DARKO, RAPTOR (FiveThirtyEight), LEBRON, RPM (ESPN)	PER, TENDEX, Points Created		
Most commonly accepted methods in use. Varying use of on/off data from using a lot to none at all.	Not adding up to anything real makes these difficult to work with.	Doesn't account for shot creation. Uses mostly box score data, not simply expandable.	It doesn't claim to need new data.

leagues where games are shorter, it may be more convenient to express things per 40 minutes or per 32 minutes, whatever the typical length of a game. But per 48 minutes of the NBA is useful because teams usually have about 100 possessions in a 48-minute game. I will tend to use per 48 minutes and per 100 possessions interchangeably.

The distribution of player values across players in the NBA with 800-plus minutes is shown in table 5. The typical values are from below −2 for the players at the fringe of staying in the league to over +4 for the superstars. If players are getting at least 800 minutes, they tend to be better players, with the exceptions being young players who are developing, veterans who may have characteristics that keep getting them time (good locker room guys, someone the coach trusts for a certain role), or the team is tanking.

If you include the players with under 800 minutes, the biggest category becomes the replacement-level players. The percentage of all minutes being played by those low-minute guys has increased from about

Table 5. Approximate distribution of players by how good they are, among those playing 800 minutes

Label (range of value)	Percentage of players	Examples
Superstars (+4 and up)	4%	LeBron, Giannis, Shaq, Jokić, Embiid, Curry, Durant, Harden, Chris Paul
Really good (+2 to +4)	10%	Khris Middleton, Donovan Mitchell, Jimmy Butler, KAT, Trae Young
Good (+0.7 to +2)	17%	De'Aaron Fox, Klay Thompson, Danilo Gallinari, Marcus Smart, Al Horford, Jaylen Brown
Average (−0.7 to +0.7)	28%	Evan Fournier, Nikola Vučević, Ian Mahinmi, Caris Levert, Daniel Gafford, Maxi Kleber, Bojan Bogdanović
Below average (−2 to −0.7)	24%	Aaron Holiday, Luke Ridnour, Ish Smith, Taurean Prince, Landry Shamet, Frank Kaminsky, Khem Birch
Replacement (below −2)	16%	Lonnie Walker IV, Cam Reddish, Kris Dunn, Austin Rivers, Bismack Biyombo, many young players developing

8–10 percent in the 1980s and '90s to about 15 percent in the era of two-way contracts. Abbreviated seasons with more back-to-backs are when you see the most minutes being played by those low-minute players.

The Need for Player Metrics

I used to think that a player metric was not a valuable tool, frankly. In general, I thought that a single number could not fully reflect the different dimensions of a player. I also thought that a player's value was dependent on how they were used and the context they played in.

I was not wrong about those reasons—they are definitely true. But as I found while working for teams, those elements are just as much reasons for *having* a metric as for not having one. I'll get back to that.

The biggest reason to have a player metric is that so much of the *language* of basketball (and other sports) is around the quality of a player.

As much as fans talk about player value, so do scouts, management, and coaches. How they talk about it is different, that is for sure, but they all talk about it. Whereas fans often discuss the best players, I really had only one conversation in fifteen years with basketball people about identifying the *best* players in the NBA. Most of our conversations were about separating the good players from the average, the average from the bad, or the "fungible" from the "nonfungible." As the people responsible for building a winning team, we didn't care whether LeBron was better than Durant, because having either would have been a blessing. Having neither was our most likely outcome, so we had to build around players who were not in that category.

Various GMs and I did go through an exercise of trying to characterize who was "nonfungible"—players you can build everything around—or identifying overall classes of players. Was Ray Allen "nonfungible"? Steve Smith? Allen Iverson? Al Jefferson? After his rookie year, was Ben Simmons tradeable or a bedrock of the franchise? What about the walking band-aids, Joel Embiid and Zion Williamson? Going through this exercise was useful in working with different people to just understand how they viewed players as a whole and how I could translate from words to numbers and back again. Maybe the conversations weren't about "nonfungible" players but about "rotation" players or "rotation players on a good team" or "starters on a good team" or "what players played terribly last night" or "why Rashard is so bad in pick-and-roll." The language that people use for describing player value was diverse, but it filled so many conversations, no matter what we were talking about or who were talking to.

We could have been talking to the trainer about how to get a player healthy, and language around player quality would show up: "How long until they are back to 100 percent?" "How is his lateral movement? He can't guard if he can't move laterally."

Or we could have been talking with coaches about players: "He just doesn't want to put the work in. He could be a lot better player if we could get him in for extra reps." "He's a selfish player. He doesn't make his teammates better."

Even talking about tactics in preparing for an opponent, the topic of how good a player is comes up. "He's better when he rolls than pops, so we want to take that away first." "We have to force James Harden to his right hand because he can't make passes as well going that way."

The Importance of Granularity

It is in that coaching context that a player value metric at one time seemed less useful to me. If it changes with different tactics or different contexts, how useful can a player metric be? That's where granularity can help.

If a metric is granular enough, it can be used to measure the value of players with different tactics or contexts. It can help identify what play types a player does best in. You can infer the impact of tactics and context somewhat from the team numbers, and that is the place to start. But coaches watch the film, and they can see on every play when a player did the right things. Even if a metric can't do that now, it is what it should strive for—to measure the contribution of a player on every play, positive or negative.

In this way, the granular part of player metrics is more important than some of the other criteria. Having even an imperfect metric to evaluate players over various slices of data can provide a way to communicate on a much broader spectrum of problems. Here are a few examples of where the granularity of Net Points provides a nice picture of players and teams.

Assists and Turnovers

The assist-to-turnover stat has been criticized by a lot of people. I won't go through all of the reasons and I won't kill the stat, because it is simple and simplicity has value in metrics. But one of the things it is generally trying to capture is a player's passing ability, and for that, Net Points and its granularity can do a little better by looking at how many a player generates through *potential* assists and just their bad pass turnovers, not turnovers from travels or illegal screens or just losing the ball. Net Points captures the value of the pass made in terms of how good it made the shot.

Table 6 shows the top ten players in the NBA in 2023 based on that metric. The first two columns show the total net points and the net points per 100 team possessions a player was on the floor for, the table being sorted by the latter column. So Jokić added +2.2 net points per 100 team possessions that he was on the floor. Tyrese Haliburton was a distant second at +1.5. That +2.2 value for Jokić worked out to be about 25 percent of his overall offensive net point rate of +8.3, shown in the far right column. To put that value of +2.2 net points per 100 team possessions into perspective, only forty players amassed that from *all* of their offensive contributions in 2023, not just passing. If we look at the more traditional assist-to-turnover statistic, Jokić's 2.7 is solid, roughly in the middle of this top ten, but it isn't capturing what the eyes—and Net Points—see in better detail.

So what is that detail that Net Points sees? A big part of it is shot quality, as shown in table 7. The shot quality on Jokić's potential assists was 61.7 percent, higher than anyone else in the top ten in overall passing, tenth overall across all players in the NBA.[5] That means the players who shot off potential Jokić assists would, on average, have an effective field goal percentage of 61.7. It turns out that they shot a little bit under that, 59.1 percent, as shown in the last column.

Trae Young had a higher shot quality on his passes, 62.4 percent, and he actually had more potential assists per game than Jokić at 16.2. But what brought him down and kept him off the list was that he committed 2.7 bad pass turnovers per game, while Jokić had just 1.6.

The point is not to get into great detail of what makes great passers. I could go a lot deeper to understand where players made passes from, whether there were multiple defenders around them, how open the shooters were, and so on. Rather, the point is to showcase the value of having a player metric that is granular enough to capture this kind of information. Even if you are skeptical of particular values for some reason, the power of a granular metric to just approach this kind of depth is valuable.

Table 6. Net points from potential assists and bad pass turnovers in 2023

Player	Total	Per 100 team possessions	Ast/TOV	Overall offensive net points per 100 team possessions
Nikola Jokić	+98	+2.2	2.7	+8.3
Tyrese Haliburton	+54	+1.5	4.1	+4.8
James Harden	+49	+1.3	3.2	+3.5
Kyle Anderson	+41	+1.1	3.3	+0.6
LaMelo Ball	+27	+1.1	2.4	+1.4
Domantas Sabonis	+57	+1.1	2.5	+3.5
Luka Dončić	+46	+1.1	2.2	+6.6
Darius Garland	+47	+1.1	2.7	+1.5
Ja Morant	+38	+1.0	2.4	+2.4
Pascal Siakam	+49	+1.0	2.4	+2.8

Note: Ast/TOV = assist-to-turnover.

Table 7. Detailed stats of top passers

	Assists per game		Bad pass	Shot	Actual
Player	Potential	Actual	TOV/G	Quality	eFG%
Nikola Jokić	15.4	9.8	1.6	61.7%	59.1%
Tyrese Haliburton	18.6	10.4	1.2	58.4%	56.4%
James Harden	15.6	10.7	1.6	59.4%	59.7%
Kyle Anderson	7.2	4.9	0.6	58.9%	57.3%
LaMelo Ball	13.0	8.4	1.4	60.2%	55.7%
Domantas Sabonis	12.2	7.3	0.7	56.8%	58.8%
Luka Dončić	14.2	8.0	1.7	61.5%	61.9%
Darius Garland	12.1	7.8	1.1	59.8%	57.4%
Ja Morant	13.5	8.1	1.5	61.4%	58.7%
Pascal Siakam	10.5	5.8	0.8	58.5%	55.4%

Note: TOV/G = turnovers per game; eFG% = effective field goal percentage.

Shot Blocks

Another example: the value of shot blockers. Jaren Jackson Jr. led the NBA in 2023 with 3.0 blocks per game. Nic Claxton, Brook Lopez, Walker Kessler, and Myles Turner rounded out the top five. But people have said that it's not just about blocking the shot but about keeping it in play and getting the defensive rebound. Table 8 ranks shot blockers based on net points per 100 team possessions, including how dangerous the shots were, their ability to keep high the chances of getting a defensive rebound, and their credit or blame for getting the defensive board or allowing an offensive board.

Table 8. Net points from blocks and ensuing rebounds by player

Player	Total	Per 100 team possessions	Blocks per game
Bismack Biyombo	+47	+2.34	1.44
Walker Kessler	+90	+1.91	2.34
Jaren Jackson Jr.	+88	+1.80	3.00
Brook Lopez	+99	+1.80	2.47
Nic Claxton	+92	+1.56	2.49
Myles Turner	+73	+1.55	2.26
Drew Eubanks	+57	+1.49	1.32
Christian Koloko	+26	+1.47	0.98
Mark Williams	+26	+1.38	1.05
Luke Kornet	+25	+1.37	0.67

Though Jackson led the league in blocks per game, he was third in terms of value of his blocks on a per-minute or per-team-possession basis. Bismack Biyombo didn't play nearly the same number of minutes, but his impact through shot blocks was the highest while on the court.

As with the previous example, this makes it easy to dig in deeper to find out why. I could pull out the shot quality on these shots or the chance of giving up an offensive rebound, for example. I could change this and look at shot contests, not just shot blocks. The number of ways to evaluate specific player skills is enormous. Net Points captures not just the blocked shots but also the shot contests and just general help on shooters.[4]

Table 9. Top offensive players in 2023 by net points and play types, per 48 minutes

Player	Pick/roll BH	Iso	Post up	Handoffs
Nikola Jokić	0.2	0.8	1.4	0.1
Luka Dončić	3.1	2.1	0.6	0.4
Damian Lillard	2.8	1.8	0.1	0.6
Kevin Durant	1.1	1.6	0.3	0.4
Jimmy Butler	1.5	1.2	0.1	0.0
Joel Embiid	−0.1	1.3	0.6	0.1
Stephen Curry	2.2	0.5	0.2	0.6
Lauri Markkanen	0.1	0.3	0.0	0.2
Tyrese Haliburton	1.7	0.4	0.0	0.2
Zion Williamson	0.6	1.4	0.5	−0.1
Donovan Mitchell	2.1	1.1	0.0	0.4
Kawhi Leonard	1.6	1.1	0.3	0.1
Giannis Antetokounmpo	1.0	0.5	−0.5	−0.2
Kristaps Porziņģis	0.0	0.6	0.9	0.1
Shai Gilgeous-Alexander	0.8	1.5	0.2	0.2

Note: Pick/roll BH = pick-and-roll ball handler; Iso = isolations; Putback = second-chance opportunity after a missed shot.

Value by Play Type

A granular player metric is also productive in evaluating players on a play-type basis, which can suggest best how to use players. Net Points does require a bit of work to do some of the detailed cake cutting, work that gets more accurate with more detailed data. Using fairly basic division of credit rules, table 9 shows a breakdown across some of the best players in the NBA in 2023.

This shows that guys like Luka Dončić, Damian Lillard, Steph Curry, and Donovan Mitchell earned a lot of their value as pick-and-roll ball handlers. Some of the same players also contributed a lot through their isos. Nikola Jokić tallied most of his offensive value in "miscellaneous" plays; these are plays not identified, plays where the player is a screener in pick-and-roll or handoffs, or plays where they may

Misc.	Transition	Putback	Overall
4.2	0.6	1.1	8.3
0.0	0.1	0.2	6.6
0.5	0.2	0.3	6.3
1.6	0.7	0.3	6.0
0.6	1.4	0.8	5.6
2.3	0.6	0.7	5.5
−0.2	1.4	0.7	5.3
2.5	0.9	1.1	5.0
0.8	1.3	0.4	4.8
0.3	0.9	1.2	4.8
−0.4	1.2	0.2	4.7
−0.2	1.4	0.1	4.5
−0.3	2.4	1.1	4.1
1.5	0.2	0.6	3.9
−0.9	1.7	0.3	3.9

be out of the action (typically they would be spacing).[5] Giannis got a sizable amount of his offensive value from transition or putbacks, which means that preparing for his half-court work is probably not as important as those other things, something that is pretty unusual across the league.

Net Points Value of Team Four Factors

Net Points allows not only additional breakdown of players but also helps at the team level. The Four Factors for teams, for example, are incredibly useful on their own, but the granularity of Net Points means that the *value* of each of those factors can be determined.

From chapter 5, the Miami Heat got a lot better in the second half of the 2017 season through their shooting as a team. Net Points paints the same picture in table 10, but it adds that it was the majority of the improvement, being worth 8.0 net points per 100 possessions.

Table 10. Improvement in Four Factors net points for Miami Heat offense, per 100 possessions, in the 2016–17 season

Factor	First half	Second half	Difference
Shots	+5.8	+13.8	+8.0
Turnovers	−15.2	−15.7	−0.5
Rebounds	−1.4	−0.4	+1.0
Free throws	+5.1	+7.3	+2.2

But it's easy to expand the picture, too, to include transition, putback situations, and where shots came from, as shown in table 11. The numbers in each of these tables aren't as intuitive as those in chapter 5 (see BOX), but they analytically measure that the improvement from the three-point line (+4.3 net points per 100) was bigger than any other half-court improvement and bigger than any improvement in transition (+0.7) or on putbacks (−0.1).

Table 11. Detailed breakdown of Four Factors net points for Miami Heat offense, per 100 possessions, in the 2016–17 season

Factor	First half	Second half	Difference
Half-court	−9.2	+0.7	+9.9
Paint shots	+1.6	+4.6	+3.0
Long twos	−2.6	−2.6	0.0
Threes	+2.3	+6.5	+4.3
Turnovers	−13.3	−13.7	−0.4
Rebounds	−1.2	0.0	+1.2
Free throws	+4.0	+5.9	+1.9
Transition	+1.9	+2.6	+0.7
Putbacks	+1.7	+1.6	−0.1

Welcome to the Argument

Despite all the rules above for how to evaluate player metrics, a lot of people are still going to base their evaluations on what they feel in their gut. Having Lonnie Walker or Austin Rivers in the replacement-level category in table 5 surely offends someone, and they'll want to throw out all the metrics. Having Trae Young higher than a lot of the guys below him is going to upset many of those people who didn't put him in the All-Star Game in 2023.

But gut feelings change. Before analytics, Carmelo Anthony was viewed as one of the top players in the NBA. With analytics having more of a voice, the broader perception of Melo came down.

My point within this section is to evaluate the various methods side by side when there are discrepancies. How you manage different viewpoints is vital to the success of an organization—you don't want to just throw some out all of the time or accept another all of the time. So it's appropriate to do that even with these metrics.

Before I get to one of these, I will point out that a lot of the informed APM metrics and Net Points are pretty well correlated with each other across historical players (see appendix 1), more so on offense than on defense. All of the methods value LeBron James and Steph Curry as among the best players historically, but they do differ on how much each one contributed.

Absolute Magnitude of LeBron and Steph on Offense

Just looking at metrics since the 2014 season—because that's the earliest that all of the metrics exist—we see some that value Steph's offense quite a bit more than LeBron's, as shown in table 12.

Table 12. LeBron James's and Steph Curry's average offensive value metrics since 2014

Method	LeBron	Steph
DARKO	+5.7	+5.6
EPM	+5.4	+7.2
LEBRON	+4.5	+5.4
Net Points	+4.8	+6.7
RAPTOR	+5.6	+8.4
RPM	+5.8	+8.5
Average	+5.3	+6.9

Only DARKO sees LeBron's offensive value as greater than Steph's in that period. Given that during this period, LeBron was on the downslope and Steph was at his peak, it makes some sense that LeBron wouldn't be above Steph.

That's just one piece of evidence. It's not conclusive, and there aren't going to be a lot of hard conclusions, but building up some evidence is what can help people resolve conflicts.

In this period, LeBron's team offensive rating when he was on the floor was 114.3, whereas Curry's was 118.0, another piece of evidence.

This kind of difference can be due to having better offensive teammates. So table 13 shows the teammates that each spent a good amount of time within this span, along with their All-Star appearances, both overall and as teammates. So Kyrie Irving had seven All-Star appearances in this period but just two while playing with LeBron.

LeBron's teammates made a total of thirty-two All-Star appearances in this time span, whereas Steph's made only eighteen. As teammates, these numbers drop to twelve for LeBron and twelve for Steph. So if there were better players with Steph, it wasn't dramatic, at least by All-Star appearances. That's a piece of evidence that the offensive difference between LeBron and Steph wasn't strongly associated with teammate quality.

The pure RAPM methods mentioned above can actually be run over much longer periods to get an overall average value, which some people consider the best metric. But it just doesn't get at what changes from season to season, so it has less use on a regular basis. The site nbashotcharts.com publishes five-year versions of a pure RAPM. Given that this is a comparison over ten years, we'll just look at each of the two five-year periods. In the first five years, both star players were incredibly valuable, LeBron adding 6.1 points on offense and Steph adding 6.7. In the second five years, LeBron added 3.4 points versus Steph's 4.2. In both periods, this method—if you place any faith in it (which some people do)—says Steph's offense was better.

Again, this is just another piece of evidence, one that suggests that Steph's offense was about 0.7 points better than LeBron's. That difference is smaller than the average difference across the metrics. The overall offensive values are also smaller in these five-year RAPM num-

Table 13. Teammates of LeBron James and Steph Curry since 2014 with at least 2,000 minutes together

LeBron teammates		Steph teammates	
All-Stars (total, with LeBron)	Not All-Stars	All-Stars (total, with Steph)	Not All-Stars
Kevin Love (3, 2)	Tristan Thompson	Draymond Green (4, 4)	Andre Iguodala
Kyrie Irving (7, 2)	J.R. Smith	Klay Thompson (4, 4)	Harrison Barnes
Anthony Davis (8, 2)	Kyle Kuzma	Kevin Durant (9, 3)	Kevon Looney
Russell Westbrook (6, 0)	Kentavious Caldwell-Pope	Andrew Wiggins (1, 1)	Shaun Livingston
Dwyane Wade (4, 4)	Iman Shumpert		Andrew Bogut
Chris Bosh (3, 1)	Matthew Dellavedova		Jordan Poole
Kyle Korver (1, 1)	Richard Jefferson		Marreese Speights
	Dennis Schröder		Damion Lee
	Timofey Mozgov		David Lee
	JaVale McGee		
	Channing Frye		
	Avery Bradley		
	Austin Reaves		
	Mario Chalmers		
	Alex Caruso		
	Rajon Rondo		

Note: In parentheses are the number of All-Star Games each player played in, then how many of those All-Star appearances occurred with LeBron or Steph.

bers than from the other metrics, where each player was considered about a point better.

Based on these pieces of evidence, Steph's offense in this time frame looks better than LeBron's. They are not the strongest pieces of evidence, but hopefully they illustrate some of the ways to track down discrepancies.

Dillon Brooks

When Dillon Brooks signed a four-year $80 million contract in the summer of 2023, there was considerable fan debate about whether he was worth a contract that size. Among the metrics, there also was a lot of discrepancy, but especially with Net Points.

Table 14 shows the different metrics over the course of Brooks's time in the league.[6] During his time as a rookie, the metrics deviated from each other by about one point. But beginning in 2020, that difference grew tremendously. A couple metrics viewed Brooks as one of the best players in the league in 2022, whereas Net Points still saw him as below average. Net Points never had Brooks as even an average player, whereas the other metrics had him at least average from the 2021 season to 2023.

Table 14. Dillon Brooks's player metrics through time across six different methods

Season	Min.	DARKO	EPM	LEBRON	Net Points	RAPTOR	RPM
2018	2,350	−2.3	−1.1	−2.3	−2.0	−1.0	−1.1
2020	2,112	−1.3	+0.4	−1.3	−2.2	−1.0	+0.8
2021	1,997	+0.4	+1.1	+0.1	−3.6	+0.2	+1.4
2022	885	+0.7	+3.6	+0.4	−1.3	+4.1	+1.1
2023	2,214	−0.1	+0.3	−0.1	−2.0	−0.1	+1.6

Most of the difference is on defense, where Net Points had him really bad in both 2021 and 2022 and the other methods had him above average (see table 15). Even in 2023, his Net Points improved to almost average, but the other methods bumped him up to +1.6 on defense. As an independent piece of evidence, Brooks made second-team All-Defense in

2023 for the first time. The increase in all stats, including net points, fits this pattern. The fact that his defensive efficiency is a good +1.6 by other metrics also fits. The Net Points number of −0.4 does not usually translate into a bid for All-Defense.

The other models are showing that the Grizzlies were at least a little better defensively with Brooks on the floor. In 2023 they were about 3 points per 100 team possessions better with him on. In 2022 they were about 2 points better. In 2021 they were essentially the same with him on versus off. These aren't huge differences, and Net Points actually uses that data in its methodology, too.

So why? What is Net Points seeing or not seeing?

Part of it is a matchup adjustment, which is not included in this version of Net Points but is implicitly included in the other metrics. Table 16 shows that he has guarded better-than-average players throughout his career, generally in the top twenty-five of toughest matchup strengths across the league. If you add those numbers into his defense, the gaps for 2021 through 2023 become −2.1, −2.7, and −1.4, respectively—still pretty big discrepancies.

Because Net Points is explainable, there is an accounting that you can use to break it down the same way that the Miami Heat were above. As a defensive stopper, Brooks is comparable to a variety of other players in the league during that particular three-year span where the differences are largest. Among them are guys like Matisse Thybulle, Marcus Smart, OG Anunoby, Jaden McDaniels, Jrue Holiday, Quentin Grimes, Herb Jones, P.J. Tucker, Mikal Bridges, Dorian Finney-Smith, Royce O'Neale, Isaac Okoro, and Gary Payton II. For example, table 17 is the Four Factors accounting between Brooks and Smart,[7] capturing how well each did in the half-court, transition, and putbacks, as well as various subcategories.

This shows that Smart was good in the half-court, worth +1.2 net points, whereas Brooks was bad at −0.8. It's not a single category in the half-court, though forcing turnovers, limiting free throws, and giving up threes are the biggest gaps. Smart was also better in transition.

Smart was just one player in this group, and it's reasonable to say that he was the best, having won Defensive Player of the Year in 2022. Rather than comparing Brooks with him alone, the collective compar-

Table 15. Net Points versus other metrics on Dillon Brooks's value

	On offense			On defense			Total		
Season	Net Points	Others	Difference	Net Points	Others	Difference	Net Points	Others	Difference
2018	−1.3	−1.6	+0.3	−0.7	+0.1	−0.8	−2.3	+0.6	−2.9
2020	−1.5	−0.6	−1.0	−0.7	+0.1	−0.8	−1.3	+1.0	−2.3
2021	−1.1	+0.1	−1.2	−2.5	+0.5	**−3.0**	+0.1	+1.6	−1.5
2022	+0.9	+1.1	−0.1	−2.2	+0.9	**−3.1**	+0.4	+1.9	−1.5
2023	−1.5	−1.3	−0.2	−0.4	+1.6	**−2.1**	−0.1	+1.1	−1.1

Note: Numbers in bold indicate large differences on defense.

Table 16. Average matchup strength for Dillon Brooks by season

Season	Matchup strength	Rank
2018	+0.4	25
2020	+0.6	24
2021	+0.9	5
2022	+0.4	59
2023	+0.7	21

Note: A higher matchup strength indicates better offensive players Brooks guarded.

Table 17. Four Factors accounting breakdown of Dillon Brooks versus Marcus Smart on defense, per 100 possessions

Factor	Brooks	Smart	Difference
Half-court	−0.8	+1.2	+2.0
Paint shots	−0.8	−0.7	+0.1
Long twos	+0.4	+0.3	−0.1
Threes	−1.0	−0.6	+0.4
Turnovers	+2.7	+3.5	+0.8
Rebounds	−0.3	−0.2	+0.1
Free throws	−1.8	−1.2	+0.6
Transition	−0.5	0.0	+0.5
Putbacks	−0.2	−0.1	+0.1
Total	−1.5	+1.2	+2.7

ison group can give a better idea of where Net Points sees Brooks as worse (see table 18).

Table 18. Four Factors accounting breakdown of Dillon Brooks versus various top defenders, per 100 possessions

Factor	Brooks	Others	Difference
Half-court	−0.8	+0.3	+1.1
Paint shots	−0.8	−0.8	0.0
Long twos	+0.4	+0.4	0.0
Threes	−1.0	−0.8	+0.2
Turnovers	+2.7	+2.9	+0.2
Rebounds	−0.3	−0.2	+0.1
Free throws	−1.8	−1.2	+0.6
Transition	−0.5	−0.2	+0.3
Putbacks	−0.2	−0.2	0.0
Total	−1.5	−0.2	+1.3

Note: "Others" were Matisse Thybulle, Marcus Smart, OG Anunoby, Jaden McDaniels, Jrue Holiday, Quentin Grimes, Herb Jones, P.J. Tucker, Mikal Bridges, Dorian Finney-Smith, Royce O'Neale, Isaac Okoro, and Gary Payton II.

The biggest difference between Brooks and the others over these three years is easily on free throws. Brooks averaged 2.4 shooting fouls per 48 minutes, second most among the comparison group, behind just Jaden McDaniels, who had the most rim protection responsibility among them, which meant that he also had the bulk of his fouls on layups. Brooks led this group in fouls on long two-point shots, the fouls that cause coaches to cringe the most. He was second to Payton in terms of nonshooting fouls and nonshooting fouls in the bonus, so he was putting players on the foul line for free points late in quarters. Overall, Brooks was fouling opposing players about 1.7 times more per 48 minutes than the comparison group, which is a lot of potential points. That's independent of the Net Points methodology.

The best defenders on this list, as based on whether they made All-Defense teams, are Smart, Thybulle, Holiday, Anunoby, and Bridges.[8] If this group is who Brooks wants to be compared with, those guys not only are fouling less but are forcing more turnovers, are better at limiting three-pointers, and are better in transition defense. These All-Defense players were overall about +1.9 net points per 48 minutes on defense, even including their non-All-Defense years in there.

The foul difference could be documented independently of net points, but what about the turnovers and three-point shots?

Among the All-Defensive players, Brooks had fewer steals over the last three years than all of them but Bridges. Brooks averaged 1.7 steals per 48 minutes, whereas the other All-Defensive guys averaged a collective 2.2. Half a steal per 48 minutes is not small.

To look at three-point shots, there are a couple of ways to imperfectly assess a defensive player's responsibility. One is by who they matched up against. Another is by when they were the closest defender. Again, neither is perfect evidence, but they are evidence. Over the last three years, Brooks allowed 36.6 percent to his matchup on threes, whereas the All-Defensive players allowed 35.5 percent. Brooks allowed just 33.8 percent in 2023, his best year, versus 41.0 percent in 2022 and 37.4 percent in 2021. Over the last three years, Brooks allowed 38.9 percent to three-point shooters when he was the closest defender, whereas the All-Defensive players allowed 35.7 percent.

That difference is huge! But three-point shooting defense has been considered lucky or unlucky, not particularly affected by defense. It can't be completely lucky because, if it were, there wouldn't be reason for players to contest them. There is some responsibility, though perhaps Net Points overemphasizes that.

One way of interpreting the combination of data above is that Memphis fully intended for Brooks to be the sacrificial lamb on defense, guarding the best perimeter players and giving up a lot, with his teammates making sure that other players didn't blow up. It's a reasonable strategy, and Memphis did finish in the top six in defense each of the last three years. Brooks could be said to have "done his job" within the defense, allowing more threes, committing fouls, and not forcing a lot of turnovers.

All of this is evidence. The evidence tells a story, one that may not convict but that must be told when a staff is faced with conflicting inputs. Hearing the evidence opens people's eyes to the details that we can evaluate, in this case about how players can affect defense. It may not resolve the issue completely, but it helps for the next conflict and the one after that.

So was Brooks worth his $80 million contract? By the time this book hits virtual shelves, there will be a little bit of further evidence. Maybe there will still be a conflict among the various numbers and amid the eyes, too, but hopefully the conversation can be productive.

The Jones Brothers: Typical Variations

The six different metrics I've used in this chapter tend to be reasonably consistent, but there is an average variation of about 1.0 point across them for the same player.

As an example, the second column of table 19 shows the specific metric values for Tre Jones for the six metrics in 2023. As you can see, the total range of estimates is about 3.0 points, but the standard deviation is 1.1. That's essentially the average variation mentioned above.

Table 19. Overall player value for Tre Jones and Tyus Jones, 2023

Method	Tre (younger)	Tyus (older)
DARKO	0.1	+0.1
EPM	−0.2	−0.2
LEBRON	+0.1	+0.1
Net Points	−0.9	+0.6
RAPTOR	+1.8	0.0
RPM	+2.1	−2.7
Average	+0.5	−0.4

As a second example, the third column of table 19 shows the metric values for Tre Jones's older brother, Tyus, also in 2023. The standard deviation across those metrics is also 1.1.

In 2023 Tre the younger played for San Antonio, one of the worst teams in the league and the league's worst defense. Tyus the older played for Memphis, one of the best teams in the league and the league's third best defense. As a whole, the metrics had Tre the younger at +0.5 and Tyus the older at −0.4 for the year, so the better player was on the worse team, but the difference was still only about 1. That isn't a lot to act on.

But what if you were in Memphis and you used the RPM metric? You're looking at a huge difference of +4.8 points between your guy and his younger brother in San Antonio. Do you try to trade Tyus the older for Tre the younger?[9]

That is the challenge with using one metric alone. You can do it, and you may gain a huge amount if you're right. But the NBA is conservative in making deals, and it has a lot of time to do so, meaning that decision-makers dig deeper. They're not going to look at only one metric or only one year. They're going to look into the why and the how around the metrics. That's why I built Net Points to be explainable. And ultimately that is how the metrics should be used, not to end an argument but to facilitate everyone's ability to know what factors go into and matter in the argument.

People want player metrics to be the simple and accurate answer to the question, "Is this guy better than that guy?" The metrics do simplify the process, but it still isn't simple. The simplest test is the eye test, but that has its own inaccuracies.

In essence, different metrics provide different summaries of the data on players; the best ones use pretty good logic to make their summaries. But both the data going into them and the logic they use can be different. They hopefully point decision-makers in a good direction—to other metrics or to specific eye tests—to help narrow the uncertainty.

Cutting the cake still requires a lot of work to dissect what the various metrics are saying about the truth. Fundamentally, there aren't a lot of simple ways to gain an advantage, even when you have good metrics. I had to dig into the metrics over and over again on examples like these during my journey through the NBA . . . which I talk about again in the next chapter.

BOX: Communication Stats and Analytical Stats

Jargon—the language of a profession—is one of the great barriers people must surmount to join that profession. I don't particularly like using it, but sometimes it is just so easy to use that I wish more people knew some of the words.

This is a common problem in our constant-communication world inside or outside of sports. The tech space brings new words and slang all the time, from "BRB" and "LOL" to "microblogging" and "artificial intelligence." But people are quick to learn, in part because there are good reasons to use those words often, especially if people are on their phones like most are.

In basketball, it's similar. The analytical stats of effective field goal percentage, turnover percentage, offensive rebounding percentage, and free throw rate are used so much within the basketball community that they're pretty well understood. But the basketball community is so much smaller than the world of basketball fans that such language can seem like jargon. The media are hesitant to talk about effective field goal percentage because they don't want to lose even one fan by saying, "effective field goal percentage is just field goal percentage adjusted for the extra point on threes."

So, to the media, the Four Factors are "analytical stats," not "communication stats." To a lot of people within basketball operations, the Four Factors are both analytical stats and communication stats.

This duality is in contrast to basic field goal percentage, which is a pure communication stat—one that everyone understands, whether a participant in the game or a fan of the game. Field goal percentage isn't really an analytical stat, because it can be so misleading. In some cases, it can give the same message, though—the Miami Heat had a higher basic field goal percentage in the second half of 2017 than in the first half (47 percent versus 44 percent), for example. In those cases, it's not bad to appeal to the broader audience. If a smart-ass asks whether the effective field goal percentage also showed a decline, you hopefully did the analysis using analytical stats, so you know the answer.

The distinction between communication stats and analytical stats is vague at times, but being conscious of it is really helpful. Being able to communicate analytical concepts to those within the basketball community is the only way to get them accepted. This is a pretty obvious statement: I generally work with analytical stats to do analysis and with communication stats to do the communication. Thus communication is imperfect, but that is the nature of almost all human communication. The benefit of more broad acceptance will eventually override the imperfection and even educate people to the more analytical language.

8

The Journey, Part 2

After all the summer league schmoozing was done in mid-July of 2004, I went to work on technical things—databases, calculations, division of credit algorithms, catching up on play-by-play data, looking into college data. I worked full days and into the nights, usually taking a break in the afternoon to get some exercise.

One afternoon in August, as I prepared to go out, I got the call that I had been waiting for. It was from Wally Walker, a co-owner of the Seattle SuperSonics. He was offering me an opportunity to consult with the team. The pay was—well, it didn't matter because I wanted my foot in the door. I had money saved to buy food; I had friends to live with; the money the Sonics would offer was a bonus. I immediately accepted, called my family, then went out to get a workout in before celebrating with my roommate that night.

I was in the NBA . . . almost.

Fate and signs and all that stuff—I had never believed in them. I wanted to make my own success, and by late September 2004 as I prepared to go to Seattle, I could say that I had done it. If there had been signs indicating that it wasn't going to happen, I didn't notice them. I still had to push to sell myself and the things that I could do. Fate wasn't going to work without my help.

And so fate or luck or Murphy's Law kicked my ass two days before I was supposed to go to Seattle for the start of my first training camp. All those databases and algorithms I had been working on came crashing down when both my laptop and the backup hard drive I was using got jolted with some sort of electric shock, rendering both useless. Two days before?!? Two days? I cursed, I may have punched a wall, but at least I didn't throw a chair before I got calm and figured out next steps. I bought a new computer and a new backup drive, and I took both of the old ones to a computer restoration specialist who made a nice bit of money by retrieving most of what I had lost.

I was on an adrenaline rush after solving that problem when I got on the plane to Seattle. I could avoid the haymaker of a crashed computer, and I knew more than anyone about what I was doing. I was going to solve all the basketball problems that awaited me.

In general, everyone is happy on the opening day of training camp. There are no win-loss records, everyone has hope, the media love you, there is food everywhere, and the carpets are clean. So when I got my key card and walked into the Furtado Center practice facility on my first day as a paid basketball analyst, the optimism was universal. I was introduced to the whole front office and the scouts that were there; then we went to the upstairs seating to observe the practice floor. I gave my quick sales pitch on what I did to each of the several new people I met. With Wally, Rich Cho, and scout Yvan Kelly, though, I could start getting to know them and learn more about how they thought I could help. Most of that discussion was around personnel—understanding the value of players in the league and in the draft. Rich showed me their still-primitive database, built by Microsoft engineers in their free time simply because they were fans of the team.

Among all the conversations I had that day, one statement struck me as the strangest. It came from Wally: "Feel free to talk to everyone here, but don't talk to the coaches. They won't know what to do with your work."

I listened and looked around to generally avoid the coaches. But then lunch began, and though I picked an empty table away from the coaches, a couple of the late-arriving coaches came and sat down next to me. I looked around for Wally, but he was nowhere to be seen.

"What you said about turnovers—that they're really important—that's exactly what I believe. There're five players, two hoops, at least twenty lines on the court, but there's only one ball. You gotta take care of it!" That was assistant coach Dean Demopoulos. We got along right away, talking about not just turnovers but three-point shooting, incentivizing players, endgame strategy, and longtime Temple coach John Chaney. We talked for half an hour. My god, I was talking not just basketball analytics but basketball! I had an ally on the coaching staff.

I had realistic expectations going into Seattle that first year—knowing that the Sonics were picked to win about thirty games and be second-to-last in the West[1]—but my first day gave me so much reason to believe that this could go really well. And it didn't end with the first day. In camp we had several players that my analysis said were better than advertised. Ray Allen was a good player. Rashard Lewis looked to be good. Antonio Daniels was dramatically underrated, as was Danny Fortson. Reggie Evans was a great offensive rebounder to go along with Fortson. We had more three-point shooters than most teams at that time, too, with Allen, Lewis, and Vladimir Radmanović. I wasn't a fan of Flip Murray, but he got hurt in the preseason, which seemed like a stroke of luck to me. Our rookie Nick Collison had some good college numbers, so maybe he could help a little. We didn't have a great center between Jerome James and Vitaly Potapenko, but maybe we could turn James into someone who could protect the rim.

I *felt* good about our guys. I felt good that I could really help, if just to better identify good players and use stats to give everyone a good dashboard for where we were as a team, tackling the real problems and maintaining our performance on the things that were already working. I could provide stock-market-like graphs on a daily, weekly, or season-long time frame to illustrate team and player trends. I could do it across the league to help with trades and free agency. I saw a bold future.

And then the season began with a thirty-point loss to a Clippers team that was picked to be worse than we were. As I said, I felt good about our guys, and I wasn't going to let a big loss in game one of an eighty-two-game season let people down. I knew right then that the best thing I could do was not break down the game but break down *history*. How many good teams had lost a game by 25 or more points early in the season? I did a quick study and found that about a third of the teams that had lost by 25 to 35 points in the first five games of the season ended the year with at least a 0.500 record, including several teams that won more than 50 games. I put together an email explaining this to the front-office personnel that I was communicating with. It was more psychological than analytical, but I was thanked for it. It made them feel a little better going forward.

What made them feel even better was that we won our next game by 21. Then we beat a really good San Antonio team by 19. Then we beat Denver by 20. As of Saturday, November 20, 2004, we were sitting at 9-1, the best team in the NBA. We were taking and making the most threes in the league. We led the league in offensive rebounding percentage. It was a formula I loved. Coincidentally or not, I even met my future wife that Saturday.[2] I was on top of the world.

I knew the success couldn't last forever, and I was working long days to prepare for that time when I'd be asked, "What's going wrong?" I was watching our games and sending out reports of where we stood in terms of the "new stats," which showed our offense was good and our defense was average. I would break it down into the Four Factors and player valuations, sometimes over the last ten games, sometimes over the season. But we were winning, so there was no crisis. We didn't lose even two in a row until January.

That gave me time to build good fast databases so that I could answer questions when they would inevitably come up. I especially had to build out one on the play-by-play level, something that I had never had access to before. At that level, I could get more information than was in traditional box scores. I could see transition and which players were good at it. I could see which shots were leading to offensive rebounds—layups or jumpers. I could see how much of offense came directly off offensive rebounds, something that we were particularly good at. I could build at least some estimates of who matched up on who to try to capture some of our defensive issues. I could use that to look at how often there were blocked shots or steals by defenders who didn't appear to be matched up, looking for ways to capture help defense.

At the All-Star break in February, we were the third best team in the West and the fourth best team in the league. My reports on how we did in each game and our trends for the season were generally meeting management's needs. I would send them new information from my exploration of the play-by-play data to give an idea of longer-term progress I was making.

I wasn't communicating with the coaches really. They were busy. They heard a little bit from me when management would pass on information based on the reports that I sent, but because we were so good, it wasn't a lot. I didn't hear anything back from management about what the coaches thought, so I had plenty of space to build and innovate.

We finally lost three in a row in early March, but two of those losses were decided by one score, and the other was to the best team in the league, the Phoenix Suns, led by Steve Nash and Mike D'Antoni, shooting quick and shooting almost as many threes as we did but at a higher percentage. There wasn't much concern at that phase.

The concern began in early April, a couple of weeks before the playoffs. Maybe it was because we had secured a spot in the playoffs and thus got lackadaisical. Maybe it was because Antonio Daniels missed a few games with a sore knee. Between April 3 and April 13, we lost six straight games, with our defense having its three worst games of the season (other than that Clippers loss in game one). As I started scouting our potential playoff opponents, this slide forced me to consider a lot more teams than I really wanted to, not just the teams probably finishing sixth through eighth but teams even better than that. One of them was our division rival the Denver Nuggets, who had hired George Karl when they were 17-25 but had gone a league-best 30-6 since then, closing to within three games of us in the standings. Not only did I get questions about what was wrong with us during that slide, but I got questions about what Denver had done to turn their season around. Our defense had slipped, our three-point shooting had slipped, and Denver had begun running and attacking the rim with abandon behind Carmelo Anthony and Kenyon Martin. Their offense had gone from twenty-fifth to fifth, and their defense had gone from twelfth to the very best. On defense, they were forcing turnovers and blocking shots at among the highest rates in the league, sacrificing a little with fouls and on the defensive glass. They had been allowing 63 percent at the rim, third worst, but were now allowing 57 percent, fifth best. All of this success started when Karl took over the team, and I was noting it in my memory banks for things that could be changed about a team.

We finished the season 52-30, a good twenty games better than we were forecast to do, winning our division, and entering the playoffs as the third seed. We were going against the sixth-seeded Sacramento Kings in the first round, who went 50-32, only a couple of games behind us. With our late slide, the pundits were focusing on our series as the one ripe for an upset, and frankly, it made me mad. I wanted to crush the Kings. I noted in playoff prep that the Kings' Brad Miller was really struggling on defense and didn't do well against us when we faced him. Maybe even our low-scoring center, Jerome James, could be an option when Miller was on him. I didn't know if anything of mine would make the final playoff preparation, but I did what I could.

We did crush the Kings, winning the series 4–1. We had one bad defensive game, Game 3, but our offense was tremendous. Ray Allen was a weapon that they couldn't deal with, but interestingly, so was Jerome James, especially early in the series. He got deep position and scored easily, frequently making Brad Miller look bad. James had four of his five highest-scoring games of the entire season in that five-game series. He became a free agent that offseason, and he got a big contract offer from New York, presumably because of that series. From the time he signed with New York, he never in his career scored more than 13 points in any single game again, despite *averaging* 17 in the Kings series and with a low of 11.

We faced the second-seeded San Antonio Spurs in the second round. They started Tony Parker at point, Manu Ginóbili and Bruce Bowen at the wing spots, then nominally Tim Duncan at power forward and Rasho Nesterović at center, back when two big men regularly played together. A big thing that came out of my preparation was to let Parker shoot anything outside the paint area, basically beg him to do so. I'm not sure my message got through to the coaches, but I was questioned by the front office about it. I told them about how the Spurs offense just got considerably worse if he was taking shots outside the paint. Statistically, he was bad at those, and he wasn't creating for other guys if he was taking them. So go under every screen and let him catch out there with space to shoot it. In the first two games, Parker scored 29 points and 22 points, getting the bulk of them off either layups or free throws. And they beat us pretty easily. After that, we accomplished more of what the numbers suggested,[3] and we held him to 18 or fewer every game, with just 6 points from layups and free throws. But when you're an underdog, you need to get an advantage early on, not starting in Game 3.

We went into Game 6 in Seattle down three games to two, but we were playing them tough. We led the first quarter and a half by as many as 9 points but went into halftime down by 5. The parade to the foul line for Tim Duncan was starting to hurt us. We were a consciously physical team, but the refs weren't having it in this game. Duncan went to the line eight times in the first half, making every single one of them despite being just a 67 percent shooter for the year. "He shouldn't get there as much, and he shouldn't make as many in the second half," I said out loud to others in our suite.

We played steady for much of the third quarter, then made a run late in the quarter to tie the game. Damien Wilkins missed two straight free throws that would have given us our first lead since the middle of the second quarter. *No problem, we'll be fine*, I thought. Parker missed a long two-point jump shot (*Yes!*). Luke Ridnour missed a fifteen-footer on our end (*cringe*), but Danny Fortson got the board and laid it in, plus the foul! "We've got the lead, but still more to do," I remember how internally excited I was, in contrast to how externally calm I remained . . . until the next possession, that is. Up by 3, we were defending the Spurs. Nazr Mohammed took a shot from the box; Ray Allen swooped in for the defensive rebound, then found Wilkins out in transition. He was ahead of the defense and was going in for a layup that would put us up 5! It looked like Bruce Bowen was trying to take the foul to stop the layup. I was ready to watch Wilkins take two more free throws that I was confident he'd make. But they called it an offensive foul? "What? That can't be right." There was no review system. Refs were only to be argued with and the entire arena was doing so loudly, but the call was not changed. My external calm was gone for about ten seconds. Finally, looking at the scoreboard and realizing that there was a whole quarter to go brought me back to calm.

Our lead was just 1 point entering the fourth quarter. It felt like it should have been at least 3 with that terrible call, if not 4 or 5. The entire fourth quarter had everyone off their seat and on the edge of either depression or exuberance. The lead never got to be more than 4 points for either team, which happens in about 2 percent of all fourth quarters. Three games before, the two teams played the entire fourth quarter with no more than a 3-point lead, which happens in under 1 percent of all fourth quarters.

I kept those stats to myself. When we ended up losing by 2 points and seeing our season end, those stats wouldn't help anyone feel better.

After the buzzer sounded on a 3-point miss by Ray Allen, I remember Wally trying to put a nice spin on our season to other people in the suite but then quickly striding out of there to go to the locker room.

I followed him to the locker room and looked around at that team, my first NBA team. I felt so frustrated at the result but so proud of those guys. I didn't go into the locker room much—it was part of the idea of staying away from the coaches—and I felt essentially helpless at that point. I shook a couple of players' hands and thanked them. I saw Wilkins crying and tried to console him. Missed free throws and offensive fouls can feel like the entire game is on you. I remember telling him that we would be back and that there would be more playoffs.[4] Then I left and milled around the training room, feeling that there was nothing I could do for tomorrow.

After all of the work, all of the analysis, all of the calm cool numbers to try to help my first team win, it took just one emotional game to wear me out entirely. I would have flown to San Antonio for Game 7, but that wasn't happening. Thinking about the past doesn't keep me awake at night; thinking about the future does. So I slept deeply that night.

No one gave me instructions to work on the 2005 draft. I just did it. My role wasn't to scout the players, though I had watched a good amount of college basketball that year. I saw North Carolina win the title that year behind Sean May, Marvin Williams, Raymond Felton, and Rashad

McCants, all of whom were first-round candidates. I had seen every first-round prospect at least a couple times, but almost nothing of all the high school kids (Martell Webster, Andrew Bynum, Gerald Green, for example) and international players (Fran Vázquez, Yaroslav Korolev, Johan Petro). There was debate over who should be the number 1 pick—Andrew Bogut or Marvin Williams—but because it was still a big man's league, Chris Paul wasn't in the conversation.

My first draft model had Paul at the top, but the model was so basic that I wasn't confident in it. The main problem was that I had only a couple years of college data. I had the recent year and the one before it. That's not much to build any kind of projection on, but I could calculate how good the players were, how strong their opposition was, then try to adjust how they'd play based on the better NBA competition. I saw that Paul was really good, but he wasn't in our pick range in the 20s. I only felt confident enough to suggest Brandon Bass as a second-round pick, based on the model and doing a whole bunch of other homework. The model didn't particularly like Deron Williams, and it liked Lawrence Roberts—both cases being ones where my eyes saw something different, so I mostly kept quiet.

That draft was where I really first ran into significant conflict between what I saw and what I could calculate. My mentality, though, was that the calculations would catch up; we just didn't know how to translate what we saw with our eyes into something we could calculate. But I knew that there was more to it. Our eyes were imperfect, too, meaning that it wasn't about catching up to the eyes, it was about *beating* them. I started working on the next year's draft a couple of weeks later, trying to build a database of historic college stats from any sources I could find. I wanted to have a voice the next year.

In those days before my first NBA draft, I was reading and hearing rumors that our head coach, Nate McMillan, was going to leave for Portland. After such a successful year, negotiations were taking place to keep him in Seattle, but those were getting stuck. In the draft room when Nate was present, it was a little bit awkward because those rumors were so loud, but talk among us was so quiet. There was one question asked of Nate about good restaurants in Portland, which he smiled at and answered, but the rest of this business stayed between his agent and our GM.

This rumor came after an announcement that Dwane Casey, Nate's lead assistant, was to be leaving for the Minnesota Timberwolves' head coaching spot. I asked Dean Demopoulos during all of this what he was going to do. He said that it was complicated, because he was close to both Nate and Dwane. Demopoulos wasn't getting consideration for the head job in Seattle, so I was going to lose my main contact within the coaching staff.

Even with such a successful season in Seattle, I could see nearly immediate instability. Even though I had made some headway in talking to the coaches (even having sat in on a couple of coaching meetings), I was going to have to start fresh. We won so much, and with the official announcement in early July that Nate agreed to join Portland, I saw the team breaking up. It wouldn't be the last time.

Summer league in 2005 was in Utah for the Sonics, and I was asked to join the coaching staff for it. Without my main contacts there, though, I felt like an outsider. I wasn't really asked to do anything, which was completely opposite of what I liked to do. As much as I hustled the year before to talk to people and get to know them, I felt like my time was wasted that year. Although I had some good contact with our summer league players, I didn't feel much like part of that team, so I went back to looking for ways to help toward the following season, including building a database of college data and preparing for the players and coaches we would have.

The coaching change was going to have Bob Weiss at the top with a staff to be filled in by people I didn't particularly know. The player change was more what I was concerned with. Antonio Daniels had helped us a lot on both ends of the court, and Jerome James was at least a big presence on defense, something that we needed—but both were gone via free agency. That meant that two defenders had gone away from a team that finished in the bottom five in defense with them. I knew that my stats hadn't reached the new coaches yet when I heard that they thought that offense, not defense, was the problem going into 2005–06. Not having a relationship there, I had to let management feed them the right stats that highlighted defense as the likely challenge going forward. I didn't know these coaches, and I remembered Wally asking me not to get involved with them, so I had to trust them.

I trusted them until we were a week or so into the season and we were 1-4 with the worst defense in the NBA. We were on track to be the worst defense in history, in fact. That forced me to shuffle what I was doing. Instead of continuing to build my college statistics history and providing the game- and season-level monitoring, I sat down to study defense. I could see that we were last in effective field goal percentage, last in defensive rebounding, fourth in forcing turnovers, and twenty-fourth in putting opponents on the line. I could see that we were allowing 73 percent at the rim, easily the worst in the league. I could rue not having Jerome James to protect the rim, but that wouldn't solve anything. I proposed simply emphasizing protecting the rim and going after shot blocks (we were twenty-ninth), which is what George Karl had seemed to change with the Nuggets.

But I also knew that I needed something at the play level to try to capture what coaches were seeing and managing. I had to create some way of tracking our defense that would lend more insight into why we were so bad. I had pulled as much as I could out of box scores and play-by-play data, and most of it left me asking more questions. I wanted deeper answers, core answers.

What I chose to do was basically torture myself by spending three hours every game to chart our defense. Not three hours to watch a game in entirety but three hours focused only on the approximately twenty-four minutes of defense that we played. I developed a tracking scheme that captured play type, who was guarding the shooter, who was helping, which defender may have needed help, and enough other things to blow up a lot of people's brains. We now have computers doing a decent job of capturing most of this, thankfully.

An important concept from the charting was that there were basically three types of defense: straight-up, help, and recovery. In that 2006 season, 47 percent of the Seattle defensive plays that I charted were straight-up, when the offensive player was defended essentially by one player. On those plays, we allowed about 99 points per 100 plays. When there was help without recovery, which was about 39 percent of the time, opponents produced 98 points per 100 plays, a little lower than against straight-up defense. But when there was any kind of recovery—which is when a defender helped and either they or a teammate had to recover back to the ball on a pass—the efficiency allowed was about 120, much worse. That happened the remaining 14 percent of the time.

The challenge with using this information was that, without universal tracking across the league, I didn't know how good we were *relative to other teams*. Were they just much better than us at playing straight-up, keeping opponents' efficiency lower or just not having to help as much? Given that our efficiency wasn't much better with help, were other teams better with their help? These questions would have required another three hours per game per team over at least a few hundred games to get a decent sample. That was already a full-time job, and we weren't hiring interns.

I could, though, identify which of *our* guys were struggling the most with needing help and with recovery. Our starting point guard, Luke Ridnour, definitely needed the most help, about 30 percent more often than any of our other guys. That fit a general narrative about him, but the fact that his usual backup, Flip Murray, was next worse was saying that point guards were generally getting us into help-and-recover mode.

I was sending regular insights that I could find on the defensive side, not just about players but what I could determine about play types. Isos were still popular, and we were okay at those if we didn't need to help, terrible if we had to recover. We were struggling against pick-and-roll, no matter what. But through all of it, I couldn't say why. Was it the players not executing a scheme? Was it bad scheme? If players were not executing, was it because the scheme was too complicated? Was it because they didn't like defense? Was it because they just didn't have the skills? Was it because they didn't like the coach? Whatever it was, we weren't getting better, still the worst in measurable history. And head coach Bob Weiss was fired.

He was replaced by Bob Hill. A coaching change meant that I needed to continue scoring games, looking for signs that we were getting better. In our first nine games with Coach Hill, we were just 2-7 and still struggling on defense. Our tenth game was on January 22, 2006. We were playing the Phoenix Suns, one of the best teams in the league.

Both teams came out on fire, making threes at nearly 50 percent. There wasn't any kind of improvement on defense, which I really wanted, but it was a fun game. At a time when the average score for a team was about 98 points, we finished regulation tied at 126. Then we played two overtimes, with Ray Allen doing just enough to give us a 152–149 victory, which would end up the highest-scoring game in the league for the whole season. I felt confident that we would at least lead *SportsCenter* on ESPN, despite the overall state of our season.

Nope. What happened that night in Los Angeles took the lead spot and held it for about ten minutes. That was the night Kobe Bryant scored 81 points, second most in history, in bringing back his Lakers team from an 18-point deficit against Toronto. The Seattle SuperSonics had their most exciting game of the year, and no one cared because Kobe had the game of a *generation*. His game was amazing, and if you've never seen it, you should; our game was merely good, but his was legendary. A few years later, I would generate the plot in graph 2, showing the timeline for Kobe's game, how his net points increased dramatically through the second half. Most of Kobe's +25 was in an epic second half that began with the Lakers down by 14. He went 18 for 28 in that half, shooting 6 of 11 from beyond the arc and 13 of 14 from the line—for a total of 55 points. At halftime, he had +3 net points, but by the end of the game, he had +25, meaning that by himself, he turned that 14-point deficit into an 8-point positive margin.

That was a fun night overall, even if we didn't get the lead spot on ESPN, and maybe the spark it generated carried through for a little while afterward. We won three of our next five games, but the defensive problems were still pretty obvious. When our offense struggled in the sixth game, it took the fight out of us. I was told to focus on the draft from then on. The defensive charting stopped, which was a dramatic help in terms of time, but I knew it had been at least a good use of time, preparing me for doing more defensive work later on.

The 2006 NBA draft prospects were highlighted at the top by Andrea Bargnani out of Italy, LaMarcus Aldridge from Texas, Adam Morrison from Gonzaga, Tyrus Thomas from LSU, Rudy Gay from UConn, and Brandon Roy out of Washington. Both Gonzaga and Washington were

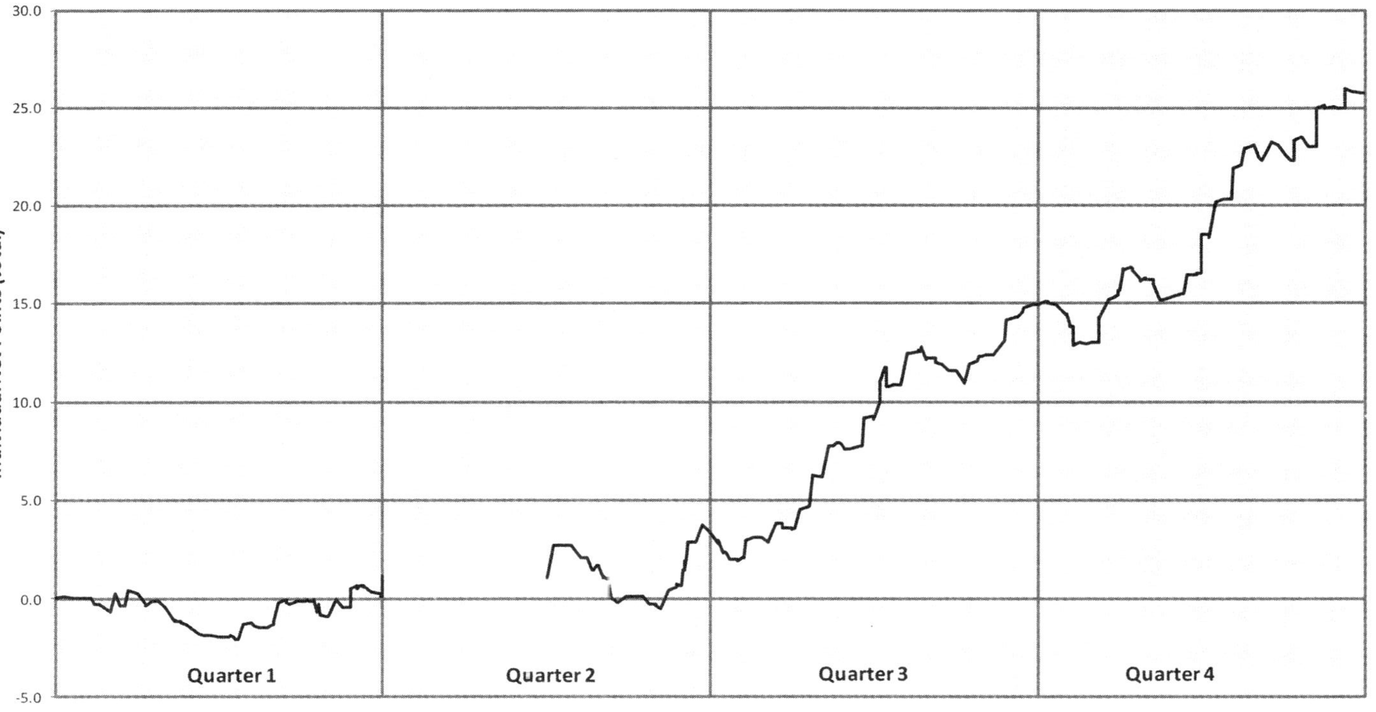

Graph 2. Total net points for Kobe Bryant as he acquired them through his 81-point game on January 22, 2006.

effectively local to the Sonics, so there were a lot of eyes on Morrison and Roy. Our pick was number 10, though, so those guys were likely to be gone by the time we were able to make our choice.

I had collected more than twenty years of college stats by the time the college basketball season was over in April. I had put a lot of that data to work in trying to fit the actual performance of the players in the draft since 1990, when Derrick Coleman was the first pick. I tried to predict who would last in the league and who would actually be good, two related but different things. When the model was done, it said that none of those top prospects was projected to be the best player and that someone else was.

The model results on previous drafts were reasonably reliable, but they hadn't gotten Steve Nash right nine years prior, which was problematic because he was now the league MVP that everyone was talking about. I spent a lot of time trying to find a model that would project him as a better-than-average player but couldn't. I ended up putting projected draft slot into the model, which felt like cheating, but it definitely helped predictions, especially in foretelling how long players would last. Even with that, the model still said another player outside the consensus top prospects was the best one in the 2006 draft.

I sent the results to the front office in late April. The top name did surprise them, but they asked me first about Adam Morrison. My model had him as a second-round pick if I didn't account for mock draft projections, still only twentieth with mock draft projections. That meant that, even if he was taken in the top five as projected, the model suggested that he was not going to be worth anywhere close to that. As always, I built the model so that I could explain why, at least to some degree. His defensive numbers looked bad—both team defense and the fact that he generated few steals, blocks, or defensive boards. Those weak college stats hadn't been a recipe for NBA playing time in the past, even if he shot well in school. Beyond that, those defensive numbers suggested that he wouldn't shoot nearly as well in the NBA anyway. We were very unlikely to have him fall into our range at any rate, but it was a useful conversation for me to test some of the analytical language around the draft.

As we progressed toward the draft, we had draft meetings during which I mostly sat silent while the traditional scouts and staff bandied about their positions and considered strategies of trading up or down. I had filed my reports and discussed results with the top people, but I was in the draft meetings more to get experience. Finally, I was actually asked what my work suggested, and I told everyone that my model's top pick was Rajon Rondo. Rondo was a sophomore point guard out of Kentucky, and I immediately heard about how he was a pain in the ass to the coaches there and couldn't shoot. My response was that, first, he was available to us at our number 10 slot. Second, the draft model wasn't perfect, but every player who ranked highest in their year ended up having substantial careers, even if they didn't end up the best player in the draft. Third, we really needed a point guard who could defend, because all the work I did that year on defense showed how much Luke Ridnour struggled. Rondo could defend—I didn't get arguments there. My final point was that we had some other shooters, so his limitation on that front wasn't as big a deal as what he could bring us.

It made people think, but it didn't change our momentum. I mentioned him enough to be heard, but no one was going to jump on board with me. We didn't take Rondo at number 10.[5] I wasn't terribly disappointed because I knew my voice was small. I was glad to have been able to use it. They asked me about other players here and there. It was a good sign that I could have conversations without people in the room hating me for having those conversations with numbers.

Less than a month later, Wally called me to say that he and his ownership group were selling the team. He and essentially everyone I worked with were likely going away. He was offering me a one-year deal with a 50 percent raise to stay on board, saying, "You won't have to actually do any work." That lack of a challenge wasn't a selling point for me.

The Nuggets had heard about me before and then heard about these changes in Seattle, so they asked for permission to formally interview me. The brass in Seattle rejected that request. I was sitting in no-man's land for a little while. I could sign the offer to stay and get paid, but I would work with no one who cared about what I'd do. I could choose not to sign the offer and hope that the Nuggets, with at least one person who wanted me there, would come through with an offer.

I took the chance, and Mark Warkentien called me on my first day of free agency to offer me a job with their front office in Denver. Some of the stories of my time with the Nuggets—the most stable five years of my career—are told elsewhere in this book.

My time with the Sonics and the Nuggets was tremendous. I gained incredible early experience and made friends, but it all should have lasted longer.

9

Respect, George Karl, and Defending a Three-Point Lead

Hall of Fame coach George Karl didn't respect me when he first met me. He was cordial, but that's different from respect. Being cordial is what you do for anyone, including people like me who had done very little in basketball.

I met Coach Karl in October 2006 after the Nuggets front office hired me, not asking for his approval. The boss who hired me, Mark Warkentien, invited the coach to sit with us over lunch. Karl was not known for subtlety, and he immediately asked me some tough questions, including what I thought about fouling when leading by three points late in a game. It was a test, one of many he would give me so that I might earn his respect. Oddly, his testing would also grow my respect for him.

We'll get back to that.

In our time working together, George often made snide comments about my work—to me, to the media. He would talk about "our analytics guy being different from other analytics guys." He didn't like some of the numbers I put in advanced scouting reports, and I would hear about it. Sometimes he would say it loudly when he knew I was in the room. He wouldn't say as much when there were things that he agreed with.

Those were the early days of basketball analytics, before teams fully appreciated the analytics of the three-point shot and definitely before they disliked the midrange shot. But this was also George playing the role of Coach Karl—a guy who would needle everyone on the team. He would do it to test your toughness. Not just me, that's for sure. He did it to players, some of whom passed the test, some of whom didn't. When you passed, Coach Karl would become George, the guy who would support you, who would care about you, who would give you the benefit of the doubt.

In testing me, Coach Karl didn't know how to evaluate numbers or "statistics" or "analytics" or "whatever you're calling them." He was a coach who looked at numbers and had figured out his way of interpreting them. If I was hired to interpret the game through a different lens, it was going to be a process for him or his staff to tell whether it was helpful or "just some crap the numbers guy came up with." The process was very much about translating numbers into words, then back again. I always took the first stab at turning it into basketball language, but sometimes it required more iterations. Usually we were in sync, though. George had an instinct for basketball that was similar to a lot of the ideas you'll see in this book.

You see, George may not have known how to evaluate numbers well, but he did understand how to evaluate players. He did it instinctively, but he did it well. We rarely had a disagreement about players. He saw rookies as bad; numbers saw them similarly. He saw Carmelo Anthony as good but frustrating and often bad at decision-making; numbers saw Melo not as good as his reputation. We never argued over Melo's value.

Not all coaches saw players the way that analytics did. Specifically, some young player development coaches (by no means *all* of them) can see only the potential upside in players, blinding themselves to what is *actually* good about those players. I heard many conversations around the league about young players who would be good "if they would get playing time." There is some truth to it—playing time does improve players. But the tendency was to see those potential skills as becoming real skills much faster than they often actually did.

George knew to let young players develop when it didn't cost him wins, when it didn't create frustration in better players who were helping him win right then and there. "Winning heals all wounds" only if the head coach is making sure that those contributing to winning are receiving the benefits of doing so.

I ultimately passed George's test of toughness, maybe because he had the same instinct about players that my analysis had. I'm not sure.

I built basketball arguments, and most of the time, we either agreed or it made him think.

One of the times I made him think was when I told him that the three-point shot across the top (the "wing three")[1] was "more important" than the shorter version in the corners (the "corner three"). This was very much against common basketball culture of the time. It is still controversial up to the point that I write this sentence because of the simple fact that the field goal percentage on corner threes is about 3 to 4 percent higher than for wing threes, 38–39 percent versus 34–35 percent in the 2020 time frame.

It's also controversial because I used the word "important," not "better." The simpler way to put this is that the wing three is shot so much *more* than the corner three that you have to get better at it offensively and prepare for it defensively. In the extreme, this is obvious. The highest percentage shot in basketball is the dunk, but saying that you should just take dunks is a lot easier said than actually done. The process to get a wing three is simpler and more common than a corner three, even if the shot is a little less accurate.

The corner three is the end of a play—you kick out to someone there (like finding an open dunker). You rarely start an offensive set from down there because the options to get something out of that are relatively limited. But a lot of plays—pick and rolls, dribble handoffs, post-ups, isolations, pin downs—can open up space at the wings. Even if the wing three were as close as the corner three, there are still a lot more shots coming from there than from the corners (which you see in college, where the line is much closer to the same distance all around). That's why wing threes were more "important."

Another way to express the "importance" of the wing three over the corner three is that it is the easiest *good* shot you can get. At 35 percent, that equates to about 52 percent from anywhere inside the arc. The only place inside the line where the average field goal percentage is that high is right around the rim. Teams got about fifteen of these layups per game in 2020 (in the half-court). If you add in free throws on shooting fouls, that brings it up to about twenty-two. The majority of the layups, of course, are contested, and they also lead to turnovers at a higher rate. Wing threes are open 85–90 percent of the time and are fairly easy to

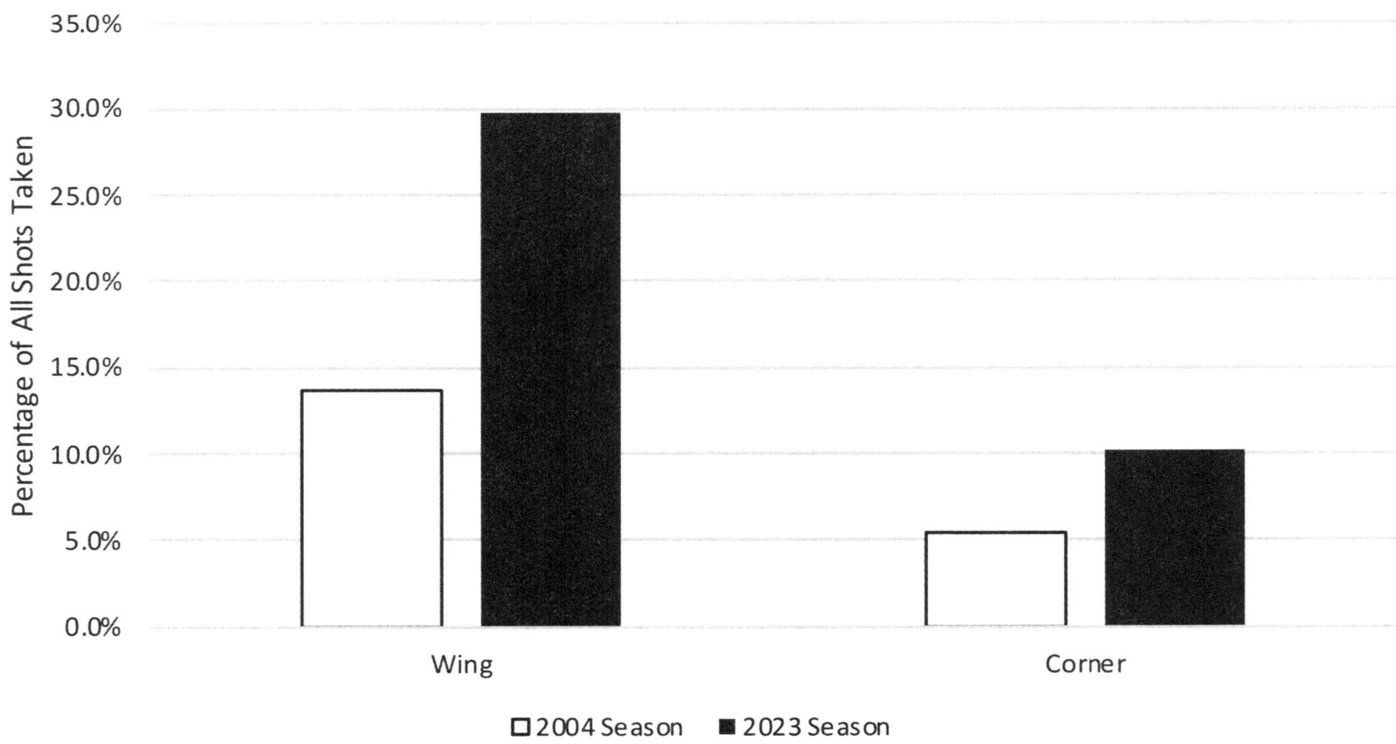

Graph 3. Percentage of shots as wing threes and corner threes in 2004 and 2023.

take at that effective 52 percent—about twenty-five per team per game (including shooting fouls). This is up from about ten in 2004 (see graph 3), but how often they're made hasn't gone down, illustrating that they were there for the taking. (Corner threes are taken about nine times per game and have gone up by about five per game since 2004.)

As I say, Coach Karl may not have fully appreciated the three at first, but he didn't dismiss it either. He was an innovative coach who wanted to maintain an advantage. After a year or two of maybe hearing me, he was telling his players this: "We like the three, but we love the rim." It was an accurate message, emphasizing the rim first, the three second. That message is still mostly true, though some teams have seen the value of shooting threes exceed the value of layups.

In that first meeting with Coach Karl, I told him that only a small part of what I did could help a coach. I told him that stats could give indicators of what a team does, but that a coach spends a lot of time with his players and should know them better. I wanted to make clear early on that I wasn't going to try to tell a legend how to do his job.

But I did take a chance on that first day, too. I told him that I had studied what he had done when he first took over the Nuggets in early 2005, taking the team from a moribund 17-25 record to 32-8 with him in charge. I had been with the Sonics at the time, and there was some risk of facing his Nuggets in the playoffs, so I knew I had to understand what changed if we were to face them. I told him that I saw the massive change in the number of layups the Nuggets took before and after his arrival. His players seemed to thrive on that, especially Melo.

After I volunteered that info, Coach Karl was silent. Instead of acknowledging my statement as accurate (which it was), that's when Coach Karl changed the subject and asked me about fouling when leading by three points late in a game.

That was 2006, and a recent study had been posted in ESPN's True Hoop section suggesting that teams should always foul. By asking me about fouling, he was implicitly telling me that he had read it or at least that someone had told him about it.

My answer was honest—I'd seen studies suggesting that you should foul, but I didn't trust the assumptions that were in them. They could be right, but there is no way that I would tell him to do it without me doing a thorough study of my own.

"Good. Because I don't think fouling works unless you practice it a lot. We don't coach our players to foul. We coach them to play defense. It's hard to have your players go forty-seven minutes of playing defense hard, then for ten seconds have them strategically foul."

I came away from our meeting with this as a long-term project that I'd aim to do the right way to capture the element of "practicing it a lot."

This wasn't easy to do, so it turned out to be a *very* long-term project. During the five years I was with Coach Karl, we saw these situations nine times and we won eight of those. It didn't affect enough games for me to prioritize this work. (In one of these cases, the Nuggets did actually employ the foul strategy, but I think it was Kenyon Martin's decision, perhaps with teammate Chauncey Billups in his ear.)

In 2012, though, when I had started working for ESPN, the question was in the public mindset for long enough that it demanded our time to dig in.

We looked at a nine-year span, including the playoffs, finding about a thousand situations (sometimes more than one in a game). In those games, committing a nonshooting foul against the team that was trailing led to winning about 94 percent of the time. Defending without fouling led to winning just 89 percent of the time. Fouling led to overtime games every eight games or so, whereas playing defense led to an extra period every five or six games. In other words, the early evidence supported fouling pretty solidly. Fouling or defending—you still won about 90 percent of the games, but there was a real enough advantage for fouling from this early look.

But that wasn't the end of the story. We needed to watch some of these games to make sure the data wasn't capturing something incorrectly. It turns out that the play-by-play *was* missing something very important—whether a defense *tried* to execute either of the strategies. In particular, the video showed cases where the defense tried to foul, but—and this is key to what Coach Karl said—they couldn't execute it. We saw cases where the defender tried to foul the ball handler and even raise their hand to acknowledge they committed a foul, but the referee didn't call it. That allowed an undefended player to get a good look at a shot. With the original data, this looked like the leading team *chose* to play defense and not foul, but they actually chose to foul and failed, leading to a good shot.

This switched some games from one column to the other, making the results more equivalent. There were also cases where a team played defense and accidentally committed a foul, which also swapped things around. In the end, we saw a 92 percent chance of winning with a foul strategy and about 91 percent when playing defense. These are essentially the same.

And the biggest reason they ended up equaling out was because of just what George told me in 2006: it takes practice to teach the foul strategy. The times that guys tried to foul and didn't, but their guy scored—those moved the results a lot.

I had to deal with George needling me for years on various things. I saw him do things that I didn't think were right. But George tried to do the right things, tried to win, tried to get his teams to play together. And he innovated, playing two point guards together in 2011, playing a deep-shooting big man in Seattle, Sam Perkins, twenty years before it became cool (later pushing DeMarcus Cousins to do the same in Sacramento), pushing his teams to run even as the NBA slowed down. He knew things about the game before analytics could be used to understand them. The biggest reason I started doing analytics was so that I could learn enough to have instincts as good as someone like George.

I'm happy to have worked with him, asked him questions, and answered his questions. I don't know if he will ever like analytics, but it doesn't matter. We could work together. He could call me Dean Oliver without adding a curse word in front, and I could call him George.

BOX: Tips to Work in Analytics with Traditional Basketball People

One of the questions I most often get asked is how to get traditional basketball people to listen to analytics. In other words, how do you work with someone who learned basketball like George Karl did? Here's a brief list of things that I'd suggest:

Speak using basketball language, not math language.

Get to know the basketball people for how they do their job.

Be very sure of what you have when you have to present something to them that is likely counterintuitive. And be prepared to support it with simple examples. Be careful of small samples. Ideally, you've built up trust through other conversations first.

Most basketball people I've known didn't particularly like graphs and charts. Talk to them, give them illustrative numbers that they understand, and provide video examples.

When working with coaches, understand that their job is to get the most out of the players they have. Most of their tools for doing so are not very well quantified—motivation, developing offensive plays and defensive coverages, and clear emphases in practice. Measurements are usually of what players do in games, which are an *indirect* reflection of what a coach does. As a result, respect that the coaches usually know what measurements say and that they're trying to get there but that there can be failure in the motivation or communication that has almost nothing to measure it.

Respect that coaches know a lot.

10

Playing Draft

The draft room in Denver was about thirty feet long and about twelve feet wide, whiteboards on much of the wall space. An elliptical table in the room was about eighteen feet by six feet. And one day, the center of that table was covered with candy. Frankly, no one was eating it, so it just stayed there while we worked with our notepads and laptops on the perimeter.

That was the actual day of the draft in 2007, and the table didn't usually have candy. I think it was there mostly for a particular person and because it added a lot of color to a bland room. Many other draft rooms around the NBA were rumored to be crazier, maybe not visually but by what happened there. I've heard stories of kids in the draft room, some getting a platform to offer serious thoughts on who the team should pick. I've heard stories of owners in the draft room calling other owners to try to make a trade during the draft without their general manager being aware. I heard a story about a coach who offered a trade without his GM's knowledge, causing the relationship to go so bad that the coach was fired not long afterward.

No, draft day in Denver wasn't crazy. It was a relatively calm day after many months of preparation. That process didn't create a script for draft day. Rather, it provided enough information to be able to improvise as things developed on that day, depending on if we wanted to make trades, if we heard about trades that other teams were making that could affect us, if a player we didn't expect fell to us, or if the top players on our list suddenly went before our slot. We were prepared for a lot of circumstances because, as our GM, Mark Warkentien, would say,

"Draft day is not about getting the best player. It's about getting your team better, whether you make a pick or trade the pick."

On that draft day in 2007, we had no pick and weren't too optimistic about our chances to get one. We were coming off a solid 45-37 year, but we were slated to get Kenyon Martin back from a season-long injury, so Mark called him "our first-round draft pick. He's going to play thirty minutes a game for us next year, and he'll be a lot better than what we can get in this draft. Maybe we get lucky and get a pick. We're prepared if we do."[1]

That year, our process resulted in no deals and no picks, but Mark insisted that we got better by not taking on any bad players or bad contracts. Other years, the process got us better in different ways.

Preseason

In preparation for the actual draft day, we met in that room almost every month of the season to discuss draft prospects. There was a comfortable rhythm to it.

In September we met there over a couple of days to discuss the huge list of prospects that we could cover during the coming year. What intel did we have from summer meetings to suggest we should see these guys? Were there particular geographic regions with more players that we should see?

In October we had both a complete list and a scouting schedule for our small staff of three or four domestic scouts, plus Mark and me. A couple of other front-office people would schedule their travel on the fly throughout the year to see prospects. These early meetings were about building the big list, whereas subsequent lists would be about cutting down that list.

I added the names, usually about two hundred of them, to our internal prospect database. Those were the players that I'd be following, not the entire ten thousand or so that played college basketball or international ball. To the degree we had important intelligence on various players, we'd talk about it and I'd take notes on things to look into through the year—a player who wasn't getting along with coaches, for example. If there were mock drafts available, I'd start collecting those to understand how the broader perspective changed over the season.

For the 2007 draft, the top prospects before the season began were

Greg Oden, Kevin Durant, Joakim Noah, Josh McRoberts, Thaddeus Young, Brandan Wright, Julian Wright, and Al Horford. Because we were supposed to be good in 2006–07, we really didn't plan in October to spend much time on these guys, but if we somehow managed to stumble onto one of them, we'd just take them.

Those guys could change, Mark cautioned. "There are only ten starters in every draft. Identifying who those are—that is success in the draft."

Exactly what is a "starter"? I had to come up with some kind of definition, so that I could test what he said. That kind of word-to-numbers translation was always a bit tricky, but if my definition came out with something different from ten starters, he'd listen and that would make the conversation worth the effort. In this case, I defined starters as players who ended up playing at least one hundred games and started at least half of available games.[2] What I showed him was basically table 20.

Table 20. Number of starters in the draft by season through 2005

	No. of starters		
Draft year	Overall	In top ten	Starter names (pick no.)
2005	8	5	Andrew Bogut (1), Marvin Williams (2), Deron Williams (3), Chris Paul (4), Raymond Felton (5), Monta Ellis (40), Ryan Gomes (50), Marcin Gortat (57)
2004	6	4	Dwight Howard (1), Emeka Okafor (2), Luol Deng (7), Andre Iguodala (9), Al Jefferson (15), Josh Smith (17)
2003	7	6	LeBron James (1), Carmelo Anthony (3), Chris Bosh (4), Dwyane Wade (5), Chris Kaman (6), Kirk Hinrich (7), David West (18)
2002	7	3	Yao Ming (1), Amar'e Stoudemire (9), Caron Butler (10), Tayshaun Prince (23), Nenad Krstić (24), Carlos Boozer (35), Luis Scola (56)
2001	11	5	Tyson Chandler (2), Pau Gasol (3), Jason Richardson (5), Shane Battier (6), Joe Johnson (10), Richard Jefferson (13), Zach Randolph (19), Samuel Dalembert (26), Tony Parker (28), Trenton Hassell (30), Mehmet Okur (38)

	No. of starters		
Draft year	Overall	In top ten	Starter names (pick no.)
2000	2	1	Kenyon Martin (1), Morris Peterson (21)
1999	9	7	Elton Brand (1), Steve Francis (2), Baron Davis (3), Lamar Odom (4), Richard Hamilton (7), Andre Miller (8), Shawn Marion (9), Metta World Peace (16), Andrei Kirilenko (24)
1998	11	7	Mike Bibby (2), Raef LaFrentz (3), Antawn Jamison (4), Vince Carter (5), Jason Williams (7), Dirk Nowitzki (9), Paul Pierce (10), Michael Dickerson (14), Rasho Nesterović (17), Rashard Lewis (32), Cuttino Mobley (41)
1997	5	4	Tim Duncan (1), Keith Van Horn (2), Chauncey Billups (3), Tracy McGrady (9), Anthony Parker (21)
1996	12	8	Allen Iverson (1), Marcus Camby (2), Shareef Abdur-Rahim (3), Stephon Marbury (4), Ray Allen (5), Antoine Walker (6), Kerry Kittles (8), Erick Dampier (10), Kobe Bryant (13), Peja Stojaković (14), Steve Nash (15), Zydrunas Ilgauskas (20)
1995	6	5	Antonio McDyess (2), Rasheed Wallace (4), Kevin Garnett (5), Bryant Reeves (6), Damon Stoudamire (7), Michael Finley (21)
1994	6	6	Glenn Robinson (1), Jason Kidd (2), Grant Hill (3), Juwan Howard (5), Brian Grant (8), Eddie Jones (10)
1993	6	4	Chris Webber (1), Jamal Mashburn (4), Isaiah Rider (5), Vin Baker (8), Allan Houston (11), Nick Van Exel (37)
1992	8	4	Shaquille O'Neal (1), Alonzo Mourning (2), Christian Laettner (3), Clarence Weatherspoon (9), Bryant Stith (13), Doug Christie (17), Latrell Sprewell (24), P.J. Brown (29)
1991	7	3	Larry Johnson (1), Dikembe Mutombo (4), Steve Smith (5), Terrell Brandon (11), Dale Davis (13), Rick Fox (24), Bobby Phills (45)
1990	4	4	Derrick Coleman (1), Gary Payton (2), Kendall Gill (5), Lionel Simmons (7)

This table showed an average of seven players per draft became starters, with as few as two and as many as twelve. That's only one out of four teams that would draft an eventual regular starter. Mark went to our next meeting and said, "Remember, there are maybe ten starters in every draft. Identifying who those are—that is success in the draft. Sometimes, there are more, like the Kobe and Nash year, but that's rare. We have to find those ten guys." He stuck to his round number of ten, instead of the seven I was finding. Given that there were good players who didn't end up starters, I was fine with the simplification.[3]

Just to fill in history since that time, table 21 shows the number of "starters" by draft year *since* 2005. There may have been an uptick in the number of starters per year,[4] but that would be partially due to adding an extra five starting spots available through the expansion team in Charlotte.

Table 21. Number of starters in the draft by season from 2006 to 2021

	No. of starters		
Draft year	Overall	In top ten	Starter names (pick no.)
2021	8	5	Jalen Green (2), Evan Mobley (3), Scottie Barnes (4), Josh Giddey (6), Franz Wagner (8), Alperen Şengün (16), Herbert Jones (35), Ayo Dosunmu (38)
2020	9	4	Anthony Edwards (1), LaMelo Ball (3), Patrick Williams (4), Isaac Okoro (5), Isaiah Stewart (16), Saddiq Bey (19), Tyrese Maxey (21), Jaden McDaniels (28), Desmond Bane (30)
2019	7	5	Zion Williamson (1), Ja Morant (2), R.J. Barrett (3), De'Andre Hunter (4), Darius Garland (5), P.J. Washington (12), Keldon Johnson (29)
2018	11	7	DeAndre Ayton (1), Luka Dončić (3), Jaren Jackson Jr. (4), Trae Young (5), Wendell Carter Jr. (7), Collin Sexton (8), Mikal Bridges (10), Shai Gilgeous-Alexander (11), Miles Bridges (12), Kevin Huerter (19), Bruce Brown (42)

	No. of starters		
Draft year	Overall	In top ten	Starter names (pick no.)
2017	11	4	Lonzo Ball (2), Jayson Tatum (3), De'Aaron Fox (5), Lauri Markkanen (7), Donovan Mitchell (13), Bam Adebayo (14), John Collins (19), Jarrett Allen (22), OG Anunoby (23), Kyle Kuzma (27), Dillon Brooks (45)
2016	8	5	Ben Simmons (1), Brandon Ingram (2), Jaylen Brown (3), Buddy Hield (6), Jamal Murray (7), Domantas Sabonis (11), Pascal Siakam (27), Dejounte Murray (29)
2015	5	3	Karl-Anthony Towns (1), D'Angelo Russell (2), Kristaps Porziņģis (4), Myles Turner (11), Devin Booker (13)
2014	10	6	Andrew Wiggins (1), Joel Embiid (3), Aaron Gordon (4), Marcus Smart (6), Julius Randle (7), Elfrid Payton (10), Zach LaVine (13), Gary Harris (19), Clint Capela (25), Nikola Jokić (41)
2013	5	2	Kentavious Caldwell-Pope (8), CJ McCollum (10), Steven Adams (12), Giannis Antetokounmpo (15), Rudy Gobert (27)
2012	8	5	Anthony Davis (1), Bradley Beal (3), Damian Lillard (6), Harrison Barnes (7), Andre Drummond (9), Evan Fournier (20), Draymond Green (35), Khris Middleton (39)
2011	11	3	Kyrie Irving (1), Jonas Valančiūnas (5), Kemba Walker (9), Klay Thompson (11), Kawhi Leonard (15), Nikola Vučević (16), Tobias Harris (19), Kenneth Faried (22), Jimmy Butler (30), Bojan Bogdanović (31), Chandler Parsons (38)
2010	5	4	John Wall (1), DeMarcus Cousins (5), Gordon Hayward (9), Paul George (10), Eric Bledsoe (18)
2009	11	5	Blake Griffin (1), James Harden (3), Ricky Rubio (5), Stephen Curry (7), DeMar DeRozan (9), Gerald Henderson Jr. (12), Jrue Holiday (17), Jeff Teague (19), Darren Collison (21), Patrick Beverley (42), Danny Green (46)

2008	11	5	O.J. Mayo (3), Russell Westbrook (4), Kevin Love (5), Danilo Gallinari (6), Brook Lopez (10), Jason Thompson (12), Robin Lopez (15), Roy Hibbert (17), Serge Ibaka (24), Nicolas Batum (25), DeAndre Jordan (35)
2007	5	3	Kevin Durant (2), Al Horford (3), Mike Conley (4), Arron Afflalo (27), Marc Gasol (48)
2006	6	3	LaMarcus Aldridge (2), Brandon Roy (6), Rudy Gay (8), Kyle Lowry (24), P.J. Tucker (35), Paul Millsap (47)

November through January

In the early part of the season, the college scouts were on the road for practices and early-season games, sometimes where prospects played against much weaker teams, sometimes where they faced really good teams. The job of the scouts was to file reports, not after every game they attended but when they had enough of a handle on a player. Mark wanted people to think through things enough to write a report but not hold themselves to the standard of being right in November or December. "We need to be right in June," he said. "Not December."

He said that because we wanted our scouts to avoid the bias of looking only for evidence to support what they had said before. At the same time, we also wanted scouts to avoid any recency bias, basing a player's evaluation most strongly on what they saw last. It was my job to highlight also whether scouts could get biased by watching only a player's best games, not their worst or their average games. Our monthly meetings in the draft room were meant to touch base and to check our process for limiting irrational biases.

One of our exercises every month was to come up with ten players we thought would be starters. People would give names, which would go on the whiteboard. Sometimes, we got to ten easily, going up to twelve or fifteen, at which point Mark would say, "Whoa! Can you name one draft that had fifteen starters in it?" Other times, we could get to only about seven names. After we named the players, we had to say why we thought they would make it, using no more than twenty-five words. It had to be short because Mark had to sell the players to the owner and to the head coach and, in those meetings, all he had time for was twenty-five words. For top prospects like Kevin Durant, the pitch was easy, "Efficient scorer from anywhere with height and mobility that are hard to match." For others, the pitch was harder, but it hopefully got easier the more we studied them.

For each of those lists, I would volunteer whether "the numbers liked them" or whether there were other players who should be on the list. Before mid-December, there wasn't a lot of data to go by for the freshmen, so I would be softer in any recommendations.

"The numbers liking" a player was a phrase that made sense in the context of Mark's decision process. In his view, there were three circles of information about players: eyes, ears, and numbers. The eyes saw what players did on the court in great detail, including some of their body language. The ears heard about players' practice habits, their ability to get along with teammates, their level of responsibility—things about them that could affect results over longer periods than just one game. The numbers saw all of the games with a cold objectiveness that provided a third pillar on which to make decisions. If all of the three circles overlapped on a player—good or bad—it was easy to classify them. If only two agreed, there was more work to do.

I was in charge of the numbers circle, but I was involved in the other circles, too. We didn't have a wall between them, because it was better to know early on about disagreements between the different circles so that they could be resolved. Those disagreements early in the process were not arguments but things that people would follow up on, whether that meant watching more of a player, finding other people to talk to, or looking through the historical data and draft models for more background.

I created my first draft model with the Sonics in 2006 and built a new one with the Nuggets. My early model hadn't really been built to work with data through November and December; rather it was built with end-of-season data, so I had to modify things. By mid-December, I ran the model on the players on our watchlist. I didn't distribute those results broadly because I knew that they were based on a subset of games, but I did look at it for surprising results, things that weren't matching what we said in meetings or what was in mock drafts. For example, Cal's

Ryan Anderson was an early-season catch by the system who was very low on our priority list in the preseason, so I brought his name up. The scouts knew he was playing well, but they went to look at him more in part because of the model.

I should say that a "draft model" is shorthand for something more complex. Most teams have some kind of mathematical toolkit to predict what the prospects will do, but that toolkit can be quite different across teams because it can try to answer a lot of questions. First of all, what is a draft model supposed to predict? It could predict a player's minutes or whether a player becomes a "starter" by the definition above, or player production via one of the metrics in chapter 7. But then the question is, When? You could care about how many minutes a player gets in his first four years or his first eight years or his career. You could care about whether he reaches starter status or an overall production level by year three or by year six. A draft model could be used to predict any of these things, so you could have a draft model to answer *all* of these things, meaning lots of draft models. If you want to have a say in the conversations, the more models you have, the better your chance of influencing those conversations.

For example, James Harden looked like a player who would be good early, playing a lot of minutes early and over the course of his career. His chance of failing without playing a few years was under 3 percent. He would probably shoot a lot and shoot efficiently, while still having assists at a rate like a combo guard. All of those details are little predictions of a draft model.

I had models to make those predictions, but one of Mark's beliefs when he hired me was that numbers helped most in *eliminating* prospects, not identifying them. If we could eliminate various players, it meant that the eyes could focus on a much smaller subset. That meant that there were "rules of elimination" that we gradually built up.

For instance, one of Mark's favorite ideas was that older players were not good bets, especially early in the first round. "If you're nineteen and doing well against twenty-two-year-olds, you're a lot better than the twenty-three-year-old who is playing at the same level against those twenty-two-year-olds." So I looked into it. Among guards who were at least twenty-two and a half at draft time, how many of them taken in the first round actually were good versus just subs versus bad? The test was looking at roughly forty players in the last couple of decades. Of those, fifteen were taken in the lottery—Andre Miller, Tim Hardaway, Greg Anthony, Derek Anderson, Lindsey Hunter, Jason Williams, Fred Jones, Pooh Richardson, Trajan Langdon, Shawn Respert, Bo Kimble, Michael Dickerson, Courtney Alexander, Rumeal Robinson, and Mateen Cleaves. Those were older guards in the lottery, and many people reading this probably don't remember those players' NBA careers particularly well because several weren't substantial. About half of these guys had careers where they were at least subs. In the lottery, about 75 percent of players end up at least as a sub, so 50 percent isn't good, showing that the age factor mattered. But it didn't fully *eliminate*. Showing that it was a poor bet was often good enough.

It was hard to find complete elimination rules. Could we eliminate guys who didn't average at least double figures in points in college? Dikembe Mutombo, Andre Iguodala, Jeff Foster, Sam Dalembert, and Greg Ostertag were among those who averaged under 10 points per game in college but had pretty good NBA careers.

What about just *perimeter* players who averaged under 10 points per game? Andre Iguodala, Jason Richardson, Charlie Ward, Matt Barnes, Eric Snow, and Randy Brown all had at least decent careers. There were a lot more who didn't make it, but most of them were second-round picks, among whom the rate of survival wasn't great to begin with.

Mark's favorite example of a guard who failed as a first-round pick and didn't average 10 points per game in college was Tate George. George was an NCAA tournament hero in 1990 whose stock shot up with his postseason play. He was also over twenty-two years old at draft day. So maybe we can eliminate low-scoring guards who were older? If you add "over twenty-two years old" to the under 10 points-per-game perimeter players, the best NBA player out of this group was Charlie Ward and a few mediocre subs. So this rule—at least twenty-two years old, under 10 points per game, a perimeter player—mostly eliminated guys from being good prospects. Even then, only five of these guys were first-round picks, so the hit rate wasn't terribly different from that of an average second-round pick.

A couple years into working on these rules, we did eliminate eventual lottery pick Joe Alexander. He was a likely first-round pick, older than twenty-one and a half years, had poor assist/turnover numbers, shot under 46 percent from the field, and didn't average even twenty-nine minutes per game for his college career. He was slated to go in the first round because he played really well late in his career, just like Tate George. We found nine first-round picks—only nine—who generally had similarly poor career numbers in college. Just five of them even played a thousand minutes in a season and never on good teams. Alexander had a very small chance of being substantial compared with other first-round picks, especially lottery picks, which is what he became.[5] We ended up calling it the Joe Alexander Rule, and it was applicable to subsequent first-round picks like Gerald Henderson Jr., Taurean Prince, Josh Heustis, and P.J. Hairston, none of whom had significant careers.

This kind of elimination test was simple to communicate, at least. I would generally check its results against what the more sophisticated draft models said, for sure, but the value of communication was huge in knocking off names from the whiteboard.

Another element of the draft process at this time was to scout the NBDL (now called the G-League). Those players didn't cost a draft pick and would likely be better in the short-term than a draft pick. Even if we didn't sign anyone from there, watching the games was a reminder to college scouts of the difference in play between that level and college. It forced scouts to think about the college players they liked in the context of this level.

February through March Madness

In February and especially March, there was a definite danger of falling in love with players who did well on the big stage, whether that was their conference tournament or the NCAA tournament, even if they were mediocre in so many games before then. As a result, we generally didn't scout the NCAA tournament. We scouted the conference tournaments for the sake of seeing players outside our normal regions. Scouts who usually worked out west would go east to watch different conference tournaments, for example.

The most extreme example of a player who got a huge bump due to late-season performance was the aforementioned Joe Alexander in 2008. Alexander was barely in mock drafts until March of his draft year but started showing up as a first-round pick based on three straight 29+ point games early that month.

Jonny Flynn was another. He played all but three minutes in a six-overtime game in the Big East tournament in 2009 that upped his draft stock from late first-round selection to the middle of the first round. It was a heroic game, one where he willed Syracuse to a legendary win. But it was just one game amid a lot of good games, games that made him a prospect but not a hero. He ended up getting drafted as a hero at number 6, one spot ahead of eventual MVP Steph Curry.

Zach Collins was a talented power forward for Gonzaga in 2017, ranked generally in the bottom half of the first round, until the team went to the NCAA Final Four for the first time in history. Many more people saw the team finally going against top competition, and they saw the talented Collins hold his own, even if he wasn't a star. He vaulted up to the number 11 pick in the draft.

All of these players saw their stock driven by a small sample on a big stage.[6] We had our rules—no scouting the NCAA tournament, seeing different players later in the season—to keep normal biases like these from affecting our eyes. A major part of a good draft process, which is nine months of a lot of voices, is about avoiding misleading human biases—the eyes-ears-numbers combination, not overscouting big events, forcing scouts to see college and higher-level games, and building statistical tests to eliminate players.

April and May

In the week after the end of the college basketball season, the Portsmouth Invitational Tournament (aka PIT) started up. This event was a few days of basketball for seniors across the country to show what they could do. Since so many of the top prospects weren't seniors anymore, the relevance of PIT declined, but it served as a convenient way to get the scouts together for a meeting. Instead of our draft room, we often met at Roger Brown's, a big sports bar that was filled with NBA personnel during that week. We'd talk about family, the Master's golf tournament that was going on at the same time, and how the playoffs were shaping up before we dove into work.

Most of the players at PIT had been eliminated by us over the course of the year, but there were a few who were on the fringe. Our job was to try to "close our eyes and imagine a way that these guys would get on the court and what those circumstances were." We were often short on three-point shooters, so we tended to look for those, but a lot of them were shorter and not particularly good athletes, meaning that they may not be able to defend anyone. It was a rough balance.

Recognition of that balance was built into the format of our scouting reports,[7] which was simple. It first asked for a description of the player and which games formed the basis for the report; then it challenged the scout to answer three questions:

1. What does this player do to get him in an NBA game (sometimes called their "piece")?
2. What causes this player to fail?
3. Who does he play like?

At PIT, we were looking for players whose piece was relevant for us. For example, our head coach had to be able to look down the bench at this player and say, "Hey, we need you to go out there and make some threes" or "get some rebounds." If they had that piece, they had to be good enough at the other things so that they wouldn't fail. Denver's Reggie Evans was a perfect example of a specialist who was really good at rebounding and just good enough at other things that he could stay on a roster, something he did for thirteen years despite not getting drafted. He became an icon that other players could get compared with in question 3 of the scouting report.

Going into PIT, I relied on a modification to my draft model, one where I looked historically for types of players who went undrafted but landed somewhere and were helpful. There were a good number of defenders who managed to get a chance, like Ben Wallace, Bruce Bowen, Bo Outlaw, Michael Curry, Chris "Birdman" Andersen, and Raja Bell. And there were point guards—David Wesley, Darrell Armstrong, JJ Barea, Chucky Atkins, Damon Jones, Earl Boykins, and Anthony Carter. I was surprised that there weren't more rebounders like Reggie Evans, but having been around Reggie enough in my career, I am comfortable saying that he was one of a kind.

PIT for me was about identifying players whose piece was either as a defender, a point guard, or, because we often needed the role, a three-point shooter whose other weaknesses could be hidden. As a group, we kept our options open beyond that, but PIT had sixty players and I couldn't focus on that many.

At the end, we had a hard time imagining most of those players for us. Even most of those we imagined having some kind of role ended up as nothing more than imagination. But we did look at Jeremy Lin, who played well enough through college that I had flagged him as a potential undrafted point guard. He played pretty well at PIT but still didn't get drafted. It took a year, during which he was waived by Golden State and Houston before his famous Linsanity season of 2012 in New York, after which he was a regular rotation player for four years.

Lin was an example of why it's useful to predict *when* a player is good. He did absolutely nothing in the NBA his first year after college, but then he was a rotation player for five years. How long it will take for a player to be good is critical to making a decision on whether to sign them, how long to keep them around, and then whether to pick them up later. Predicting timing is particularly hard, though, because even Lin had lucky circumstances to get the minutes he got in his second year (see chapter 19).

One of the players that Mark noticed at PIT was Brian Cusworth, a seven-foot center out of Harvard. "He's a Harvard guy. He can probably run every drill to perfection, but he's a stiff!" Mark was telling the harsh truth in his joking way. "He's too slow, he's too mechanical. But after he makes money in Europe for a few years, he'll make a great doctor!" And Mark laughed as Cusworth missed a layup, then got the offensive rebound, then missed again. As of this writing, Cusworth did indeed play four years in Europe and a year in the G-League. He is now a doctor in St. Louis. Whether he's a "great doctor," I don't know, but Mark's prediction was accurate, even about the timing.

PIT was just the beginning of two months of refining our evaluations of players. We keyed in on players that were realistic for us and tried to understand what we didn't understand. This meant filling in the gaps in prospect profiles but also understanding what the other options were out there—whether coming from the G-League or international players (which Mark called "spies"). A bad draft pick just sits on your bench and on your cap, preventing you from getting better.

June: Draft Month

The NBA draft is on a Thursday in late June, and those of us responsible for making decisions were together for at least the two weeks leading into it. We ate a lot of lunches and a good number of dinners together. Most of us were living at a hotel, away from our family, so Father's Day was celebrated by phone.

The work was meant to be efficient, not all-consuming. We weren't going to gain a lot of knowledge about the players in June, though maybe a few last-minute interviews could modify things a little. In those interviews, we tried to ask the players what we asked our scouts—what was their piece, what would cause them to fail, and who they played like. We could gauge their answers for how well their perceptions matched ours, usually a good sign that we could work with them.

We asked one prospect, "Have you done anything bad that we should know about? We're serious about bringing you in, so we will look into your past. Is there something we may find that we should know now?" The prospect looked at all of us in turn around the room to try to get a read on us, then got sheepish and answered slowly, "I'm pretty clean, but I stole a bike when I was ten years old. My mom never knew because I told her a friend gave it to me." We all laughed and assured him that we wouldn't tell his mother.

The workouts that accompanied the interviews were for the coaches to get to know a bit about potential players joining us, but those tests could be problematic. Sometimes, good prospects had poor workouts. Sometimes, nondraftable players who came in just to go against good prospects played great and impressed the coaches. When I was on the coaching side and hadn't seen much of these prospects, I could like how attentive one was to details, how he spoke our language, and how he executed our defensive schemes, but he could be a player who had no realistic chance. Workouts were dangerous because there was no part of them that could affect the main decision-makers or the draft models, even though coaches could get a voice based on them. At least the workouts gave our medical team time to study the players. Good body type or bad signs for injury potentially had long-term relevance if we acquired the player at the draft or later.

What also happened at this time were discussions with other teams on trades. There were a lot of phone calls to determine which teams may want our picks, which ones were willing to shuffle their picks, and which existing players could possibly be thrown into deals with picks. With our goal to simply get the team better, that last part—players already in the league—could be quite relevant.

What we didn't have for trade negotiations was a draft value chart, like the one that has existed publicly in the NFL for decades. If a team was offering the twenty-eighth pick and the eighteenth pick for the eighth pick, was that a reasonable trade? In the NFL, the draft value chart gave both teams an approximate answer. In the NBA, the chart may have existed for one team in a discussion but not the other. Having a public version—even flawed, as the NFL's was—greases the wheels for trades.

A simple version of a draft value chart for the NBA looks like what's in table 22. This version looks only at player value in the first four years in the NBA, not career value, because four years is a common benchmark for young players.[8]

The "values" shown in this chart are the average value of points above replacement at these draft picks,[9] along with some error bars on the estimates. They have a real meaning, so that a team can consider not only trading pick number 8 for number 28 and number 18, but it can also consider trading number 8 for number 28 and a player who would be forecast to add another 130 points above replacement in the next four years. If you equate points to dollar figures, then this can also account for selling picks, which definitely happens.

There are lots of other versions of this chart out there.[10] Most of them are quite similar philosophically, having a high value early on, then dropping a good amount past pick 20 or so. Sometimes they account for career value instead of the first four years. Sometimes they consider the chance that a pick will get an extension, which tends to raise the value of the highest picks because they're more likely to get one.

Table 22. NBA draft value chart: Points above replacement after four years, with standard deviation

Pick	Value	Pick	Value	Pick	Value	Pick	Value
1	371 (±72)	16	121 (±26)	31	62 (±15)	46	26 (±9)
2	309 (±61)	17	116 (±25)	32	59 (±15)	47	24 (±8)
3	272 (±54)	18	111 (±24)	33	56 (±14)	48	23 (±8)
4	246 (±49)	19	106 (±24)	34	54 (±14)	49	21 (±8)
5	226 (±46)	20	101 (±23)	35	51 (±13)	50	19 (±7)
6	210 (±43)	21	97 (±22)	36	48 (±13)	51	17 (±7)
7	196 (±40)	22	93 (±21)	37	46 (±12)	52	15 (±7)
8	184 (±38)	23	89 (±20)	38	44 (±12)	53	14 (±6)
9	173 (±36)	24	85 (±20)	39	41 (±12)	54	12 (±6)
10	164 (±34)	25	81 (±19)	40	39 (±11)	55	10 (±6)
11	155 (±33)	26	78 (±18)	41	37 (±11)	56	9 (±6)
12	147 (±31)	27	74 (±18)	42	35 (±10)	57	7 (±5)
13	140 (±30)	28	71 (±17)	43	32 (±10)	58	6 (±5)
14	133 (±29)	29	68 (±17)	44	30 (±10)	59	4 (±5)
15	127 (±27)	30	65 (±16)	45	28 (±9)	60	3 (±4)

Those things make sense and are reasonable to discuss in negotiations, especially when a draft class is considered stronger or weaker. What doesn't make sense is that some charts use values that are arbitrary, like 4,000 or 57,000 as a maximum. I don't know what the values mean or how to work with them. But public draft charts like any of these do help with discussions.

Mark used to talk about general managers around the league who "loved to play draft," meaning that they loved the pursuit of finding the young kid who could be a star. Those were GMs that we could sell or trade our picks to, he said. We sold a couple of picks while we were together.

We made just one first-round selection while I was there. Even though I was brought in originally to eliminate prospects, I had earned enough trust that I could advocate for a prospect by that point. We narrowed it down to two players about a week before the draft. The eyes liked them both. The ears were hearing that one was not much of a practice player, but the numbers were pretty strongly in favor of that player. We talked about both players again but figured we needed more information. At that stage, there weren't a lot more games to watch and it was hard to get new answers out of the data, so we reached out to coaches who had worked with the players. For the player with the potential work ethic issue, we heard confirmation of the issue but also that he was the most talented point guard that coach had ever been around. That was enough for us to go for that player, grabbing Ty Lawson in 2009. He, by my calculations, ended up with a career as good as any player taken after him, which is what you aim for.[11]

Afterthought: Chase Budinger

The 2009 draft had a kid from the University of Arizona named Chase Budinger. Budinger was an athletic small forward with versatility—able to pass, shoot, and drive. Hailing from Southern California, he was also an elite high school volleyball player, though he didn't play in college so that he could focus on basketball. We talked about him during our draft meetings in a variety of ways—whether he could play fast like we did in Denver, whether he would solve our problems shooting from deep, and then about something I had never heard in the draft room. Mark had recruited a lot of kids from Southern California when he was in college, so he had built up a lot of experience with talented kids who played multiple sports. Basketball was a nice path for them because they could make a lot of money and have a long career, but was it their true love? Mark was concerned about that with Budinger. Budinger was so good as a volleyball player that he "didn't need basketball." If times got tough in basketball, would he just resume practicing volleyball to prepare for his next move? The guys who needed basketball would fight through the challenges because they had no backup plan. Budinger, Mark thought, had a backup plan.

We crossed Budinger off our list because of this backup plan. None of us—not the scouts or the analytics—loved his game, so the story was just the clincher. I continued to think about the story as Budinger became a journeyman over seven years in the NBA. Was Budinger working as hard as he could on being an NBA pro? I couldn't see that firsthand, and no one I talked to spoke poorly of his work ethic. Was he working on his volleyball game on the side? I potentially could have found his agent and asked, but they wouldn't have told me the truth. It turned out that Budinger would retire in 2017 from professional basketball and immediately begin his second career on the professional beach volleyball tour.

But I still think about the Budinger story now because maybe that wisdom can apply beyond basketball and volleyball. Do you have to *need* your job in order to work at it? Not just love it but *need* it. How much does that motivation matter?

11

Emotion

You know what really goes beyond being on paper? Emotion. Heart. Courage. Drive. All of those supposedly unmeasurable things that the old-school scouts felt couldn't be captured by the new-school guys in *Moneyball.*

But you know what? You can measure them. If they're real, you can measure them. That's what we're going to do.

And you're going to like it, dammit (see BOX, "The Curse").

The first time I had a discussion on the importance of heart was with regard to Adam Morrison. Morrison was in the 2006 NBA draft, a 6-foot-8-inch junior out of Gonzaga who had played high-level basketball the previous seven years of his life despite having type 1 diabetes. He was tough and competed incredibly hard, building his skills despite fighting his own body. He was the collegiate player of the year (with JJ Redick) and carried the Bulldogs to a top five ranking and to the Sweet Sixteen in the NCAA tournament, in some ways establishing Gonzaga as a legitimate top basketball program, not just the eternal Cinderella that they were previously.

Morrison had heart, even if my method of projecting him as an NBA player said that he wasn't a good NBA prospect. At the time, I wasn't going to argue his courage, his ability to fight through challenges, or his heart. Frankly, I couldn't measure it then and I wasn't even sure what it meant to measure it.

I have come to think that what people talk about when they refer to heart is a player's ability to reach his potential. There is some natural level of ability and . . .

. . . Okay, it's time to stop dancing around the words. I may use the following words interchangeably: heart, character, drive, motivation, self-starter. They probably have subtle differences in meaning, and I kinda have a feel for that, but the words are vague. In part, the purpose of this chapter is to assign some concreteness to this vague concept. Maybe we will end up with different forms of what it means, and we can assign those different forms to different words.

And now we return to our regularly scheduled chapter.

I think what people are seeing when they refer to heart is a player's psychological ability to push himself to reach his physical potential. The danger with Morrison was believing that his internal drive could carry him *beyond* his physical potential. When evaluating draft picks, it's important to distinguish between players' potential upside and whether they will reach it. What mathematical models typically capture is an average projected level of performance, not the upside, but they are related. My model was suggesting that his average projected performance was not what other people believed "he was worth." I was with the Sonics then, and our pick was low enough that it was unlikely that Morrison would fall to us, so our discussions were not overly important and thus not very heated. That distance was useful because we could actually think about each other's perspective without the pressure of the decision.

That all happened a long time ago. With the methods that have evolved over many years, we can actually look for periods when players exceed or underperform expectations, seemingly because of emotion.

The most obvious place to start is garbage time.

Garbage time is not something that has its own clear definition, but it is said to happen when the winner of a game is already decided and the players are not trying hard. The concept itself implies that the drive to play hard is not there, but there is more to it.

Ryan Bowen was a career backup in the NBA who became an assistant coach in retirement, and he didn't like the term "garbage time." As he explained it to me, he always looked at times when the game was out of reach as opportunities for him to get minutes to show the coaches he could play and that he deserved more time. So he called it "show-me time."

This perspective gets at the concept that subs have something to prove by playing hard but the starters and regular rotation players don't. If this internal drive impacts performance, then performance stats should show that regular players play below their normal level during garbage time but that bench players play closer to their peak.

Graph 4 generally supports the idea. It shows that the good players play about 1 point per 48 minutes worse during garbage time, mostly on the defensive side of the ball because that's when they aren't particularly motivated. Average players aren't all that different, and poor players are a bit better in garbage time, especially on defense, because their motivation to impress still exists.[1]

This finding shouldn't be controversial. It doesn't overturn conventional wisdom or go against years of non-basketball-related scientific literature. People, including basketball players, respond to incentives. The graph is simply evidence of that fact.

In the last several years, Kevin Pelton of ESPN and Ben Falk of CleaningTheGlass.com pointed out that Las Vegas oddsmakers had noticed something weird about "desperate" playoff teams that suggests the impact of motivation. Home teams that lose Game 1 of a seven-game series tend to be favored by more in Game 2 because losing would mean that they have to win four out of five, with four of those games on the road, so they *need* to win to avoid long odds. For instance, in 2018 the Portland Trail Blazers lost Game 1 of their series against the New Orleans Pelicans when they had home court advantage. Before Game 2, the oddsmakers actually increased the line toward the Blazers by one point.

Oddsmakers aren't perfect—and the Blazers did indeed lose Game 2 in 2018—but they are usually capturing something real. In this case, the record for playoff teams over the last eighteen years or so reflects what the oddsmakers saw. The home team losing Game 1 did win 79 percent of their Game 2s, whereas home teams that won Game 1 were victorious in just 74 percent of their Game 2s. The home teams that lost actually did better than those that won by about 1.5 points per game, close to the increase in the line. Falk found similar numbers when he did the study in 2017. He also ran a statistical algorithm that showed that the result of Game 1—win or loss—was predictive of Game 2 on

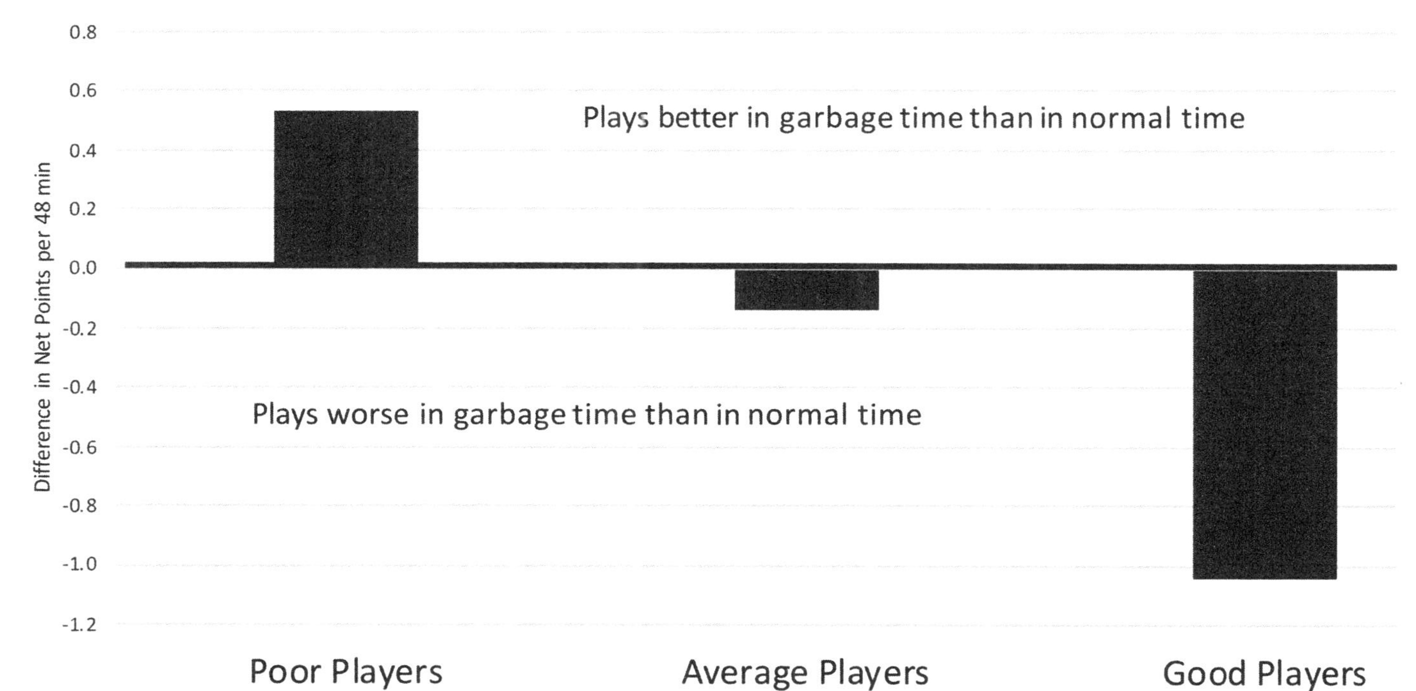

Graph 4. Difference in how well players play in garbage time versus normal time.

top of both teams' season performance, in a way that is consistent with teams being desperate.

Frankly, though, it's not clear that desperation is a real effect. Falk's results weren't particularly strong then, and the effect has weakened since 2017 to the point that it's reasonable to question whether it matters at all.

We want to believe the story. There is some evidence, and it definitely makes some psychological sense. The fact that we can't quite make a conclusion about the desperation effect doesn't mean that it doesn't exist (like the hot hand,[2] as noted in *Basketball on Paper*). Maybe the lack of proof so far means that the effect is just harder to find (and the hot hand has been found in some refined studies since *Basketball on Paper*). There isn't enough evidence to prove or disprove it. We just don't know.

Measurement of whether desperation affects play is so noisy, but it probably won't affect our innate belief that the emotion does matter. So measurement doesn't matter for that. It does matter in gambling, however, because if the line is changing based on this effect, you want to know whether that effect is real. Or, if you can't *know*, you want to understand if it's as big as other factors—like player injuries, history of coaching adjustments, schedule challenges, and, frankly, whether those players care because some circumstances make it so that they don't.

In the summer of 2010, Carmelo Anthony refused to sign an extension with the Denver Nuggets. The Nuggets were good, but Melo wanted to go to a bigger market for personal and professional reasons. He wanted out, everyone knew it, and that knowledge cast a cloud over all that happened in Denver. Through the summer, the Nuggets held discussions with him and with other teams about the future, but nothing cleared up and the team headed into the season with Melo on the active roster and uncertainty in the air.

You can imagine the mentality of Melo. Did he want to play hard for a team that he couldn't see himself with long term? You can imagine the mentality of teammates whose names were getting tossed around as parts of potential trades. Did they want to play hard for teammates they may not be with for very long?

From game 1 to game 57 of that season, the lack of motivation was evident inside the building and on the court. But from the time of the trade before game 58 to the end of the season, everyone wanted to play and the numbers echoed it.

Table 23 shows the players for the Nuggets before and after the trade. The boldface entries indicate when the player got better after the trade.

Table 23. Nuggets 2011 player performance before and after the Carmelo Anthony trade

Player	Playing time	Offense	Defense	Total
Ty Lawson	Starter	**1.8 → 3.4**	**−1.6 → 0.1**	**0.2 → 3.5**
Nenê	Starter	2.6 → −0.5	**0.5 → 3.3**	3.1 → 2.8
Kenyon Martin	Injured starter	**−1.7 → −1.0**	**−0.1 → 1.2**	**−1.8 → 0.2**
J.R. Smith	Rotation	**1.3 → 3.4**	**−0.5 → 0.2**	**0.7 → 3.6**
Al Harrington	Rotation	**0.0 → 0.5**	−0.6 → −1.1	−0.6 → −0.6
Arron Afflalo	Starter	1.8 → 0.4	**−1.6 → −0.7**	0.2 → −0.3
Chris Andersen	Rotation	**−1.2 → 3.4**	**1.7 → 3.1**	**0.5 → 6.4**
Gary Forbes	Bench/rotation	**−0.1 → −0.4**	**−2.1 → −0.6**	**−2.2 → −1.0**
Melvin Ely	Bench	**−1.8 → 1.4**	**−1.9 → 1.0**	**−3.6 → 2.4**
All players		**1.0 → 1.2**	**−0.8 → 0.9**	**0.2 → 2.1**

Note: Bold entries are cases where the player improved. Performance is measured in net points per 48 minutes.

Every player but Al Harrington got better on defense after the trade. Every player but Harrington, Nenê, and Arron Afflalo got better overall after the trade, and all of those guys were essentially the equivalent before and after. After the trade, all players knew they were going to be there the rest of the way, for each other, for the coach, for the fans. The impact was about 1–2 points per 48 minutes *per player*, which is 4–8 points for a team of five guys. For reference, the team improved by a total of 7.7 points per game.

Just the improvement of the Nuggets players—not the acquisitions—goes a long way toward explaining why the Nuggets won 56 percent of their games before the trade, going 32-25, and 72 percent of their games afterward, going 18-7. You might ask, "What about the players they got?" So let's take a quick look.

The Nuggets received Raymond Felton, Danilo Gallinari, Wilson Chandler, and Timofey Mozgov in the deal. All but Mozgov played real minutes during that posttrade period. On the whole, they played solidly, especially Felton and Gallinari. But they were replacing Melo and Chauncey Billups, both good offensive players (as well as Anthony Carter, Renaldo Balkman, and Shelden Williams). The total production of the new players was actually about 1.6 points per game *worse* than what Melo and Billups would have provided using the same minutes (assuming pretrade production).

Masai Ujiri, GM of the Nuggets at the time, said, "We feel like we got killed" in the Melo trade. He was speaking about losing the offensive talent of Melo and Billups, but a lot of the killing happened before the deal—in the motivation of players.

Finally, an anecdote illustrates the power of emotion and the lack of power we have over it in basketball. I'll leave out the player's name, because it was his personal story and it can happen to anyone. We'll call him Kirk.

I noticed that Kirk was having a series of really bad games. One bad game would never really capture my attention. Two bad games in a row would capture my attention for good players. Multiple bad games would make me think that perhaps we could find a pattern, which may mean a solution.

In this case, Kirk was shooting more, but definitely worse, from inside and from outside. I thought maybe he was trying to do too much in the offense, taking more shots, pushing it too aggressively in transition. His assist rate was up a little, too—maybe a sign that he was trying to grow his skills. But his defense was down a lot, as well. These were all signs that he was trying to step too quickly into a bigger role.

It sounded like a good story, and I prepared all of this information into a concise form to talk to Coach Karl about it. I walked into his office and said something like the following: "I have noticed that Kirk has been struggling the last two weeks. Not sure if you asked him to try to do more, but it may be costing him and us on both sides. He's taking tougher shots and making a lot less. His defense . . ."

"Wait. When did this start?"

"About two weeks ago, it looks like."

"That's when his girlfriend broke up with him. He's been a bit unfocused since."

"Okay. I have nothing more to say then."

This was a player who was hurting emotionally. It was reflected on the court, but associating that on-court play with tactical decisions or his own decision to play differently was going too far. He simply had to be human for a little while. The data represented symptoms, but in this case the symptoms couldn't differentiate between tactics and an underlying emotional cause.

And for reference, he was worse by about 3.5 net points per 48 minutes, a bit more than what the previous examples showed, but the sample size was the smallest, just one player.

This is all great. It shows what I said it would show—that we can measure the impact of heart or emotion or motivation. It's a big effect, far bigger than anything you can get by drawing up a play. But it all came from studies where we *knew* the motivation was different—garbage time, being down in a playoff series, trade rumors. On a day-by-day basis or minute-by-minute basis, that data doesn't exist. I'm not sure we want it to.

Reality Box: The Curse

"But is he a motherfucker?"

That question was part of one of the draft rooms I worked in. We said it in reference to players, not in a derogatory way. No, there were good players in the draft, there were great players in the draft. And then there were "motherfuckers." These were the guys that would end up being real franchise-changers: talented but also fierce enough that they wanted to rip an opponent's heart out.

It wasn't officially a category we wrote down, but we talked about it, and we talked about it using bad language.

It's part of fucking sports, frankly. The players curse, the coaches curse, the players and coaches curse at each other to the point that it doesn't get taken too seriously. They know it means something, but they also know the tone when the curse is intended to really mean something to really give a shit about.

Female athletes curse. Female coaches curse at female athletes, and vice versa. I haven't seen men and women curse at each other in sports, but I haven't been in many situations that would allow me to see that.

If you are thinking it's a racial thing, it's not. It's passion that runs in all colors and, frankly, in at least several foreign languages.

I personally rarely curse, but in a sports environment, I found times that it was useful to do so. On the other hand, it just rolls out of some other people's mouths, like it's a test to see if I can decipher what they're saying because the meaning is hidden behind every three words being "shit," "fuck," or "asshole." I definitely learned to translate.

I understand why it's not part of a regular office. I worked in a few. In an office, the people are often told to fill a role dispassionately as part of the process. Drama that is expressed with cursing gets in the way of their role.

In the NBA, there is no secretary, there is no mailroom guy, and no editor (though editors have been known to curse, by the way, and my editor is probably cursing at this section). Every player has to play when they're on the court. Every one of them has a physical job to do, even if they are on the bench behind LeBron. They all have to be passionate. They have to love the job and hate the losses. The coaches do, too. They're all on TV, and TV doesn't like boring. Despite the passion, TV doesn't like cursing, which is why they bleep it out and add a seven-second delay. That's also why the NBA, which relies on TV, gives out technicals to players and coaches for some cursing—the kind of cursing that is aimed at a ref or just to demean a person, not the kind designed to inspire teammates.

Cursing is an expression of passion, *passion* being something we supposedly treasure. Passion gives us the drama we love, teams battling as hard as they can for the simple love of a victory. Money makes it dispassionate, money makes it into an office, where everyone reports for their role. That's why we don't want players to fight over money—we want them to be simply passionate because so few of us outside of sports can be. We want them to care so much that they can't help but curse here and there.

But as passion creates helpful drama for spectators and can help a coach convey a point, it can also tear apart those involved in it on a regular basis. Ripping into a person with too much fire or too often, even if well intended, can shatter nerves. Player-player relationships and player-coach relationships have definitely been hurt when the emotion of cursing goes beyond helpful. Passion is great because it can motivate people to go beyond what they believe they can do. But it can also take people to the point of high stress, which affects the ability to be calm and solve problems.

Cursing may be the language of passion, but know your audience and use cursing for good, not evil.

12

The Problem with Nonscorers

In February 2009 the *New York Times* ran an article by Michael Lewis, the author of *Moneyball*, about Houston Rockets forward Shane Battier, calling him "the no-stats All-Star." Battier was averaging 7 points per game at the time and taking an average of just seven shots in his 32 minutes on the court. That's the "no-stats" part. But as Lewis wrote, Battier was "a player widely regarded as a replaceable cog . . . yet every team he has ever played on has acquired some magical ability to win."

The article was as much about Rockets general manager Daryl Morey as it was about Battier. Morey was like Oakland A's GM Billy Beane in *Moneyball*, making analytical decisions about players, and Battier was like Scott Hatteberg, the A's first baseman whose value wasn't captured by traditional baseball stats. Morey talked about the secret sauce he used to identify Battier in this article, but he didn't give away the recipe, as has been said about Beane in baseball.

The article became basketball analytics' biggest advertisement, nudging those teams that hadn't invested in it by illustrating that numbers had that "magical ability." In a passage that gave the article even more weight, Lewis wrote that the subculture of analytics in basketball is different from that in other sports because "it happens to be the sport that is most like life." I didn't know exactly what he meant, but I loved it.

This chapter is not about Battier so much as the whole class of players who just don't shoot a lot, Battier being the most hyped example. This type of player can be efficient, as the *Times* claimed Battier to be, but how much do they really contribute? Conventional wisdom has generally discarded these players from any discussion of greatness. They have been complementary players, not All-Stars. They have been the guys standing in the corner without the ball, making occasional shots when someone else created an open look. Opposing teams didn't develop their game plan around these guys, so how good could they be?

Here's another player from that class who, like Battier, had a long career despite really not shooting much: Nick Collison. Collison played his entire fourteen-year career with the same franchise. His first year with the Sonics was also my first year in the league, so I was around him a little bit. He was a great team guy, his teammates liked him, he did the dirty work on the court, like screening and boxing out. He averaged 6 points per game for his career, never more than 9.8 in a season. He took under 12 total shots (field goal attempts and equivalent free throws) per 48 minutes, thirty-ninth lowest in recent league history (Battier was thirty-seventh lowest).

Bismack Biyombo is another great team guy still in the league as of 2023, setting screens, rolling to the rim, doing what he's supposed to, having some intimidation factor on the defensive side. He has been in the league twelve years, averaging 5 points per game, never more than 7.4. He has averaged 11 total shots per 48 minutes, twenty-second lowest.

Bruce Bowen took 10 total shots per 48 minutes in his long career, eleventh lowest. He was the model for the "three-and-D player,"[1] shooting three-pointers when left open on offense and guarding the opponent's best player on defense. He was the model for what Battier became but was a little too early for Michael Lewis to do a story on him. Thabo Sefolosha (thirty-second lowest total shots per minute) and Trenton Hassell (twenty-fourth) were along this line. Royce O'Neale (thirteenth) and P.J. Tucker (fifteenth) fit this mold currently.

To be clear, not a single one of these players ever made an NBA All-Star Game. So the "no-stats" part has generally been winning, keeping these guys off the prominent award rolls.

If the conventional way to measure players was to look at the points they scored per game, the Morey way was to look at the plus-minus statistic, how much the team outscored the opponent with a player on the floor. It was added to NBA box scores around that time but was lurking throughout the analytics subculture for years. If the team

Table 24. Selected nonscorers and their composite offensive values by experience in the NBA

Experience (y)	Battier	Biyombo	Bowen	Collison
1	−0.2	−3.6	−1.0	−0.5
2	0.9	−2.9	−2.7	−0.2
3	0.8	−2.7	−2.2	−1.0
4	0.3	−1.9	−2.0	−0.6
5	−0.2	−2.0	−2.1	−0.8
6	−0.3	−2.9	−1.2	−0.6
7	−0.2	−3.4	−2.1	−0.6
8	−0.7	−2.4	−1.9	0.0
9	−0.7	−1.7	−2.1	0.2
10	0.3	−3.5	−2.2	−0.1
11	−0.5	−1.2	−3.0	−1.1
12	−0.4	−2.8	−3.7	−3.0
13	−0.8			−1.6
14				−2.7
Average	−0.1	−2.6	−2.2	−0.9

did well when you were on the floor, it was a piece of evidence that you were good. The analytics subculture never said it was a perfect stat or even the equivalent of on-base percentage in baseball, which became much more prominent after *Moneyball*. But the metric was simple, and it said something to balance out the message of points per game.

It was not Morey's secret sauce. Rather, Morey and his staff would adjust plus-minus to account for who else was on the floor—that was more the secret. He had an adjusted plus-minus metric like what is discussed in chapter 7, "Cutting the Cake," which isn't secret now and wasn't secret to the analytics subculture back then.

If that was at least secret to other teams, what wasn't secret was Morey's breakdown of Battier's game to help explain why Battier could be so helpful. Morey talked about Battier tipping rebounds to teammates, getting his hands on the ball before Kobe Bryant could prepare

Hassell	O'Neale	Sefolosha	Tucker
−1.4	−1.1	−2.6	−1.1
−3.6	−1.8	−1.8	−0.7
−1.8	−0.6	−1.7	−0.1
−1.9	−0.7	−1.9	−0.8
−1.8	−0.7	−1.1	−1.1
−1.6	−1.5	−1.6	−1.4
−3.7		0.1	−1.4
−3.2		−1.4	−1.7
−3.7		−0.7	−1.9
		−1.5	−3.3
		−1.7	−1.3
		−0.7	−3.3
		−1.6	
		−1.9	
−2.5	−1.1	−1.4	−1.5

for a shot, and knowing opponents' tendencies extremely well. Notably, Morey didn't mention anything about Battier's offense.

It's time to look at the player value metrics for this class of eight players. There are a lot of metrics, as mentioned in chapter 7, and some have only a partial history of data, so a composite of them makes sense here.[2] Table 24 shows the above players and their *offensive* value according to a composite metric. This analysis is not about their defense, just what they appeared to create on the offensive side of the ball. From that table, it's easy to see that none of these guys really ever reached positive offensive values for any extended period. Collison and Sefolosha had a couple of years slightly better than average.

Battier had three years of positive offensive numbers and, frankly, one metric among the composite particularly dragged him down (RPM). If you throw out that metric (and many in the analytics subculture don't like it), he was slightly positive in years 2 through 8 of his career (year 8 being when Michael Lewis wrote about him). He wasn't ever great on offense, but he was solid to good in at least years 2 through 4, which is more than can be said of the rest of the players on this chart. Those guys were pretty bad. So what made Battier different?

Table 25 compiles all of these guys to show their career effective shooting percentages, the percentage of team field goals that they attempted, and how often they turned it over. These three stats explain a lot here, and the fact that Battier is the only player on this list who ranks in the top four in all of them is a big part of the reason why he came out as the most valuable offensively. Specifically, among the players on this list, Battier actually took the highest percentage of his teams' shots, he shot the ball pretty well,[3] and he turned it over the least.

The story on Battier came out in 2009. Morey would pull off the biggest deal of his career about three years later when he acquired James Harden from Oklahoma City for Jeremy Lamb, Kevin Martin, two first-round picks, and a second-round pick. Whereas Battier was making about $6 million in salary from the Rockets in 2009 (about 11 percent of the salary cap), Harden's starting salary on his extension was nearly $14 million (about 22 percent of the cap).

Harden was a scorer. Whereas Battier was thirty-seventh lowest in terms of shots per 48 minutes, Harden was twenty-fifth *highest* as of this writing. Whereas Battier never actually made an All-Star team, Harden was a ten-time big-stats All-Star. Whereas Houston's offense ranked an average of sixteenth with Battier on the team, the Rockets averaged the fourth best offense in the eight full seasons with Harden, never finishing worse than sixth.

Don't get me wrong; there was no trade here of Battier for Harden. I'm not saying that the only change in those teams was those two players. Not at all. But the point is that Morey went from highly valuing a no-stats guy to much more highly valuing a big-stats guy with whom the offense got a lot better because he did blossom into an actual All-Star.

It's kind of a secret of the analytics subculture that a player's points scored average actually is a pretty solid indicator of player value. As

Table 25. Low-usage players by various values

Player	Offensive net points per 48 min.	Effective field goal percentage	Percentage of team field goals attempted	Turnovers per possession used
Battier	−0.1	52.9% (4)	13.8% (1)	12.2% (1)
Collison	−0.9	53.6% (2)	13.1% (2)	17.2% (7)
O'Neale	−1.1	55.4% (1)	11.4% (7)	15.0% (4)
Sefolosha	−1.4	50.9% (6)	13.1% (3)	16.0% (6)
Tucker	−1.5	51.3% (5)	11.4% (6)	14.2% (3)
Bowen	−2.2	49.4% (7)	12.2% (5)	13.1% (2)
Hassell	−2.5	45.9% (8)	13.0% (4)	15.4% (5)
Biyombo	−2.6	53.3% (3)	10.8% (8)	18.8% (8)

Note: Ranks are in parentheses.

much as basketball analytics may have wanted to minimize conversations around points per game the same way that baseball minimized use of batting average, the subculture knew that it still mattered. The informed plus-minus metrics were better, of course, but even they had points scored per minute as a pretty important input to some of them. Beyond that, if you look at the correlation between game-by-game offensive value (using net points) and all the box score statistics, the strongest correlation is with points scored, not shooting percentage, not assists, not turnovers, not three-pointers made.[4] So it's not surprising that, of this class of eight players, Battier easily had the most points per game, 8.6 versus fewer than 7 for everyone else.

Another secret of the basketball analytics subculture is something called the Pue equation, which relates a player's overall offensive productivity to their possession usage and to their individual efficiency.[5] So the offensive productivity measures shown for these eight players in table 26 relate to their overall usage and efficiency in a clear way.[6] The productivity values are from above, the usage numbers are from Basketball-Reference, and then the Pue equation gives the individual efficiency values. Of these, Battier is the only player among them with an efficiency above the league average efficiency for their career (compare the fourth and fifth columns). Even though there were other low-usage

Table 26. Low-usage players, their offensive productivity, usage, and efficiency

Player	Offensive net points per 48 min.	Usage	Efficiency	League average rating	Points per game
Battier	−0.1	12.9%	109.5	105.9	8.6
Collison	−0.9	13.4%	103.9	106.5	5.9
O'Neale	−1.1	11.1%	109.2	111.8	6.6
Sefolosha	−1.4	12.7%	100.5	106.9	5.7
Tucker	−1.5	11.0%	102.4	109.0	6.8
Bowen	−2.2	11.4%	92.5	105.3	6.1
Hassell	−2.5	12.5%	90.5	105.5	5.8
Biyombo	−2.6	12.6%	92.7	108.1	5.1

players like Battier, in this class of eight guys, none of them scored as much or as efficiently as he did.

Regarding Lewis's article about Battier, it's not clear whether Lewis reached out to Morey or vice versa, but there was clearly a synergy between what Lewis had done in baseball and football (*The Blind Side*) and what Morey was doing in basketball. Lewis was frequently writing about the hidden edge in his books (even his nonsports ones), so Morey's use of stats was a logical extension. For Morey, inviting Lewis in to interview his staff and watch a game would make sense. Doing so would help the young Morey's profile and put him in line to be the Billy Beane of basketball, at least.

That's a pretty unique angle with the press. Most general managers would have no shot at getting that kind of parallel. Most general managers either avoid the press or use it selectively to push a team agenda. In Morey's case, he could well have also been pushing a team agenda on top of raising his personal brand. Trade value on guys scoring under 10 points per game is generally not too good, so a story on his no-stats All-Star could only help. Battier was in the middle of his contract at the time, so there was essentially no risk of the good publicity being used against Morey in a contract negotiation. For Morey, it only served to raise the league value of Battier, not his internal value.

That angle of promoting your own players is common. It's partially a bias; being around players naturally makes you like them a little more (in most cases). But it's also a marketing ploy. Morey definitely did it with Battier. Every other GM would have done similarly, even if they weren't on Michael Lewis's contact list.

·

If the above numbers show that Battier was above the league efficiency, why didn't he shoot more than he did? Wouldn't he have helped the team more by doing so?

The answer to the latter question is, "Yes, he would have helped the team more if he could maintain his efficiency while taking more shots."

The answer to the first question is more like, "He would likely have sacrificed efficiency by taking more shots." That's what the chapter "The Problem with Scorers" in *Basketball on Paper* looked at more than twenty years ago. Different players had different abilities to take shots and keep making them. Kobe Bryant and Shaquille O'Neal could take a lot of shots before their efficiency went down. Other guys like Jerry Stackhouse and Allen Iverson had gradual declines in efficiency as they took more shots. Role players like Battier tended to not be able to take many shots at all before their efficiency declined significantly. Battier was only a few months into his NBA career at the time the chapter was written, so there was nothing specifically written about him in that chapter, but that was the general message. And it's probably correct.

But I re-created Battier's "skill curve" from that no-stats All-Star season, and it tells a slightly different story. He used only about 12 percent of the team possessions that year, but the curve suggests that he could probably have used about 16 percent before going below average in efficiency,[7] which would have maintained or improved his overall productivity while doing so. Why would he have taken so few shots that year? In fact, that season was Battier's lowest usage year of his career, but it started out pretty normally. After he did the interview with Michael Lewis about being a "no-stats All-Star," Battier shot less, as though he were trying to live up to the message of the piece. That difference was significant, too, not just a small decline, going from about 10.8 field goal attempts per 48 minutes to about 7.7 the rest of the year. It is only circumstantial evidence, but it does look like that article itself kept Battier from playing optimally. It's amazing what you can do to a player by messing with their head.

The Usage Gap

The Battier story is from 2009, and the league has changed a bit since then. Three-point shooting has exploded. Kobe Bryant, who was master of the midrange, retired, and so did Battier. There has not been another article about no-stats All-Stars, but there have been blog postings and tweets.

One particular thing has changed even more in the post-COVID NBA: star players got a lot more productive and even more ball-dominant, especially in 2023. Luka Dončić and Giannis Antetokounmpo were as dominant with the ball as anyone, controlling the game, running sets and either shooting or passing based on what the defense did—things done also by LeBron and Dame and Ja and Trae and Tatum, guys good enough to be known by one name like Brazilian *futebol* players. There were sixty-four players who both played 800 minutes and averaged a usage of at least 25 percent in 2023, basically controlling one of every four possessions for the team. That was more players than in any other season.

What happened at the same time was that seventy-seven players had both 800 minutes and averaged *under* a 15 percent usage—using less than one in every six possessions. That seventy-seven figure is also the most in history, representing a growing divide, having more ball dominance by single individuals and more players essentially just screening and spacing. Of those seventy-seven nonscorers, a composite metric of their offensive performance said that only nine of them were better than average offensively. Those nine were Kevon Looney (a big), Robert Williams (a big), Josh Hart (a wing who is great in transition), Delon Wright (a point guard), Walker Kessler (a big), Steven Adams (a big), Quentin Grimes (a wing), Sam Hauser (a wing), and Luke Kennard (a wing). Only Grimes averaged in double figures (with 11). All but the last two were considered to have a pretty good defensive component to them.

Only nine of seventy-seven nonscorers were above average in overall offensive productivity! It's not surprising, though, right? These guys weren't major threats or the top of the scouting report. Nine of seventy-seven means about 12 percent of nonscorers were at least good with their offense. That's pretty average historically and, frankly, that is essentially exactly the percentage of one Battier being above average versus the seven other guys compared with him above. As much as people wanted to praise Battier, his best composite offensive value in a season was +0.9 points per 48 minutes. Among the nine players in 2023 who were positive offensively, their best was Hauser at +0.6.

So nonscorers aren't good offensive players, as a rule. They can be a little bit above average, but not many of them are. That is the conventional wisdom, but it is also analytical.

Coincidentally or not, Morey once said of analytics that a lot of it ended up confirming conventional wisdom, this case being that, duh, players who score more points are generally better. Efficiency matters, and there are other ways to create value besides scoring. We're trying to measure more of those ways all the time, but no matter how much data we get on screening or spacing through new technology, scoring points is going to remain valuable.

Why Is This Important?

So if the above study on nonscorers is simply confirming conventional wisdom, why is this important?

For one thing, you should be leery of claims of "no-stats All-Stars," Shane Battier or otherwise. Of players since 2008 with a usage rate under 15 percent, Kyle Korver in 2015 had the best offensive season, his composite offensive value being +3.0, which is essentially All-Star level. And you know what? He actually did make the All-Star Game that year. He also shot 49 percent from beyond the arc and 90 percent from the foul line, led the league in true shooting percentage, scored 12 points per game, and started for the best team in the NBA.

Second, the Pue relationship puts nonscorers and scorers onto a common measuring grid. For example, those nine players from 2023 who used under 15 percent of possessions but were slightly positive

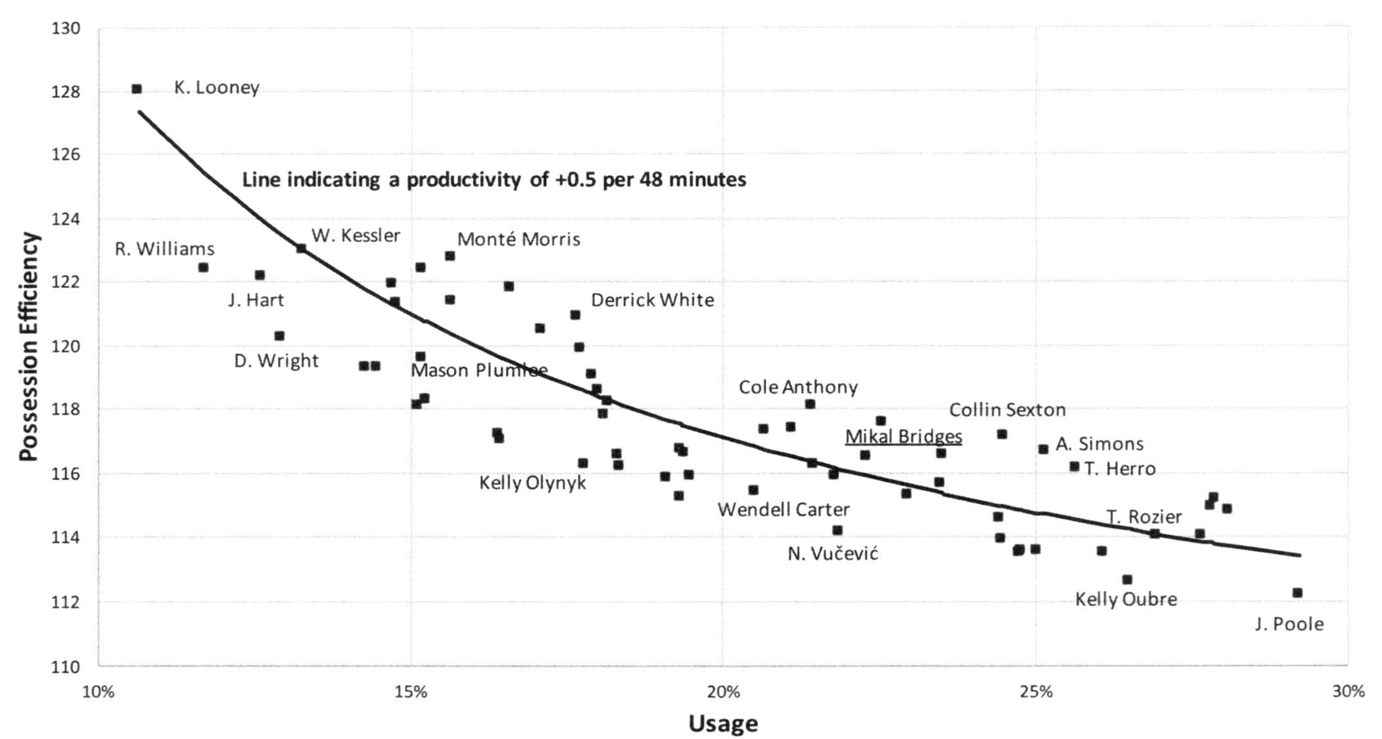

Graph 5. Efficiency versus usage for various players in 2023, all having an overall offensive productivity of about +0.5.

offensively can be put on a graph with guys who used possessions at higher rates and were essentially at the same productivity level (graph 5). Jordan Poole, Anfernee Simons, Tyler Herro, and Terry Rozier are just some of the higher-usage players whose overall offensive contribution wasn't particularly different from that of low-usage guys like Looney, Robert Williams, Kessler, and Hart. Guys more in the middle range of usage who generated similar productivity were Monté Morris, Derrick White, Kelly Olynyk, Cole Anthony, Nikola Vučević, and Collin Sexton. All of these guys, despite a range of usage between 11 percent and 29 percent, produced about the same amount of offensive benefit to their teams. Some were bigger offensive rebounders, some were cautious point guards, some were gunners who weren't the most accurate.

Maybe you think that some of these guys are better than others. It's fair to question them, since metrics aren't perfect. But I'm guessing that a lot of that subjectivity is a belief that the guys on the right are better than the guys on the left, reflecting the typical bias toward higher scorers.

Note particularly where Mikal Bridges is in graph 5, having a usage of about 22 percent along with his composite productivity of +0.9. This was the year that Bridges was traded from Phoenix, where he was mostly a nonscorer, to Brooklyn, where he had to become a scorer. His usage increased from about 19 percent to 29 percent after the trade. Do you know what his overall productivity was in the prior couple of years when his usage was really low, at 15 percent? From the same composite, it was +0.8 in 2022 and +1.3 in 2021, essentially the same as in 2023 after he used so many more possessions. So him ramping up how much he scored was effectively offset by a decline in efficiency. Not all players will do that, but Bridges did.[8]

Understanding the relationship between how much players *can do* and how much they *actually do* is not a secret of the analytics subculture, because the subculture doesn't do it right yet. The work of twenty years ago in "The Problem with Scorers" aimed to address it, but it should be done better with some of the modern tracking data. Data that captures how good players are in specific roles can suggest which roles they take on more often or less often. That knowledge affects as much as anything whether they are a scorer or a nonscorer. That and some degree of player development.

Reality Box: Implications of the Pue Equation

Remember, it was Michael Lewis who said this, not me: basketball is the sport that is most like life.

He didn't elaborate on that statement at all. He left it hanging, so let me try to fill it in.

Basketball is about competing against opposing teams and competing for credit among teammates. Life is a bit like that. Everyone wants to win as a team, but everyone wants to be the hero of that team.

Basketball is about making decisions to help the team. Decisions about who is in the best position to succeed, who is needed for what role—those go beyond basketball.

Basketball is about the efficiency of a team and the productivity of the teammates. How big a role a person gets means taking on a risk of being the hero or being the scapegoat. That's life and that's also the Pue equation, which has been referenced a couple times in the main part of this chapter.

The Pue equation was derived because I needed it for basketball, but it is not built on things specific to the game. It just looks at a group of people as a team and how to reward players for the size of their roles. It is then relevant for teams outside sports—teams in corporate America, teams in grade schools in Japan.

So that equation actually lends insight into why basketball is more like life.

It says that the size of the team actually matters, for instance. The more players on a team, the smaller the cost to any one of them for just participating. Someone who doesn't have a role on a two-person team is more costly to the team than someone on a five- or ten-person team.

The equation also says that the difficulty of finding other talent also matters. If it's relatively easy to find solid talent, better players can take a smaller role and be as effective. If it's harder to find talent or if the range in talent is much broader, then better players need to take on a bigger role. This is partially why players in college tend to have higher usage numbers than when they get to the NBA. But it also suggests that firms built around high-end talent should be a bit more balanced.

Finally, it says that individual efficiency is a bit more important to overall value than how big a role is. The two bits of data are often correlated, as they are in basketball, where the most efficient players get the most opportunities. But if you're in a smaller role, do it efficiently and maybe it will grow like it did for Mikal Bridges. Or maybe just be like Shane Battier, the complementary piece that everyone wants around.

13

Make 'Em Better

After working a lot of years in a front office, I spent four years as a coach. I worked with a lot of good coaches and I listened to them often, but I also asked questions, like "Why do we do so many shooting drills without defense?"

"A lot of coaching is about building habits. Shooting does that," they'd say. "Sometimes players also just want to talk, and casual shooting is a good time to do that."

"But does it make them better shooters?"

"Practice helps. More reps help. We know that. It's the ten thousand hours thing."

"By the time they've gotten to the NBA, they've easily gotten ten thousand hours. I'm just wondering what helps in the NBA, now that they're here."

"I don't know. It's your job to sort that out."

So I spent a lot of time just trying to identify what worked and what didn't. Data told me that players are 5–10 percent worse on the first shot at a spot in a drill. And I'd ask, "Why don't we incentivize making the first shot at a spot in a drill? If they're supposed to make five, but they make the first one, they only have to make three, for example."

"That's not a bad idea."

"Can we contest more of their shots then, too?"

"We already do some of that, but if you want more, you're going to have to do it."

"Deal."

I became the guy running out to world-class shooters to give them more realistic closeouts. As one of the players told me, though, I was working too hard on it, and as a result, I pulled my groin once, then tore a part of me that I didn't know existed, which kept me out for months. I loved the idea, but my body didn't love that I was the one implementing the idea. Did the idea work? I think it did, but it would take more controlled testing to know.

We tested the Kornet Eclipse contest, too. It's named after Boston big man Luke Kornet, who would play ten to fifteen feet off his man but jump early with his arms up to limit the shooter's view of the rim. To test it in practice, we couldn't get a big man to jump over and over again, so we held up a long pad to block the view of the rim for a couple of shooters. We got a solid sample size, and the test showed evidence of the move working for at least a couple of shooters. One thing we saw is that the shooters seemed to get better against it the more they saw it. Again, it wasn't enough to *know*.

Many right-handed shooters like to go left to shoot a jumper. Terry Rozier, for example, does it often, shooting 4–5 percent better drifting left than drifting right, whether off the catch or off the dribble (see table 27). Julius Randle is a lefty who tends to drift right on his jumper off the catch or off the dribble and almost never drifts left. Many shooters don't have much directional tendency, but keeping those that do from going in their preferred direction helps the defense.[1] The data is actually pretty good for that finding. But in a game, a defender might sell out completely to that preferred side. Even though anticipating the drift direction worked great for me in practice, doing that in a game can open a defender up to allowing a drive. So despite *knowing* that this observation of a directional tendency can help in defending a jump shot, there is a tradeoff in games that isn't measured (or at least not analyzed), which keeps us from knowing whether it works overall.

Flipping the previous paragraph from defense to offense, if we know one of our shooters has this tendency, what should we do about it? Should we defend on that side more in practice to get them used to it? Should we try to get them to go that direction less often? The possible solutions make some sense, but I wasn't able to study them to know.

In general, I can't *know* the answers here without better testing than I was able to do. As coaches we do what we *think* is right because we have to. We have to teach something, and it's going to work sometimes.

Table 27. Players who shoot more or better on three-point shots drifting the opposite direction of shooting hand

	Off catch 3-pointer makes/attempts (3pt%)			Off dribble 3-pointer makes/attempts (3pt%)		
Player	Going left	Going right	%Drift	Going left	Going right	%Drift
Righties						
Terry Rozier	97/256 (37.9%)	39/118 (33.1%)	48%	95/293 (32.4%)	28/97 (28.9%)	74%
Caris LeVert	15/54 (27.8%)	0/2 (0.0%)	15%	49/155 (31.6%)	1/5 (20.0%)	41%
Donovan Mitchell	37/121 (30.6%)	23/68 (33.8%)	31%	178/475 (37.5%)	60/176 (34.1%)	56%
Lefties						
Julius Randle	4/12 (33.3%)	91/240 (37.9%)	28%	0/2 (0.0%)	124/349 (35.5%)	74%
James Harden	0/1 (0.0%)	7/24 (29.2%)	12%	2/23 (8.7%)	145/399 (36.3%)	39%
Kelly Oubre Jr.	1/4 (25.0%)	59/189 (31.2%)	24%	1/1 (100.0%)	30/98 (30.6%)	49%

Note: %Drift indicates the percentage of their three-point attempts that have a drift in either direction.

But we probably do it for too long without testing it adequately to *know* if it's right. And I say that because, as coaches, we sometimes forget that we can make players worse.

Shaquille O'Neal came into the NBA making 57 percent of his foul shots in college at LSU. In his rookie year, he made 59 percent. In his second year, it was 55 percent. In his third year, it dropped to 53 percent, which is when the stats were clear that he was worse than he was in college. It then dropped to 49 percent, then to 48 percent. He was shooting a lot of free throws, taking about ten per game, so an extra 10 percent on his percentage would add a lot of value.[2] He ended up reaching his college free throw percentage of 57 percent in only three seasons of his nineteen in the league. We don't know what coaches did with him, but we know that there were a lot of voices. Many people would try to remove the kryptonite weakness of Shaq, because doing so would make him unstoppable.

Then there is Ben Simmons, a number 1 pick out of LSU like Shaq. In his first year in the league, he shot 56 percent from the free throw line, well below the 67 percent that he shot in college. Did someone try to improve it? His high school coach, for whom Simmons shot better, thought so:[3] "When he first got to Philly, I don't know what really happened, but his form changed—really, technically not correct—I think maybe trying to straighten him out too much with his arm, ended up opening his arm up. It didn't look good, and I think he lost confidence—the way it appeared, and also the result." We don't know what was done or who did what, but his free throw percentage clearly declined, like Shaq's.

From the outside, it is essentially impossible to know the interaction and, hence, when to look for results. For the cases above, we just know that results changed from one year to another with an assumption that the players were coached in these areas. Maybe coaches knew the right form Shaq should take on free throws but taught it poorly. Maybe they taught it well, but Shaq couldn't get past his own mental hurdles. Maybe they coached him regularly, or maybe it was periodic fixing. Maybe they actually did nothing, but I doubt it. We don't *know*.

That's why we want to *know* what works and what doesn't—because it is possible for coaching to hurt a player. Until we can know, though, these are some of the things that I *think* can help, based on my interactions and analyses of data.

Make sure players are building skills, not just habits. A lot of times, when trying to build a skill, we're practicing something that a player isn't good at, like midrange pull-up two-point shots. To build that skill, players need to do it a lot, but if they're doing it in a game while they're bad, they're going to hurt the team. They're not going to get as many reps in a game as they can get in practice, so the value of game shots isn't huge to building their skill. But if they take a lot of shots in practice, they're also building the mental *habit* of taking the shot. Until it's good enough, it's just a habit and not a skill. Monitoring that habit until it's good enough to be considered a skill is then critical. For example, for NBA players' midrange shot to be worth taking, they need to make it at about 48–49 percent in games.[4] By my experience, that means that they need to make it at about 80 percent in practice.[5]

Incentivize making the first free throw. Players tend to shoot 2–4 percent worse on the first shot at the foul line. On the first one, they don't have the muscle memory from the previous shot, and their heartbeat may still be elevated. Being better at the first one helps in making the next one. If players have to make twenty-five free throws to finish practice, they should only have to make twenty if they make the first one, for example.

Similarly, we should *incentivize the first shot at a spot in a shooting drill.* Players tend to shoot 5–10 percent worse on the first shot at a spot in a shooting drill, but that's the one that is most representative of game situations. If they have to make five at a spot to move on in a drill, reduce the number to three or four if they make the first one, for example. This change can be annoying for coaches who usually count shots up to five or ten. But if they count *down* instead of up, it gets easier.

Practice shooting with distractions. These distractions are not just having coaches contest shots but also shooting when the player has to make a decision about shooting, passing, or dribbling or having to think about the shot clock. Decision-making is one of the biggest distractions a player faces. Shooters don't get enough of all those distractions through spot-up drills or live scrimmages. I'm pretty sure that the reason the NBA average shooting percentage rises through the course of the year is that jump shooters get less distracted by what else is going on as they get used to teammates and their offense. It's not layups or free throws that improve during the NBA season. It's the three-point shots and midrange jumpers. Layups are short and happen fast. Free throws are farther but have no distractions.[6] It's those jump shots where there is a *decision* to shoot—that's what gets better, so try to get better at it sooner.[7]

Clearly define what is spot shooting for getting reps versus what is a drill to improve. Spot shooting drills at the end of practice to just wind down or have some fun—those are needed for connection between players and staff. We don't want to take fun and connection away—that's part of how you get players to play for you—but them knowing that certain segments are more serious also builds connection, especially if skills, not just habits, are being built.

Emphasize the ability to set screens on the ball, but emphasize the ability to use screens off the ball. Setting and using screens are both fundamental to the success of a screen, so both should be taught. What I've found through the screen effectiveness data of the NBA, however, is that the effectiveness of screens is more often dictated by who is setting the screen when it's on the ball but more often dictated by who is using the screen when it's off the ball. That means you should not ignore the other responsibility but be clear with the emphasis.

Teach defenders that offensive players tend to drive more to their shooting hand side and pull up for jumpers to their off-hand side. Depending on the offensive player's strength, you can then favor one versus the other. It just gives a defender an extra half second of advantage to be able to keep up with a driver or to close out on a pull-up. There are occasional exceptions to this rule but not many. Alec Burks, Tyler Herro, Immanuel Quickley, and Landry Shamet are the primary exceptions I've run into.

Rebounds tend to go opposite of where they were shot or back toward the shooter or stick around the rim. Players should position themselves according to those rules, filling in where their teammates aren't. I heard something like this while growing up, but it was simpler—just that shots go opposite or back toward the shooter. The NBA data confirms that fact. What happens a lot, though, is that players won't go to fill one of the open areas, whether it's the opposite side, the shooter's side, or just around the rim.

I would love to *confirm* these recommendations, but I feel good enough about them to say that I believe in them. That assurance is partly because coaches do some of these things already. And I'm hoping that coaches can do their own studies to confirm that they work.

Do You Develop Their Strengths or Weaknesses?

Even outside the drills that coaches run, there is still guesswork in what gets emphasized for players. Usually, at the end of a season, a staff will come up with priorities for various players to work on in the off-season. Those priorities usually come down to building various weaknesses, but they can cover a lot. Sometimes, they cover so much that the emphasis seems like, "Work on everything." And fundamentally, a lot of these off-season plans aren't documented well enough to see how they're executed, a problem of coordination and resources.

Without evidence of what was emphasized historically, it's again hard to *know* what works. But as coaches say frequently, "You are what you emphasize," which suggests that what results is a consequence of what gets emphasized. So what should you emphasize to build the best version of a player?

There are a couple of rules of thumb here. Shooting is the most fundamental skill of the game, so the first such rule is to work on that; only the players who rarely touch the ball can get away with not working on shooting. This rule is well known. Second, emphasizing the skills that define a player's role is also important. For example, working on ball handling makes sense for a point guard but not for a big man, because the latter won't handle the ball much as part of their role. That rule is also well known.

Roles, however, are often a little vague, and players don't always fit into a specific position. As a result, you have to ask questions like this: Do you work on a big man's three-point shot when he's already pretty good with his inside game, or do you try to make what he's already good at even better?

This is a philosophical question for most, but the NBA has enough statistical history to go beyond theory. There is an especially large collection of data on player development in the NBA: thousands of players got better, got worse, or stayed the same. That history, if used right, can suggest what to emphasize for a player.

You can start with a tool that is used widely in sports: similarity scores. Developed in baseball and often used to make predictions about the future, similarity scores are a tool to quickly identify a class of players similar to each other. Nate Silver, for example, used similarity scores to predict the future of a basketball player by taking an average of the futures of players who are most similar.[8] But you can do far more than that.

You can generate a list of similar players, then look not only at the average of the most similar players but also which ones got better versus which ones got worse in the long run. From those who got better, you can test which of the stats were apparently driving that improvement.

For example, in the summer of 2022, Lauri Markkanen's career was in flux. He was traded to Utah, which would be his third team in three years. He was a big man with perimeter skills, and up to that summer, his role had been gradually constrained to being more and more of a perimeter player, shooting a higher rate of shots from beyond the arc, shooting less, and getting fewer defensive boards. What should he emphasize for his first year in Utah?

The group of players similar to Markkanen was an eclectic mix, reflecting the difficulty of assigning him a position. The best players were some old-school guys like Brad Daugherty, Rasheed Wallace, Tom Chambers, and Andrew Bogut, as well as more new-school guys like Danilo Gallinari, Jonas Valančiūnas, LaMarcus Aldridge, Al Horford, Brook Lopez, and Kelly Olynyk. The worst players were mostly those whose careers had ended, like Vlade Radmanović, Wayman Tisdale, Andrea Bargnani, Andrés Nocioni, Vin Baker, Pat Garrity, Kevin Duckworth, and Lorenzen Wright. And then the guys in the middle were a mix: Aaron Gordon, Thaddeus Young, Harrison Barnes, Tristan Thompson, Charlie Villanueva, Keith Van Horn, Mike Miller, and Raef LaFrentz, among others.

What did the best players in the group do in the sixth year of their career that the worst players didn't? Or that the middle-of-the-road players didn't? Again, we don't know from the outside what was emphasized, and we don't know which drills they ran, but we can see which stats differentiated these classes of players in their sixth years. For these groups, the best players dramatically improved their effective shooting, going up by one percentage point, whereas the worst players declined by 2–3 percent. The best players particularly shot the three better, whereas middle-of-the-road players got better inside the arc, and the worst players got worse in both. The worst players didn't get to the line as much in year six, whereas the best players got there at least as much as their career average. Notably, there wasn't any differentiation in turnovers, so that wouldn't be an emphasis.

Table 28 highlights all of the stats where there was differentiation across the three comparison groups for Markkanen. The line labeled "Danger sign" shows the statistical average of the players in the worst comparison group. The line labeled "Middle end" has the average stats

Table 28. Goals and danger signs for Lauri Markkanen entering his sixth year, 2022–23

Goal	Games	Min./G	eFG%	FG2%	FG3%	DR%
Danger sign	42.0	27.3	51%	49%	34%	20%
Middle end	51.5	29.1	**54%**	**55%**	37%	22%
High end	**57.3**	**30.4**	**54%**	**52%**	**39%**	22%
Actual	66	34.4	59%	59%	39%	21%

Note: Bold numbers indicate goals he met or danger signs. Abbreviations are defined in a list at the beginning of the book.

for the group in the middle. The line labeled "High end" has the stats in year 6 for the players who maximized the rest of their careers.

For Markkanen, the first two statistical goals were simply games and minutes per game. Markkanen needed on-court playing time. If he played only forty-two games in his sixth year, that would be a danger sign. If he played fifty-seven or more, that would be a good sign. He ended up playing sixty-six, so he exceeded both the high- and middle-end goals. He also exceeded the minutes goals. He exceeded a lot of his offensive goals, as highlighted in bold in table 28, missing only on the rate at which he took threes, then missing on steals on the defensive side.

Markkanen exceeded his shooting goals by so much that he won the Most Improved Player award in 2023. Not surprisingly, his career projections also improved. His comparison groups also changed but not a lot. Karl-Anthony Towns, Domantas Sabonis, and Pau Gasol all got added on the good side. Kiki VanDeWeghe and Eddy Curry got added on the bad side. Sean Elliott, Rudy Gay, Antonio McDyess, and Nic Batum got added in the middle. From these new comparison groups, Markkanen's goals for year seven (2023–24) changed to a smaller collection than he had in year six, as seen in table 29. An important thing with this list is that it is mostly suggesting he keep doing what he has done for his *career*—not what he did *last year*. He still needs to shoot a lot—26 percent while he's on the floor. He needs to assist on 9 percent of teammates' made shots and keep blocking 0.9 percent of opponent's attempts. He should be close to 40 percent from the arc and continue to get to the foul line. But he doesn't have to shoot 59 percent from inside the arc as he did in 2023. That was 5 percent higher than he had ever

FTr	FG use	ASTr	FG3r	BLKr	STLr
15%	22%	6.5%	**49%**	0.8%	**1.0%**
19%	23%	8.0%	53%	0.8%	1.1%
18%	**25%**	**8.2%**	54%	1.1%	1.2%
30%	27%	8.6%	45%	0.9%	0.9%

shot before, and expecting the exception is asking for disappointment. Even if his goals for 2024 are less than what he did in 2023, they should still keep him on the positive end of projections going forward.

Table 29. Goals and danger signs for Lauri Markkanen entering his seventh year, 2023–24

Goal	FG3%	FTr	FG use	ASTr	BLKr
Danger sign	32%	18%	23%	7.1%	0.6%
Middle end	33%	23%	24%	8.7%	0.7%
High end	40%	21%	26%	9.4%	0.9%
Prior year	39%	30%	27%	8.6%	0.9%

This is using just Markkanen as an example. The approach can be applied to almost anyone, as long as you can find other players who are somewhat similar. The method applies to players as they get older, too, though it often finds fewer things to work on besides staying healthy, not surprisingly.

Table 30 has the goal summary for the last six recipients of the Most Improved Player award, who were all in their third to seventh seasons in the league. You can see that all of them achieved at least half of their high-end goals, and none of them had more than 20 percent of their danger signs triggered in the year they won. Most of them triggered no danger signs.

To show that something like this analysis is relevant, you have to talk about the players who didn't improve, too, like Jarrett Culver, a 2019

Table 30. Goal summary for recent Most Improved Player recipients

Season	Most improved	Danger signs	Middle end	High end	Goals
2023	Lauri Markkanen	17%	75%	67%	G, MPG, eFG%, DR%, FTr, FG use, ASTr, **FG3r**, BLKr, **STLr**, FG2%, FG3%
2022	Ja Morant	0%	50%	63%	MPG, eFG%, DR%, FG use, ASTr, STLr, PF/48 min., FG3%
2021	Julius Randle	0%	100%	100%	MPG, TO%, FG use, ASTr, PF/48 min.
2020	Brandon Ingram	0%	83%	67%	MPG, OR%, FTr, FG use, ASTr, STLr
2019	Pascal Siakam	20%	80%	80%	G, MPG, eFG%, **BLKr**, FG2%
2018	Victor Oladipo	0%	88%	63%	G, MPG, eFG%, OR%, TO%, FTr, FG use, PF/48 min.

Note: Bold stats indicate that they hit the danger sign for that stat. All hit at least 50 percent of high-end goals. Most had no danger signs. Abbreviations are defined in a list at the beginning of the book.

top-ten draft pick who appears to have fallen out of the league as of the end of 2023. Year by year, he failed to achieve a good percentage of the goals recommended by this method, as shown in table 31.

After Culver's first year, the method recommended eight different goals for year 2, and he triggered danger signs on three of them—games played (he played just thirty-four games with a danger sign at fifty games), minutes per game (he played just 15 mpg with a danger sign at about 22 mpg), and field goal use (he took 18 percent of field goals while on the floor with a danger sign of 19 percent). This was a guy who needed time on the court and game shots to reach his potential. He didn't get them in his second year.

He didn't get them partly because he got hurt, but the Wolves weren't giving him the time anyway. As a result, at the end of the year, they traded him to Memphis. Memphis saw enough of him before he played

Table 31. Jarrett Culver's year-by-year goal achievement

Year of goal	Danger signs	Middle end	High end	Goals
2	38%	50%	50%	**G**, **MPG**, eFG%, DR%, FTr, **FG use**, ASTr, *BLKr*
3	60%	20%	20%	G, **MPG**, **eFG%**, ASTr, FG3r, **BLKr**, **PF/48 min.**, **FG2%**, FG3%, **TR%**
4	75%	25%	25%	**G**, **MPG**, **eFG%**, FG2%

Note: Bold stats indicate that these triggered a danger sign. Italicized stats are ones where being worse in that stat was actually a positive. Abbreviations are defined in a list at the beginning of the book.

a real game for them to not pick up his fourth-year option. So they didn't have a lot of incentive to give him minutes either. Culver had a list of ten goals in that Memphis year, and he triggered danger signs in six of those ten.

By his fourth year, Culver just needed to play and shoot passably (aiming for an effective 48 percent). He probably needed to sign with a bad team and get minutes, but there weren't many interested. Instead, he got a two-way contract with Atlanta and played ten games and under 14 mpg, below the danger sign indicators of thirty-three games and 15 mpg, well below the goals of forty-five games and 20 mpg to be a little optimistic. Plus, he shot only an effective 41 percent, so he wasn't earning time.

Would Culver have been better by emphasizing the stats identified here? Possibly. Maybe the coaches did emphasize those specific things. I doubt it, but it's possible. Maybe Culver had other issues and couldn't stick with the emphases. From the outside, all we know is that Culver didn't get better in the details or in the big picture.

And that's the job—make 'em better. That's the job not just of the player development staff, not just of the coach, but also of management. Management's responsibilities don't stop when they draft a player. Their responsibilities may be fewer because the coaching staff has the daily contact with a player like Culver, but making sure everyone is on the same page regarding priorities for someone like Culver is huge. A failed top-ten draft pick is a big cost.

When we don't know the steps that failed—whether it was choosing Culver to begin with, whether it was not developing him the right way as a rookie or in his second year or whenever—almost everyone feels the pain of the overall failure. The Timberwolves changed coaches and GM around the time that they realized Culver was failing. That's not the best way to do things, but it is what often happens because ownership can't keep track of who had the most responsibility with a player.

This chapter used similarity scores to build specific statistical goals, those statistics being mostly traditional ones involving shooting, passing, rebounding, and getting to the line. With increasingly detailed NBA data, there is potential to do even more. For example, R.J. Barrett loved to go left when he entered the league and Deni Avdija loved going right, so should we develop their weak hand or improve their strong hand? The data hasn't been there to do that analysis, but it probably is there now. I can tell you that coaches don't know the answer on this because we debated it.

The tracking data now allows you to ask whether to emphasize pick-and-roll versus isolations for a ball handler, spotting up versus running off screens for shooters, or rolling versus popping for a big man setting a screen. These questions are relevant from the best players to the worst ones, and they have traditionally been answered by what we *think*. Even if this method doesn't get us to the point that we *know* the answer, it can at least improve what we think. And a lot of coaching is still about what we think, not what we know.

As an endnote, I intentionally did not try to go through the construction of similarity scores here because there are resources online for how to build them. I also didn't spell it out because they are mostly a tool to an end. They are a versatile tool, though, including answering the question that we had to answer when scouting players for the draft: Who do they play like? If you do that for Jarrett Culver based on his college stats, you end up with a list of interesting players, the top ten being Josh Jackson, Khris Middleton, Jordan Hamilton, Marcus Williams (the forward from

Arizona), Jayson Tatum, Paul Pierce, Joe Forte, Chase Budinger, Henry Walker, and Kelly Oubre Jr. Some players failed as first-rounders (Jackson, Forte), and two major successes were Tatum and Pierce. That list, though, could have formed the basis for identifying the development goals even before Culver hit the NBA. What did Tatum, Pierce, and Middleton do that was different from the other guys who got a chance and did a lot less?

14

Game Planning 'Em

It was pregame in a visiting coaches locker room somewhere, in the middle of the season. A couple of coaches were out on the floor running through pregame rituals for the players they worked out, but the rest of us were in the locker room eating peanut-butter-and-jelly sandwiches and taking a mental break.[1] We would normally chat about basketball trivia or news or celebrities or shoes, but that night brought a question the other coaches had to twist my arm to answer: "What is the most important stat in a game?"

One danger in responding to that question was that they wanted a simple answer, not the complex one that painted a better picture. They could keep the simple answer in their head and forget the rest. If I used other parts of the answer later on, they would still remember the simple part. No matter what I said, I would be setting myself up for problems.

The answer the coaches wanted to hear was "points in the paint." So much of what coaches think about on defense is how to limit opportunities in the paint, so that answer would validate the time spent.

I've generally defined "important" as something that, if accomplished, helps you win but, if not accomplished, could lead to losing. That definition is a bit simplistic and there are better ways to do it, but in the world of communication stats—which is what a lot of coaching is—it goes a long way.

For points in the paint, which is defined in the NBA as points scored off made baskets within the rectangular painted region only, the team that "wins" this stat in a game also wins the game about 60 percent of the time. That means that they lose the game about 40 percent of the time they win the stat, so it's better than fifty-fifty, but it's not a big advantage.[2]

The intent of the question was to give coaches a key stat to look at in postgame evaluation and to perhaps focus their emphases. After a game, it's great to get statistical validation for the game plan, something that gives a talking point like this: "We focused on attacking their paint and protecting ours. We did that and we won! Great job, people!"

But if you say that after one win, then after five more, but don't mention it after four games where you won the stat and lost the game, the players notice. That inconsistency could eat away at the credibility of the coach and the game plan. That's also why I hesitated to answer the question.

But giving coaches a better answer has its own problems. The stat that has the most importance, as defined here, is effective field goal percentage, because winning that stat means an 81 percent chance of winning the game. That's a big impact, but it has a few issues. First, there is always reluctance to use an advanced analytical stat like effective field goal percentage with players. I hate that reason because I believe players are plenty smart enough,[3] but I have seen enough reluctance around basketball to know that it's real. Second, the importance is almost too big. If a stat is so important that besting the opponent at it means that winning the game is nearly automatic, it suggests that rebounding, turnovers, and drawing fouls don't matter. That, of course, is not true, but when the numbers get this extreme, it can feel true. Lastly, effective field goal percentage doesn't exactly focus the emphasis beyond this edict: "Make shots and force the bad guys to miss theirs."

A stat that solves all of these problems is three-point percentage, which wins about 70 percent of the time. This is the answer I went with, but it was an answer they didn't want. They wanted points in the paint, and three-point percentage is essentially the opposite of that. It *suggests* that all of their time thinking about protecting the paint is better spent thinking about protecting the three-point arc.

But here again is why I didn't like the question: the link between that answer and what you should do is not so simple. Emphasizing the paint or emphasizing the three-point shot implies that players should take *more* of those shots. But having more attempts in the paint or more attempts from beyond the arc wins the game only about 51 percent of the time. Pretty weak.

It's not about *taking* the shots. It's about *making* the shots. It's not about giving up attempts in the paint or at the arc; it's about challenging those attempts enough so that the bad guys miss more. What matters is that brief second between when a player gets into the shooting motion and when they actually release the shot. It's one second where focus or distraction wipes out the relevance of what happened during the rest of the possession.

All of the available player tracking data doesn't capture well that one second of focus or distraction. It doesn't see the players' eyes or read their minds to tell how comfortable they are. As of 2024, a new tracking technology was introduced to capture shoulder position and wrist position, and that data may help, but the best shot quality metrics available in 2023 captured players only as moving dots without evidence of focus or distraction. If a team wins the shot quality on three-point shots, they win about 58 percent of games. If a team wins the shot quality on shots in the paint, they win also about 58 percent of games.[4] With numbers like that, there is no simple emphasis.

All of this ambiguity is why I didn't want to answer that question.

If basketball can be simplified to just making shots, not taking shots, the first part of coaching the sport is making your own guys better shooters, which I covered in chapter 13. But there is also a component of coaching associated with the team in the other locker room. Knowing those players' tendencies and their style of playing the game can highlight little weaknesses.

I'm not going to use the rest of this chapter to give every possible breakdown of stats that can tell you about a team's tendencies. You would hate me.[5] I've seen thirty-page reports on opponents' tendencies without a summary, and it takes a few hours of hard work to condense that information into something that only might get incorporated into a coach's pregame plan. There are often a few things in a report that various players will want to know, but a head coach has little bandwidth for the big data dump.

And a lot of data dumps don't actually get at what matters. They can spit out statistics about how well players shoot, who rebounds well, which players like to go right when dribbling, which plays they run, how well they run them, and so forth. Those are fine *descriptions* of what a team is, but there is a fundamental question that underlies this picture, and it's not really in the data dump. That question is this: If we do X, does it help us win? X may be a lot of things, including:

Making LeBron James a scorer instead of a passer
In pick-and-roll where Damian Lillard is handling the ball, having his defender go over the screen, rather than under the screen, to stay more closely attached to him.

Unfortunately, we don't have great cause-and-effect data to fully answer these questions. We don't know which other teams tried to make LeBron a scorer and which teams tried to make him a passer. From the outside, we don't know who tried and failed and who didn't even try.

But *trying* to answer these questions is more relevant for game planning than just regurgitating stats.

LeBron James: Scorer or Passer?

Philosophically, should you defend in such a way that encourages LeBron James to be more of a scorer or more of a passer? He is so good doing both, but is there a general strategy that a defense should take to try to minimize his impact on the game?

One approach to this problem is to look at how well the Lakers have done with LeBron scoring more than his average versus scoring less. Over the course of his career with the Lakers, when LeBron scores 27 points (his average) or more, the Lakers win 61 percent of the time, but if he scores fewer than 27, they win 57 percent of the time. Scoring more has helped them win an extra 4 percent of games.

But if you look at assists, a simple measure of LeBron's passing in a game, there is a bigger difference, about 15 percent: When LeBron had at least eight assists in a game (his average), the team won 67 percent of the time, but it won only 52 percent of the time if he didn't. That paints a broad-brush picture which says that, as a defense, you'd prefer LeBron to be a scorer rather than a passer.[6]

It's really broad-brush and it's a philosophical guideline, not a game plan. Sometimes players respond to the philosophical guidelines, but you have to make sure that they know it's not perfect. This specific philosophy doesn't mean to just give LeBron open shots or to stay completely at home on shooters without helping on his drives. It means something like staying a half step closer to the shooters that he would pass to, rather than a half step closer to him.

That's an attempt at answering the question. Giving a suggested action makes it *analytics*, not just statistics in a big report.

Damian Lillard: Over or Under the Screen?

First of all, what does it mean to go over or under a screen in pick-and-roll? Pick-and-roll is a specific play that forces a defender into an offensive player who is setting a screen or a pick. To stay with his responsibility, the defender can go over the screen—farther from the rim—or under the screen—closer to the rim. For our purpose in this section, just view going under and going over as opposite tactics, but I felt the need to explain a little more of the technical aspects in this situation.

This breakdown of pick-and-roll defense is a fairly standard stat that shows up in those thirty-page pregame packets. It captures how well Damian Lillard's team does when a defender goes over versus under the screen when Lillard has the ball. In 2023, for example, the Portland Trail Blazers scored 135 points per 100 possessions when defenders went over the screen, far higher than when defenders went under the screen, where the efficiency was 106. That pattern was true in prior seasons, too.

This difference reflects an action by the defense and a response by the offense. It is getting at a cause-and-effect relationship, and it strongly suggests that going under the screen works far better for a defense trying to limit Lillard and the Blazers.

But defenses across the league went over the screen *six times* as often as going under! Were they just dumb? Maybe, but scared is more like it. Lillard is a great shooter off the dribble, and going under the screen opens that shot up for him. That's why teams don't do it very often against him. Given that other teams aren't doing it, it would take a lot of guts to go with the stat over what your peers are doing, but it would also mean that defenses would be getting away from what they normally do.

Be the Best Version of Yourself

One of my top recommendations in preparing for an opponent is to actually just be the best version of who you are. Defenses go over screens four times as much as they go under screens, in general. Going over is what they practice, it's what they're used to. And getting better at what you do is at least as important as adjusting to your opponent, especially in a regular season where you play a new opponent in a new arena every two nights. It's a lot easier to be you than to be some team that goes all out to go under just to take away Lillard's pick-and-roll.

In fact, you know what the best overall defenses have done to slow down Lillard? They've just been who they are. They are actually better against him by going over screens rather than going under. The bad defenses, in contrast, have been horrible going over the screen against Lillard, so going under helps them.

Focusing on yourself and less on the opponent is a risk. It means acknowledging that you don't know something. Someone else may know more about the opponent's eighth man than you, the coach. But that's all right. The mental energy that players save by focusing on themselves can make them better.[7] And a coach's job is the big picture of maximizing the team, not knowing the little details about the other guys.

Rules of Thumb

Part of game planning is building your defense to handle a lot of scenarios, things like pick-and-roll with a shooter like Lillard versus pick-and-roll with a nonshooter handling the ball, pick-and-roll with a big man who can shoot, and so on. Setting up your rules for those situations helps so that you aren't teaching new things every game, just changing which of your own rules to emphasize.

But it makes sense to include here a few rules of thumb in building that defense and preparing for an opponent's offense.

Layups and threes are the most important shots to take away. Just as you encourage your own players to take those shots more often, it's important to build a defense that best prevents the opponents' shots from succeeding. The worst thing for a defense is having a bunch of defenders sitting in the midrange between these two shots and covering nothing important. This analytics rule is one of the oldest in the book, so people should already be doing it.

The defensive impact of being closer to a shooter is greatest on layups, less on floaters, and smallest on jump shots. Every foot closer to someone shooting a layup is worth about 2.5 percent on their percentage, but the percentage falls to about 0.5–0.8 on jump shots.

Contesting a layup with a hand up can cut percentages 10–20 percent, but contesting a jump shot in that way cuts only 3–7 percent.[8]

Being taller has a much bigger impact on cutting shooting percentages on layups than it has on doing the same on jump shots. Every six inches taller cuts the field goal percentage on layups about 5 percent, but it has just a 1 percent effect on jump shots. This difference encourages big men to remain closer to the rim. "Bigs in, guards out," is a phrase I heard more than once relating to this.

Distance from the rim matters a lot for shooting, roughly every foot farther lowering shooting percentage about 1 percent. Some players, including Lillard, will take really deep shots. They make enough to instill fear, but even Lillard shows a clear decline in ability to make shots as he gets farther away. Off the dribble from 2021 to 2023, he shot 45 percent on threes up to 26 feet from the rim, 34 percent on threes 26–30 feet away, and 29 percent on farther shots.

Jump shooters tend to drift toward their off hand, especially off the dribble, so contest on that side (as mentioned in chapter 12). Off the dribble, lefties shoot only about one in ten of their jumpers going left—the rest split evenly between going right and being stationary. Right-handed shooters are not as extreme, taking about 15 percent of their shots going to their right and taking about a third of their shots going left, the rest having no direction. On catch-and-shoot jumpers, players take eight in ten shots without drifting either direction, and they're pretty good at it. If they drift, it is more likely to the off hand, but it's more important to just contest than having a direction.

Don't stress pregame matchups too much. In general, trying to micromanage who is guarding who isn't worth the effort. If you look through all the data on matchups, you'll find occasional situations where one player knows a star's tendencies better and has done a good job on them, but it's not a lot. Hiding a bad defender on a lesser scorer only works so well with all the switching that happens on defense. There may be players who are good defenders on the ball but bad off the ball, and vice versa; in such cases, managing matchups can help. As an example, Milwaukee has tried to allow Giannis to guard lesser players because he is such a good off-ball defender, even though he is also good on the ball. That strategy allows his teammates, who aren't as good off-the-ball defenders, to do what they do better.

Beyond these guidelines, don't stress the opponent too much. It's 80 percent about you doing what you always do—and that is the most important stat . . . at least until the playoffs.[9] That situation changes things a bit.

15

The Journey, Part 3

Mark Warkentien was the NBA executive of the year in 2009. He was let go in 2010, despite having another fifty-win season. There were business reasons.

George Karl was the NBA coach of the year in 2013. He was let go two weeks later with a full year left on his contract. There were business reasons.

Success does not breed stability.

I couldn't control a lot of things in the job. The math may have helped win games and influence people, but winning games and influencing people only get you so far.

There were people who didn't like my work or maybe just me—sometimes it's hard to tell. I discussed that with other people around the league, both analytics personnel and otherwise, and I heard things like, "You only have one hater? That's pretty good," or "Being hated is better than being ignored."

The people business of basketball made me friends but also forced me to watch those friends move on. Instability is common in the league, and everyone in the league knows that it is part of the price of the competition that we love. I saw it in Seattle originally, and it continued in Denver.

After Warkentien was let go in Denver, I left to join ESPN to build their analytics group. They had the foresight to tell sports stories in a new, analytical way. I told them that I had been telling stories with numbers for years, just with a smaller audience—the people within a basketball organization. The analytics group I helped build still exists, telling stories about the quality of college basketball teams, college football teams, NFL quarterbacks, pass rushers, pass blockers, and now receivers. It has influence with people like Rece Davis and Jay Bilas. The tools the group uses are great for building lists, like the top quarterbacks in clutch situations, the top receivers for getting open, and the at-large teams for the NCAA tournament with the best chance to win.

But there have been analytics stories that are tougher to tell, ones that I think are valuable and profitable because they make readers think. Those stories are intimidating to some, and they go beyond the easy headlines. You see, news coverage is motivated by clicks and eyeballs—the more of those, the more money that comes in. We as readers and watchers may *say* that we want a story about Kevon Looney and his rebounding technique or the third assistant coach for the Portland Trail Blazers and his journey to the league, but most readers and watchers don't actually click on those or watch them. A few people do, but most want to hear about LeBron James and Steph Curry, whose names instantly create interest. Most people don't particularly want a story about Gregg Popovich, a Hall of Fame coach, a natural leader, someone with a journey to the league that involved the military, the Olympics, and some small basketball program in Los Angeles nicknamed the Sagehens.[1] The business of sports is still quantity of eyes, not quality of the content.

It's not just sports, though. The media beyond is a reflection of us. It may at times try to be a reflection of the better version of us, the one that builds the better story, but the public pulls the media right back to reflecting us in both our best and our worst. The numbers tell the media that we want LeBron and Steph and lists of the top ten scorers in clutch time. The numbers tell the media that few people want to hear about Kevon Looney's way of worming in for an offensive rebound or about assistant coach Joseph Blair's favorite vegan restaurants while on the road.

Anyway, I had occasional haters in media, too, not just working with a team. The same people who would accuse me of just looking at the numbers and not watching the game—they were the ones who would be on their phone throughout the first half of a game, then go into the studio at half-time to talk about the first half using—guess what—the stat sheet, because they hadn't had their eyes on the game. One on-air analyst went so far as to tell me, Al Gore–style, that he "invented analytics" and that no one should be telling him how to use numbers.

There were people in the media who created a narrative with their eyes and wanted numbers only to support that narrative. If the numbers didn't support the narrative, a couple would make them up and be proud of it. Others would proceed without citing numbers, not changing their narrative.

I was able to survive in both the team and media worlds because I could withstand a few individual defeats for the purpose of a bigger-picture victory. I also knew that I was an educator and that teaching is nowhere close to being 100 percent successful.

One of the biggest challenges in doing this job is, as someone described it to me, "You're the math person in a business filled with people who wanted to avoid math." Or, as another put it, "The starting point in analytics is that you've lost, because everyone on your own team is against you."

Those things were said by two of the many people I talked to in order to try to capture the roadblocks of doing the job. Some of what I heard was true on both the team side and the media side. Some of the things I heard were true only on the team side. Some of the things I heard were things that I experienced. Some of the things I heard don't need to be told because they are just gossip. But some of the things can be helpful to ensure that people in the analytics profession do not get pigeonholed in sports, to show that analytics is just part of the way that decisions get made. There isn't an "analytics specialist"; there is just decision-making, and analytics should be part of it.

These are some of the things that I hope can be useful.

Early on, it was often the owners who wanted to hire someone to do analytics. Many of the owners had a background of using numbers to guide their decisions, as Wally Walker had had in Seattle when he first hired me in 2004. Bring in someone who knows how to quantify what is going on in the game—a basketball accountant, if you will—and put them in the mix, see how they affect things. At least they can tell the big boss what's going right and what's going wrong.

And that there was a problem. If you're hired by one person to work for another, you can be viewed as having two masters, each one questioning whether you're a "spy" for the other, passing on private knowledge. Being an owner's spy on the staff or being a general manager's spy on the coaching staff—those are problems of perception at least. Overcoming the paranoia around being a spy is an investment of one year, maybe two, maybe three, according to those I talked to. And in some situations, that paranoia never gets fully overcome. If an owner or a boss in general wants to be cc'd on emails, an analyst is in a position where they can't win, getting yelled at by the staff if the boss yells at them, or getting yelled at by the boss if the emails don't give them something to yell about.

Stop. "Analyst"—this is a terrible name for the position. This issue is something else that came up in different ways when I talked to people who used analytics in helping to make basketball decisions. Often, just getting the job title of "analyst" or any title with "analytics" in it limited career options relative to other people who were just interns with less basketball experience and knowledge. But because they didn't have the label, they got more opportunities. It's a little like that person in the office who knows how to fix the printer when it breaks—pressing reset, opening up a tray, sliding something one way or another—that person knows how to fix the printer better than even tech support, so they become "the tech expert," even if their skills would be better used on twenty other things. The person in the office who knows how to do analytics ends up not being seen for all the other things they do really well because, hell, it's helpful to have someone who knows how to calculate effective field goal percentage. Then they also have to answer questions like, "And, oh yeah, why do they call it effective field goal percentage anyway? Can we call it adjusted field goal percentage? I like that better." Don't call them "analysts"; call them "director of basketball operations" or "manager of basketball strategy" or "assistant general manager" or even "general manager."

If the front office and coaching staff are at least partially about making better decisions, everyone on the staff should understand the logic that goes into "analytics." For the person who knows it best, their job is not really to be the voice of analytics but to facilitate an environment where everyone is comfortable with thinking logically and clearly and knowing all the tools that help in making those decisions.

And that brings us back to the boss that hired ya. That boss sets the environment for you. Or they better give you the authority to mess around with that environment. Because, if they don't, then you're the spy or you're the mother-in-law giving advice on how to do their laundry the right way, so they avoid you. A boss placing a single person with analytic expertise into the middle of an organization that doesn't have the mentality to work with analytics—that's not going to work, at least not fast.

If the organization is good, then there is consistency and intellectual humility around the processes that everyone respects. Being rigorous and self-reflecting—that's what you want. Do anything you can to check yourself, giving people the freedom to speak but the responsibility to check themselves when they do so. Then there is no "analyst," just a group of people who want to do things better for themselves and for others. That is a "step change" from an organization with one analytics person in the midst of twenty people who use only their eyes and ears.

A lot of people go into a front office or coaching staff merely wanting to help. The satisfaction comes in feeling like you're contributing to winning. But the perception of analytics to others can be that you're there to tell people how to do their job. Without the step change, without the collective will to be rigorous and reflecting, that perception will win out.

The Houston Rockets had that step change when they hired Daryl Morey to be general manager. Houston embraced these values, and Daryl's hiring simply signaled to everyone inside and outside the franchise that they were doing it.

But the story was told in the media mostly about Daryl because that's the reflection of us, the public—we like stories about heroes. Daryl got to be the hero for the basketball analytics movement. He enforced that the team would focus on layups and threes. He turned Jeremy Lamb and Kevin Martin into James Harden, who would become MVP and the rock of the franchise for a decade.

But some around the league also called Daryl, in a derogatory sense, "the smartest guy in the room," an allusion to the movie about Enron, the energy company whose most senior people exploited shareholders and consumers through its position in the marketplace and its accounting practices. That slur got used against individuals doing analytics in other organizations, not just Daryl, to suggest that analytics was some kind of shell game.

Some of the analytics people, though, responded to this by saying, "If I'm the smartest person in the room, it's time to change rooms. I like to have people in the room that I can learn from."

And learning is a big part of analytics—learning from mistakes in the draft, learning from coaches about how they make decisions, learning because that is how to stay ahead. The advantage of shooting layups and threes, the advantage of recognizing early that Harden was a superstar—those advantages that the Rockets had, they came and have now gone. The advantage of thinking logically, rigorously, and with humility—those advantage don't go away because irrational behavior is common, laziness is easy to succumb to, and stepping up to take responsibility is hard.

That's what people told me.

And then there is fear, or what psychologists call "anxiety" because fear is instant and often helpful, whereas anxiety is wasting time thinking about potential fear. Anxiety about losing your job is a huge part of what motivates poor decisions in the NBA. I've personally felt that anxiety is higher at the NBA level than at lower levels because there is no place to go but down. A coach or a general manager at that level—their upside is winning a championship, but their downside is not being in the NBA anymore, losing the status of being at the top of the mountain. Yeah, a championship is the real top, but being in the league feels like the top.

Anxiety drives coaches not to innovate because innovation can fail, leading to their failure. If the median lifespan of a coach at his job is two years, the anxiety is real because fear is proximate. In the short time that they have, a coach wants to succeed on their own merits, not fail by listening to the smartest guy in the room over there. That would be the worst—failing because you weren't yourself.

Anxiety drives general managers to listen to the language of traditional scouts, without trying to check it. If a prospect has "good feel for the game," ask the damn question, "What the hell does 'good feel' even mean? Can we check that? Who else had good feel when they entered the league? Do we have that written down? Can we check all the players who had 'good feel' and all the players who had 'no feel' (because no one ever says a player has 'bad feel') and see how well they've done? I'm being serious here, and I'm not being personal. When you say a player has 'good feel,' you better not be saying it because it's hard to check it. You better be saying it because we have four months until the draft and we need to check it out."

No one gives that damn speech. It has too many questions in it. Questions open up the floor to answers, and opening up the floor often means giving up control. But I heard this more than once: coaches and management should *manage* communication, not control it, not dominate it. The scouts and the assistants and the players and the staff shouldn't be trying to guess what the boss wants so that they can echo it back to them. They should be able to say what they think without worrying about their job but know the responsibility of saying it.

I simultaneously love and hate what one person told me: "The NBA is an emotionally violent league." I have a whole chapter on emotion and how important it is to the performance of players and the team as a whole. Emotion makes us all go, staff, players, and fans alike. We love the game, but then some people use that love as a club, threatening other people's relationship with the game if they don't like what the others are doing or saying. The responsibility of doing the job does not mean that the job should be at risk of disappearing every time you open your mouth.

Getting past the emotional violence allows you to get to the simple biases. "Cognitive bias" has become a buzzword, a good one because, once you have emotionally nonviolent people, they are still subject to making natural human errors. What they saw last about a player tends to influence them too much—recency bias. Or they will accept evidence that supports their own preconceived notion more strongly than the evidence that doesn't—confirmation bias. These little biases aren't intentional but are merely human. Overcoming them is not as simple as pointing them out. People hate it when you point out that they're ordinary humans falling for a trick of nature.

But sometimes those human biases are short-term beneficial. When a scout suddenly likes the numbers because they support their notions about a player, that feels gooood. That scout will be your buddy now. You've got someone to watch film with and have longer conversations with. A lot of analytical people look for those wins by knowing when they can use confirmation bias to get someone on their side. Doing it enough—that can build a relationship.

It's still bias, and it may help you now but bite you later. Overcoming bias is part of that bigger process involving integrity, consistency, and rigor. Hopefully, the relationship becomes part of that process.

Communication has changed in this business. It used to be that the audience for any analytical work was small—a couple people to whom you could explain things simply in the language of basketball. But now it's a bigger audience, one that can look at tables of numbers and even graphs of data. A lot of basketball people know not only what effective field goal percentage is but also why it's better.

The language has evolved to incorporate some of the analytical concepts from this book and its predecessor. For the teams with rigor and consistency, the language of uncertainty has developed. The tests that Mark Warkentien created for the draft—to understand how many twenty-one-plus-year-olds with bad stats have survived, for example—capture the idea that we are playing the odds here. Almost nothing is a sure thing, so playing the odds means quantifying the odds. Doing so leaves room for talk of "good feel," but you better keep track of it so that it can be referenced down the road.

Playing the odds also opens up decisions based on a balance between risk and reward. The Houston Rockets drafted Cam Whitmore at number 20 in the 2023 draft because every other team above them got nervous about a medical report. Or they got nervous about a questionable attitude; it wasn't clear. Whether it was medical or attitude, the risk went up suddenly on draft day after every mock draft prior to that day had him between the second and the tenth pick in the draft. Traditional language would basically red-flag Whitmore, whereas the language now would consider "the right tail of his predicted outcomes" and potentially weight that higher against his "risk of failure," depending on the team situation. Houston had the opportunity at number 20 to take a chance. Maybe other teams didn't feel their situation was right for that specific risk at that time. Maybe they didn't like the risk-versus-reward ratio, or maybe they red-flagged him. Regardless of what happens with Whitmore, some teams will learn something from Whitmore's future performance about the balance between talent and a bad medical or attitude report. And some won't.

The language of uncertainty, though, has historically been viewed as a weakness. Corporate landscapes have often rewarded the overly confident, not the ones with the intellectual humility to say it's not 100 percent guaranteed. That has affected the NBA, too, where going into a draft room with probabilities between 5 percent and 95 percent pushes the probability that anyone will listen to you down to 50 percent.

But true confidence comes from doing the process the right way. You shouldn't walk into a draft room on draft day in June with those numbers; you should walk into a draft room in December or January, six months before the actual decision, with those numbers. And you should be prepared to update those numbers over the next six months, edging toward a clearer decision in the way those Superforecasters do.

Out of this presentation of numbers, arguments will happen. It's normal, and you want it to be so. Stats are far more stable than emotions, so the rate at which numerical decisions change is far slower than that of decisions made with eyes and ears. That difference can cause conflict. But it's not the argument itself that is the problem; it's that some people will use the argument to kill relationships and the process itself. The process is to build a "shared truth," as a couple of my contacts said. It's hard to reach a shared truth if those relationships get killed.

That's what people told me.

There are many diversely talented people doing this job now, evolving the job and evolving the environment around it, but evolution is slow. As hard as the technical parts of the job can be, the mentally hard part is that it is slow to make a difference. Building an environment means changing a lot of people's minds or just changing a lot of people, neither of which goes quickly.

A rather dreary Nobel Prize winner once said, "Science advances one funeral at a time. . . . Scientific truth does not triumph by convincing its opponents and making them see the light, but rather because its opponents die, and a new generation grows up that is familiar with it." The business of sports is going that way. Not only are young staffers being raised with analytical knowledge, but veteran players who have been in the league ten years now have heard about what analytics can do. If they're the ones getting the next front-office and coaching jobs, they are exactly what that Nobel Prize winner said—the new generation.

Unlike science, though, which is a collaborative field, there is an advantage in sports to having the knowledge and the environment even before the new generation arrives. Do it faster. There are business reasons.

16

What Does Frescobol Have to Do with It?

It is called beach paddleball or, when I first played it, *frescobol*, according to my Brazilian girlfriend. The point of the game is simply for two people to hit a ball with wooden paddles back and forth as long as possible. We played it on the beach, of course, usually on that fringe of damp, semifirm sand where the waves would occasionally touch. My girlfriend was generally a more consistent hitter than I was, since she played a bit growing up. But when she hit one astray, I would dive onto the sand or into the waves to try to hit it back. I may not have been as consistent in my shots as she was, but I could make some dramatic saves.

So why am I talking about frescobol when you're here to read about basketball? Let me tell you a little basketball story.

One of my biggest basketball influences growing up was the John Stockton-to-Karl Malone pick-and-roll play. It worked incredibly well in an era where pick-and-roll wasn't nearly as common. Malone would come up to screen Stockton's man, then he'd either retreat toward the basket or go off to the side or up to the top of the three-point arc. Stockton would read Malone and the defense to either take advantage of the screen and get by his man or use some of the confusion of the defenders to get separation or find Malone and his great hands. Those details don't matter much for this story, but everyone talked about how good Stockton and Malone were *together*. They could read each other, they knew what each other was doing, the Malone ability to catch and finish complemented Stockton's ability to read the situation and pass. They fit well together.

That was a subjective take on it. Broadcasters and coaches talked about it; fans believed it. I believed it.

And I still do believe in it, in part because of frescobol. The general description of how Stockton and Malone fit—Stockton's ability to read and pass, along with Malone's ability to screen, catch, and finish—is of simple complementary skills between two players. In frescobol, the skills are simpler, even more basic: the consistency of hitting the ball accurately and the athleticism to go save an errant shot. Because frescobol is a lot simpler than basketball and because it has a couple different relevant skills, it serves in a general way to study the impact of teammate fit on performance.

To be clear, this is not about whether players *like* each other personally. I clearly liked my girlfriend, but it's not clear how much Stockton and Malone actually spent time together hanging out, talking about country music.[1] Let's separate whether teammates like each other personally—which I call "chemistry"—from whether their skills fit. In a nutshell, the question for this chapter is, Did my athleticism fit my girlfriend's consistency? And the question is not, Did whether we liked each other make us a better frescobol team?

Because frescobol is simple, you can "solve frescobol," meaning that you can predict how many times back and forth the ball will go based on simple measures of consistency and athleticism.[2] Because of that predictability, you can actually come out with a few clear conclusions on the importance of fit on teams.

The basic conclusion of this work is that the whole is not the same as the sum of the parts when there are at least two skills and at least two players teaming up. "Positive fit" would be when the whole is greater than the sum of the parts, and "negative fit" would be when the whole is less than the sum of the parts. The most extreme example of positive fit in frescobol arose when two players were both consistent in hitting the ball back to the sweet spot of the other. They were two players who were not athletic at all but could simply hit the ball back and forth together. The sum of their parts would only be about eleven hits, but they averaged almost thirty-eight as a team because of their positive fit. In contrast, the math said that my athleticism was not a great fit for my girlfriend's consistency.[3]

Another conclusion of the work is that you can make trades that are mutually beneficial due to fit considerations. Team A could trade a player to Team B for another, and both teams could get better if the new fit was bigger than the change in skill.

Related to this positive-fit trading is that acquiring a player with the same skills as another can make your team a lot better or only a little better, depending on the skills of the teammate. In one frescobol situation, there were just four player types: athletic and consistent (which we'll label "Superman"), athletic and inconsistent ("Homecoming King"), nonathletic and consistent ("Accountant"), and nonathletic and inconsistent ("Slug"). If there was a team of two Slugs (the worst players, in general), replacing one with a Superman (the best player) improved the team a little bit, but replacing both Slugs with Supermen improved the team a lot (several times more than one)! That was because Superman fit better with another Superman than with a Slug. The apparent value of Superman relative to a slug depended on context.

And that lesson is relevant for basketball, right? How valuable Steph Curry is depends on who he's playing with. It's not just that the players he's around are better, it's that the fit is better. This is particularly relevant for someone like Draymond Green, whose offensive value has often been in debate. He played with Curry, and Draymond's style of waiting to make the right pass really helped Curry and helped himself. But if Green had to make more shots or if he was playing with a great player who needed the ball in their hands more often (Chris Paul, for example), would his ability to pass be as valuable? Probably not. We can't easily quantify it now, but the frescobol analysis strongly suggests it.

The frescobol article also addressed how fit affected player metrics and, as a result, likely salaries. It did this by simulating seasons and various teams and looking for differences between apparent value in those seasons versus actual value based on players' skills (essentially, if they played on all possible teams). The leagues were simulated so that players were traded or kept together based on how successful the team was. If the team was good, there was a smaller chance of it being broken up than if the team was bad, just like what is seen in the NBA.[4] This variability created some player movement, but super-teams tended to stay together. In this simulation, players would "get paid" based on their adjusted plus-minus metric—the same tool mentioned in chapter 7 for evaluating basketball players. With that metric, those players who just fit well with their teammate got paid a ton, even though their overall value was just solid or good when playing with all possible teammates. Good fit could result in players being overpaid in some sense. Their value to one team was much higher than it was to other teams, at least.

The implication is that fit makes player metrics inaccurate. All of the basketball player metrics in use are just looking at the value of players in light of their context. So LEBRON, DARKO, and Net Points all measure the results and assign all credit to the players, not to fit. Normal player movement tended to inflate player value metrics across the frescobol league (and the presumed salaries associated) relative to a league where everyone has to play a little alongside everyone else.[5] Even the best player metrics in use for the NBA can get "fooled" by context if other information is not incorporated.

Back to basketball.

Table 32 lists the five best defensive five-man units in the NBA in 2023 that played at least five hundred possessions, the equivalent of about five full games.

Table 32. The top five-man lineups on defense in 2023

			Four Factors			
Team	Lineup	DRTG	eFG%	TO%	DR%	FTr
Chicago	Beverley-LaVine-Caruso-DeRozan-Vučević	104.1	52.7%	16.1%	81.5%	0.169
Minnesota	Russell-Edwards-Anderson-McDaniels-Gobert	105.0	50.2%	15.1%	75.3%	0.168
Minnesota	Russell-Edwards-McDaniels-Towns-Gobert	108.0	48.7%	12.5%	74.5%	0.133
Golden State	Curry-Thompson-Wiggins-Green-Looney	109.3	51.3%	12.9%	77.7%	0.184
Miami	Lowry-Herro-Butler-Martin-Adebayo	110.7	55.3%	17.8%	78.1%	0.150

Note: Abbreviations are defined in a list at the beginning of the book.

Chicago's lineup of Patrick Beverley, Zach LaVine, Alex Caruso, DeMar DeRozan, and Nikola Vučević was the best. Minnesota had two good ones, differing only in that Kyle Anderson played in the better one, Karl-Anthony Towns in the slightly less good one. Those first two lineups may be thought of as a little like that frescobol team that could stand and bounce the ball back and forth thirty-eight times, never having to make a tough save. They stood out, about 10 points better than the league average defense.

Table 33 has the best *offensive* five-man units in the NBA: Golden State's lineup with Steph Curry, Klay Thompson, Andrew Wiggins, Draymond Green, and Kevon Looney was more than 15 points better than league average on offense. Sacramento's lineup was almost as good.

Table 33. The top five-man lineups on offense in 2023

			Four Factors			
Team	Lineup	ORTG	eFG%	TO%	OR%	FTr
Golden State	Curry-Thompson-Wiggins-Green-Looney	131.0	65.0%	12.8%	22.7%	0.150
Sacramento	Mitchell-Huerter-Barnes-Murray-Sabonis	129.8	64.9%	10.6%	15.2%	0.167
Boston	Smart-White-Brown-Tatum-Horford	127.6	61.5%	11.0%	14.7%	0.190
Denver	Murray–Caldwell-Pope–Gordon–Porter–Jokić	127.0	61.3%	12.6%	24.8%	0.160
New York Knicks	Brunson-Grimes-Barrett-Randle-Robinson	125.2	58.4%	11.8%	27.8%	0.202

People in the NBA love to stare at tables like these, looking for patterns to explain why these lineups are so good. They may think that maybe you need to have at least one good defensive player to have an elite five-man lineup—Beverley and Caruso for Chicago, Gobert for Minnesota, Draymond for Golden State, then Adebayo and Butler for Miami. That rule would seemingly explain it. And maybe you need an elite offensive player for a five-man offensive lineup to stand out: Curry for Golden State, Sabonis for Sacramento, Tatum for Boston, Jokić for Denver, and Brunson and Randle for the Knicks.

People are good at finding patterns, including ones that aren't there, unfortunately. The rationale about having one critical piece seems to explain the offensive leaderboard, but it would imply that *every* lineup with those guys in it was good, which is definitely not true. No, what's helping these extremely good lineups is the same thing that helped that frescobol team: good fit. Their results are better than the sum of the parts. The parts aren't bad, but greatness implies that fit is good.

That's the last result that came from the frescobol study: extremely good results imply good fit.[6] The fit itself may not be spectacular like those two players who could just hit back to each other constantly, but it needs to be *good*. The difference in calculated fit between the *top ten teams* in the frescobol leagues and the other hundred-plus teams was highly significant. But between the top half and the bottom half of frescobol teams, there was no difference in fit—that was a difference in *talent*.[7]

So these really good NBA lineups probably fit together better than most teams. The skills that the players had were complementary, like Draymond's passing patience with Steph and Klay.[8] There were talented players on these units, too—don't get me wrong—but greatness seems to require both talent and fit. Fit *has* to happen with greatness, whereas good players can lead to less than great results. Good fit can happen with lesser teams, too; it's just harder to detect.

Fit among NBA Lineups

Working with five-man lineups is not recommended. Over sixteen thousand unique lineups were used in 2023, over five hundred per team, so you can kill your brain looking for those that have good fit. And because it's a flawed human brain, it will see patterns that don't exist.

But if you're working for a team, someone is going to ask you to look into five-man lineups anyway. People really want to know what lineups to play, as though the right lineup has magic to make everything work. The Warriors had their Death Lineup and their Hamptons Five lineup, lineups that were given names as though they were magical. But the magic was partly ability and partly fit.

The original Warriors Death Lineup was Steph Curry, Klay Thompson, Harrison Barnes, Andre Iguodala, and Draymond Green. Despite not having anyone taller than 6 feet 8 inches, they could guard almost anyone, and they were fast. When Barnes left and the Warriors acquired Kevin Durant, Durant became the other part of the lineup, and it was renamed the Hamptons Five. Durant, at 6 feet 11 inches, added height without losing much in terms of quickness. And of course, Durant had Hall of Fame talent, too.

When you talk about elite, those lineups indeed met the standards. The 2019 version of the Hamptons Five had an offensive efficiency of 136 and a defensive efficiency of 102, basically outscoring their opponents by more than 30 points per game. They didn't use the lineup much, a little more than two minutes per game, due to injury and maybe some sense of mercy. The 2017 version outscored opponents by a slightly more modest 24 points per game and was used about three minutes per game.

The original Death Lineup in 2015, though, was merely good, outscoring opponents by about 12 points per game and playing just one hundred minutes together. But what got the unit labeled the Death Lineup was its use in the NBA Finals against the Cleveland Cavaliers. After the Warriors fell behind, two games to one, when using a starting lineup with classic center Andrew Bogut, they said, "Screw it, I definitely see a pattern," and started the Death Lineup the rest of the way, sweeping the next three games to take the title. What happened then was not only good *fit* but also good *matchups*, which is like fitting well but *against* the players on the other side. If you thought it was hard analyzing teammate fit, analyzing matchups is harder.

For the sake of giving your human brain something to spin its wheels on, table 34 has a list of those thirty-one lineups that actually played five hundred possessions together in 2023, along with a few numbers on the right. First are the lineups' offensive and defensive ratings, then their net ratings. The final two columns are estimates of "smoothed fit" for offense and defense, that is, how many points were added to their offensive rating (and subtracted from their defensive rating) based on the complementarity of player skills. An overview of how the method works is in appendix 3.

Table 34. All five-man lineups that played at least 500 possessions on offense in 2023, ordered best to worst

					Smoothed fit	
Team	Lineup	ORTG	DRTG	Net Rtg	Offense	Defense
Golden State	Curry-Thompson-Wiggins-Green-Looney	131.0	109.3	21.7	1.8	1.5
Chicago	Beverley-LaVine-Caruso-DeRozan-Vučević	118.1	104.1	14.0	0.1	0.9
Denver	Murray-Caldwell-Pope-Gordon-Porter-Jokić	127.0	113.9	13.2	3.2	0.8
Philadelphia	Maxey-Harden-Harris-Tucker-Embiid	124.0	111.4	12.6	1.1	0.8
Minnesota	Russell-Edwards-Anderson-McDaniels-Gobert	117.0	105.0	12.0	0.2	1.0
Boston	Smart-White-Brown-Tatum-Horford	127.6	115.6	11.9	0.9	−0.8
Denver	Murray-Brown-Caldwell-Pope-Gordon-Jokić	123.3	113.1	10.2	2.6	1.0
Toronto	VanVleet-Anunoby-Barnes-Siakam-Poeltl	122.2	112.1	10.1	1.6	0.8
Sacramento	Mitchell-Huerter-Barnes-Murray-Sabonis	129.8	120.6	9.2	1.5	0.0
Minnesota	Conley-Edwards-Anderson-McDaniels-Gobert	122.1	114.7	7.5	0.9	0.8
Philadelphia	Melton-Harden-Harris-Tucker-Embiid	122.7	115.5	7.2	1.0	−0.1
Atlanta	Young-Murray-Hunter-Collins-Capela	119.3	113.0	6.3	0.6	1.2

					Smoothed fit	
Team	Lineup	ORTG	DRTG	Net Rtg	Offense	Defense
Cleveland	Garland-Mitchell-Okoro-Mobley-Allen	123.1	117.8	5.3	1.4	−0.7
Atlanta	Young-Murray-Hunter-Collins-Okongwu	116.8	111.5	5.2	0.1	1.3
New York Knicks	Brunson-Grimes-Barrett-Randle-Robinson	125.2	120.1	5.1	0.8	−2.0
Sacramento	Fox-Huerter-Barnes-Murray-Sabonis	122.6	117.5	5.1	2.0	0.0
Miami	Lowry-Herro-Butler-Martin-Adebayo	114.8	110.7	4.0	1.4	1.0
Indiana	Nembhard-Haliburton-Hield-Nesmith-Turner	122.2	118.3	3.8	1.8	0.1
Brooklyn	Dinwiddie-Bridges-Finney-Smith-Johnson-Claxton	113.7	111.6	2.0	−0.2	1.1
Toronto	VanVleet-Trent-Anunoby-Barnes-Siakam	117.5	115.7	1.8	1.0	0.5
Minnesota	Russell-Edwards-McDaniels-Towns-Gobert	109.6	108.0	1.6	−0.8	0.8
Chicago	Dosunmu-LaVine-DeRozan-Williams-Vučević	113.7	112.2	1.6	−1.0	−0.6
Orlando	Fultz-Harris-Wagner-Banchero-Carter	115.5	114.6	0.9	1.2	−0.4
Utah	Conley-Clarkson-Vanderbilt-Markkanen-Olynyk	114.9	114.9	−0.1	0.9	−0.3
Portland	Lillard-Simons-Hart-Grant-Nurkić	117.8	118.1	−0.3	0.7	0.5

Portland	Lillard-Simons-Hart-Grant-Eubanks	119.3	121.1	−1.9	1.4	0.2
New Orleans	McCollum-Ingram-Murphy-Jones-Valančiūnas	119.7	121.6	−2.0	1.2	−0.9
Oklahoma City	Gilgeous-Alexander-Giddey-Dort-Williams-Williams	111.6	114.0	−2.5	−0.7	−0.5
Houston	Porter-Green-Martin-Smith-Şengün	115.5	123.2	−7.7	0.4	−0.5
Houston	Gordon-Porter-Green-Smith-Şengün	110.7	121.1	−10.5	0.3	−0.4
Detroit	Ivey-Hayes-Bogdanović-Stewart-Duren	112.3	125.7	−13.4	−0.4	−0.7

A couple things you probably won't notice in table 34, even if you do study it for patterns, follow:

Denver's starting unit had the highest offensive fit with +3.2. Their other unit listed had the second highest offensive fit with +2.6. Adding 2–3 points per game is like adding 5–8 wins in a season.

Frankly, Nikola Jokić is just a perfect fit. The fact that the fit is highest for two lineups with him in them is no coincidence. He really does make everyone better. There is a way to aggregate how much a player fits on average, and Jokić was at +2.6 on offense alone in 2023. LeBron was around +2.0 in some of his best years.

And here are some things you reasonably would have noticed if you studied it at all:

Most lineups in this list of thirty-one had positive net ratings, twenty-three to be precise. Only seven of those lineups had negative overall fit, with four of those having multiple young players.

The average offensive rating here is about 119, above the 114.6 league average that year. The average defensive rating is pretty much the league average at the time.

- Almost all of them had a center. There was a Toronto lineup with Siakam being the big and a Utah lineup with Olynyk as the big, the only two lineups shown without a real center listed. The league may be trending toward playing small, but even the Warriors played with big man Kevon Looney a lot.
- The worst offensive lineup here was the Wolves' Russell-Edwards-McDaniels-Towns-Gobert. Together, that group counted five All-NBA awards, nine All-Star Games, and three All-Rookie teams. The Wolves traded away Russell midseason to get Mike Conley. With Conley, the team's offensive got a lot better, but the defense was worse, though some of that is associated with the NBA as a whole always getting worse defensively as the season proceeds.
- The worst defensive unit on this list was Detroit's, which had four of those players on rookie contracts.

In the end, fit is a relevant factor. It makes some sense for coaching analysts to spend hours looking for fit (because those people don't sleep anyway), especially between player pairs, as looking at five-man units is asking for pain.

And it's especially true if they want to be great, not just good.

17

Draymond with a *D*

His name is Draymond Green. Not Raymond. It is Draymond, with a *D*.

I honestly don't know how history is going to look upon him, so it's probably a good idea to summarize him here in case he is forgotten like far too many basketball players.

Draymond was a 6-foot-7 center and power forward for the dynasty that was the 2015+ Golden State Warriors. At that height, he was considered too small by traditional standards to play center or power forward, but he played both positions brilliantly. Without great shooting skills or even average athleticism, he was not supposed to be able to play the small forward position, but he also did that well.

At this writing, in 2023, Draymond has won just a single Defensive Player of the Year award, but he has been named to eight all-defense teams. He was second team all-NBA once and third team once.

On the other hand, he also kicked LeBron James in the groin and kneed a lot of players when he thought the cameras weren't watching, and his suspension for Game 5 of the 2016 Finals was prominently blamed for the Warriors losing that series after a record-setting regular season.

Some people consider Draymond dirty. Some people love Draymond. Either way, he wasn't supposed to have such an impact when he was coming out of college.

Entering the draft as a senior out of Michigan State in 2012, Draymond didn't pass the traditional eye test. He was slow, overweight, not athletic, and too small for his skill set. He was a player "without an NBA position" (which is a little like the baseball players who "didn't look good in a uniform" in *Moneyball*). He was generally considered a good passer and a good rebounder with a high basketball IQ, so he got drafted in the second round by Golden State.

During that draft process, the website DraftExpress shared various content related to Draymond, including videos, opinions of him as a player, and news items that still exist. The collection of content wasn't huge because he wasn't a highly rated prospect, but what was there was eye-opening for both how spot-on it was and how off the mark it was.

Draymond himself was the spot-on part. In a video linked on the site, an interviewer asked Draymond where he saw himself after the draft process and in five years. He confidently said, "Just on an NBA team, hopefully with a couple world championships under my belt." Draymond was his own draft oracle.

On the other hand, the experts at DraftExpress echoed what was being said in many NBA personnel departments:

> Green's physical limitations make it quite difficult to project him as being anything more than a liability on this end [the defensive end] of the floor in the NBA. His lack of size means he's quite easy to post up and just shoot over the top of even at the NCAA level, and his poor lateral quickness makes it tough to envision him being able to guard most power forwards on the perimeter or even less likely small forwards, which his height suggests he'd have to. This will be a major hurdle for Green to overcome, and it's not quite clear whether a[n] NBA team will be able to get past this issue, despite what he contributes in various other facets of the game.[1]

I am not reproducing this quotation to criticize the people who wrote it. The sentiment expressed in it was common in the league. In fact, this passage followed a segment in a longer article that praised Draymond for his defense in college. People saw his skills in college but just couldn't see that those skills would translate to the NBA.

There are a couple of ways that NBA draft evaluators can do better in looking for the next Draymond Green, not that anyone will ever be perfect. First, there needs to be a better evaluation of defense throughout basketball and better ways of predicting success at it. Division of blame in chapter 3 and the concepts of chapter 6 get at some of the ideas for better tracking defense. Second, the classification of players and positions can use an upgrade. "Not having a position" is a wonderful phrase in how compact it is, implying that the team that drafts him wouldn't know how to use him, but it is also a frustratingly vague part of the misleading narrative on Draymond. Draymond himself addressed the problem by going to the other extreme, discarding positions entirely: "I don't like classifying myself. . . . I'm just a basketball player," which seems like something you'd see in an online dating profile, but that is kind of what the draft is.

The traditional positions—point guard, shooting guard, small forward, power forward, and center (also labeled 1 through 5)—have always been used as a guide to help simplify the game. If draft evaluators oversimplify it to the point of misevaluation, though, they are being counterproductive. But they aren't going away, and we'll have to live with them.

If you google "Draymond Green position," you will find the phrase "Power Forward and Center." If you look him up at Basketball-Reference.com, it tells you "Small Forward and Power Forward." Because he has also been the team's leader in assists for several years, he has characteristics of a point guard, which is why there are references to him as a "point forward," a combination of point guard and some kind of forward.

The label "point forward" is actually getting at a classification scheme that is useful for Draymond and other basketball players. The "forward" part is referencing his *defensive* role, him being a bigger player who can protect the rim but also guard some players away from it. The "point" part is referencing his *offensive* role as a passer. That dual classification is what I've tried to build into a classification scheme for players. Here are the main concepts behind that scheme:

Defense gets categorized by which part of the floor a player is most responsible for, the inside or the perimeter, as well as the general size of players they guard.

Offense gets categorized by a player's passing responsibilities, how often they shoot, and where they shoot. These characteristics essentially capture the way they are a threat on offense.

Instead of having positions 1 through 5, as the traditional system goes, the positions are designated by a two-digit number, with the first digit indicating their defensive role (called the "defensive series"), and the second digit, the offensive role ("offensive series"). For instance, a point guard who mainly defends on the perimeter is an 11, where the first 1 is for guarding on the perimeter and the second 1 is for having the primary offensive role of distributing the ball. A big man who mostly defends the paint but whose offensive role is mostly shooting from deep (think of Channing Frye or latter-day Brook Lopez, for example) would be a 52, the 5 meaning he defends the paint and the 2 indicating the shooting of a lot of three-point shots. A point forward—as Draymond is often labeled now—would be a 31, where the 3 is for defending bigger players on the perimeter with some inside responsibility and the 1 is for being the distributor. A point center—another label seen at times for Draymond—would be a 51. One small benefit of this numbering system is that it still allows players to be ordered from low to high, as in the traditional system.

The details of how the method works are in appendix 4, but note that those details aren't etched in stone. It's reasonable to expect that the details can be improved or modified at different levels of basketball.

Before looking at Draymond, see table 35, which shows a general overview of the system and its results.

The method I used to put players into the above bins is not perfect. Some of the examples resulting from use of the method don't necessarily fit what I believe. For example, James Harden typically comes out as a 33. I have no problem with him being a versatile scorer (a 3-series on offense), but I don't think of him as defending a lot of bigger players (the 30-series on defense). On the other hand, his general manager has pointed out several times how well Harden defends in the post, so perhaps it makes sense.

Rather, the point of this scheme is the *mentality* of classifying players by both their offensive and defensive roles and not being stuck to an overly concise concept of what a power forward should be.

Table 35. Player types, percentage of players in that type from 2019 to 2023, and examples

	Player type	Percentage of players	Examples
Perimeter defenders (aka the 10-series)			
11	Point guard	12%	Chris Paul, John Wall, Tony Parker, Tim Frazier
12	Shooting guard, jump shooting guard	8%	JJ Redick, Wesley Matthews, Eric Gordon, Gary Harris
13	Versatile scoring guard	5%	Bradley Beal, Kyrie Irving, Jamal Crawford, Dwyane Wade, Monta Ellis, Brandon Knight
14	Inside scoring guard	1%	Tony Allen, Courtney Lee
15	No offense, perimeter defense	3%	Terrence Ferguson, older Keith Bogans
Wing/versatile defenders (30-series)			
31	Point forward	7%	Andre Iguodala, Draymond Green, Lance Stephenson
32	Shooting forward	17%	Trevor Ariza, Luke Babbitt, DeMarre Carroll, Danny Green, Kyle Korver
33	Versatile scoring forward	7%	Paul George, Melo, DeMar DeRozan, Tobias Harris
34	Inside scoring forward	5%	Thaddeus Young, Paul Millsap, Michael Kidd-Gilchrist, Trevor Booker, Brandon Bass
35	No offense wing defender, limited wing defender	6%	Thabo Sefolosha, André Roberson, Luc Mbah a Moute, Dante Cunningham

	Player type	Percentage of players	Examples
Big/paint defenders (50-series)			
51	Point center	2%	Josh McRoberts, Ben Simmons; at times: Gasol brothers, Al Horford, Andrew Bogut, Draymond Green, Nikola Jokić
52	Shooting big	6%	Channing Frye, Danilo Gallinari, Ryan Anderson, Matt Bonner
53	Versatile big	2%	Kevin Durant, Dirk Nowitzki, Joel Embiid, Andrea Bargnani, Nikola Jokić
54	Inside big	14%	LaMarcus Aldridge, Jonas Valančiūnas, David West, Derrick Favors, Rudy Gobert, Javale McGee
55	No offense big, limited big	5%	Tyson Chandler, DeAndre Jordan, Ian Mahinmi, Bismack Biyombo

If Draymond Green is a point forward, the scheme assigns a 31. If he defends more on the interior, as he has done fairly often, he is effectively a point center, which is a 51. This classification system labeled him a 51 in the 2015 and 2016 seasons, for example. In 2017, though, Kevin Durant joined the team and took some of Draymond's interior responsibility, so the system saw him as a 31. For his career thus far (the system can be applied over various time spans), he is labeled as a 31.

Table 35 shows that both of these positions are pretty unusual. The point forward, 31, shows up on only about 7 percent of player seasons. The point center, 51, shows up on only about 2 percent of player seasons.

When you look through the list of seasons (since 2009) where a player was classified as a point center, there have been a lot of pretty good players. These are some of the best players on that list: Giannis, Marc Gasol, Andrew Bogut, Al Horford, Nikola Jokić, older LeBron James (as he got older, LeBron defended more bigs), Andrei Kirilenko, Joakim Noah, Lamar Odom. There are several Hall of Famers on that list and more than a few good players. The worst players on the list are Spencer Hawes, Ronny Turiaf, and Larry Nance Jr. Ben Simmons and Josh McRoberts are the players most commonly assigned to this position, and they weren't bad in those years. If you're looking at Draymond coming out of college as a big man who was a really good passer, this is not a bad list to use as a reference.

But when Draymond came out of college, there were even fewer of these guys. Odom and Kirilenko were established at this classification (if the classification existed), but they also were quite a bit taller than Draymond.

So if we look at the point forwards instead of the point centers, what was *that* list like in Draymond's draft year of 2012? Not bad either. At the top of the list was LeBron, who had a few seasons playing this way before moving inside. Beyond him, Andre Iguodala was already established, for example, and he wasn't much of a shooter, like Draymond. Chuck Hayes showed up as the freakishly small center that Houston used to bolster their defense. But the most established of the point forwards was 6-foot-8-inch Boris Diaw.

Diaw was drafted in 2003 out of France as some weird combination of point guard and power forward. As of this writing, Basketball-Reference oddly lists him as "Power Forward and Shooting Guard." He, like Green, was criticized for having a "bad body" and not being a great shooter but was praised for having a good basketball IQ. Diaw started his career in Atlanta, but after two years he was traded to Phoenix, where he would join the Steve Nash/Mike D'Antoni duo that was opening eyes for how fast the team played and how explosive the offense was. The offense seemed to be about playing fast, with Nash creating good shots for outside shooters and for Amar'e Stoudemire inside. It wasn't clear where Diaw, with his slow pace but good passing ability, would fit. But he did fit, and the team continued to be among the best offenses ever seen, despite Diaw not "having a position."

Diaw would later move on and play for one of the worst teams in history, the Charlotte Bobcats of 2012—the year that Draymond got drafted. Diaw was awful that year. Actually, saying that Diaw played "for" the Bobcats is probably not accurate, given that he seemed to be trying to get cut and the Bobcats accommodated him midway through the season. He got picked up by San Antonio, where his friend Tony Parker was playing, and Diaw miraculously got good again (another example of the impact of motivation), defending well and distributing the ball. So when Draymond was drafted, maybe people forgot that Diaw—with his passing and lack of athleticism—could be effective and then didn't see the comparison. It's hard to know.

There is also an analogy in the attitude between the two players. Just as Diaw packed it in when he played on that poor Charlotte team, Draymond has been known to not play as hard at times during the regular season in less significant games but then ramp it up fiercely in the playoffs. When Steph Curry missed the 2020 season, we didn't have the motivation meter, but it sure looked like Draymond wasn't going 100 percent.

Some of this classification analysis is retrospection inspection—building a narrative that we should have known better about Draymond. In fact, analytical NBA draft models did rank Draymond quite high even at that time, but those are only one part of the draft discussion. Lots of conversations occur in the draft room, and one part of them was clearly his lack of position. This kind of player classification scheme would at least have been helpful in those conversations. He had a position, and there were examples of other point forwards, ones who could contribute positively to teams.

A better player classification system can also help with analysis in the NBA. For example, the Hamptons Five lineup that the Warriors used to destroy teams had an unusual combination of players. It had Draymond and Iguodala both as 31s (point forwards), then Steph Curry as a 13 (a versatile scoring guard), Klay Thompson as a 33 (a versatile scoring wing), and Kevin Durant as a 53 (a versatile big, all using their career classifications). In the 2017 and 2018 seasons, no other team had that combination of players *on their entire roster*. Even if you took Durant off the lineup—as he didn't join them until 2017—no team in those years had the combination of the other four player types.

Not a lot of lineups are given an actual nickname, but the Hamptons Five lineup had one because it was so good. Over the three years of its existence, it dominated opponents. Were there any opposing lineup combinations that actually did decently against it? Of the combinations that played thirty or more possessions against the Hamptons Five, shown in table 36, only three broke even or did better.

Table 36. Combinations of player types going against the Hamptons Five lineup

Combination	Possessions	ORTG	DRTG	Net
11-33-12-32-35	35	146	111	35
11-13-12-52-34	33	109	87	22
11-33-12-32-35	32	116	111	5
11-33-32-35-54	49	116	117	−1
11-33-12-35-54	121	102	115	−13
11-11-33-12-35	42	100	131	−31
11-33-33-32-54	38	92	133	−41
11-11-14-52-54	98	81	122	−42

Though these results don't show a lot of possessions, there were at least some intriguing differences between the more successful lineups and the unsuccessful ones. First, the top three lineups all had two players in the 2-offensive series: shooters. None of the really bad lineups had two of those. Probably a stronger finding is that the top three lineups all had three players in the 2- or 3-offensive series, which includes shooters and versatile scorers. Across all the Warriors lineups historically, not having at least two of these kinds of players has meant that opponents really had a hard time scoring against the Warriors.

On the defensive side, stopping them was difficult regardless, but playing a second 50-series defender (two bigger defenders) made it even more difficult. For this reason, the Hamptons Five lineup forced opponents to go small in trying to defend them, just as was the conventional wisdom.

Another thing you can do with this classification system is just look at how the distribution of players has changed over time. Over the 2009–23 time frame, the number of shooters—offensive series 2—has skyrocketed from about 60 minutes in a game to about 160. Nonscoring players and players who get most of their points on the inside—offensive series 5 and 4, respectively—have declined the most. At the same time, players who are in defensive series 3—the more versatile defenders—have increased.

This isn't telling a particularly new story. It fits with what people have observed without the numbers, which means that the numbers-to-words translation is fairly easy.

Even with these changes in the league, the number of players classified as either point forward (31) or point center (51), like Draymond, hasn't changed a lot, implying that his combination of skills and size is hard to master.

There may also be another subtle benefit to having players like Draymond, guys who play the forward or center position but pass a lot. It's not as strong a trend, but it fits with something I heard a smart person say once: good passing bigs tend to be correlated with good defense. Over this recent history, the team defense has indeed been best around those players.

As an endnote, the name "Draymond" literally starts and ends with D and has twice as much "D" in it as "O"—just the way he plays.

18

Coach 'Em Up

The offseason of 2023 was hard on NBA coaches. First, Detroit's head coach, Dwane Casey, resigned after five seasons and compiling a losing record with a lot of young players. On the same day, Houston fired Stephen Silas, who was the coach of the NBA's youngest team. A couple of weeks later, Toronto fired the coach that won them a championship in Nick Nurse. Next, Milwaukee fired their head coach, Mike Budenholzer, after five seasons of great success, including an NBA championship and two Coach of the Year awards from the National Basketball Coaches Association (the award voted on by his peers, not the media). The media even voted him coach of the month two months before he was fired. About a week after Budenholzer's firing, Phoenix's new owner, Matt Ishbia, reportedly made the call to fire head coach Monty Williams because Ishbia "never really took to him"; Williams had been named coach of the year by both his peers and the media the year before. A few days later, Doc Rivers was fired by the Sixers after three years of losing in the second round of the playoffs.

Within six weeks of the end of the year, four of the prior six winners of Coach of the Year awards were gone. Rivers wasn't one of them, but he had been named by the NBA a year before as one of the fifteen greatest coaches in history. Only Casey and Silas in this group had a losing record in 2023, with both teams being in development mode with very young players.

In general, after being named coach of the year, a coach has a typical life span with his team of two years and 164 games. There is no job security in being the best in this profession.

Is it any wonder that some people call coaching the hardest job in sports?

One day after practice with the Wizards, I was sitting with a couple other coaches on the sidelines, talking about who-knows-what when Bradley Beal came over to sit with us. It's not uncommon for players to just come over to sit and talk after practice. It's part of what you do when you're with people for six months almost continually.

The conversation shifted at some point to talking about players around the league. That's when Brad said, "I would never want to be a coach. We as players watch film, but you all are crazy." We laughed because it was true—coaching is crazy. We can watch the same play over and over again to understand who did what and why. Then we often simplify the story of what happened so that we can watch it again with the players.

In my role, I didn't watch film the same way as others, but I still watched a lot to make the numbers as cohesive with my eyes as possible. That process is extensive and can take away from all of the other work I had to do to answer questions from numbers. I had to be more efficient in watching film, pulling clips from parts of games rather than watching entire games straight through.

But it's natural among coaches to sacrifice a lot of their life to watch film and be in the gym. It's natural among NBA *head* coaches to add on to that by meeting with the media, having discussions with the front office, and doing public events. The stories of head coaches who sleep only three hours a night aren't exaggerations.

In 2010, when I was with the Denver Nuggets, our head coach, George Karl, was given a diagnosis of throat cancer. He would undergo serious treatment that would take him away from the team at times, but the prognosis for survival was good. The news was a jolt to everyone on the team, a reminder of the world outside gyms, hotels, buses, and planes.

After the news sank in for a week or two, we in the front office did have to consider what we would do if George couldn't return to the team. Who would take over? In the interim, it was Adrian Dantley, one of the assistant coaches. But considering who to hire for the long term was a big decision, one that forced us to sit down and think hard about it.

We first made a list of names, many of which wouldn't be recognizable to the readers here. The list wasn't particularly productive, especially since we weren't actively looking to make a change, so our conversations shifted more toward the philosophical side. What did we want from a coach? What are the characteristics of a good coach?

A coach, we decided, was first about knowing What to Do, then about Communicating It. A coach had to know how to judge personnel, how to build strategies and adjust tactics in-game, how to delegate, and then how to determine what analytics had to contribute (which was my addition to the list). With all of that, a coach also needed to be able to convey the relevant parts of what they knew to the players, then listen to them for their feedback and other contributions.

Then Herb Livsey—the old-school scout from chapter 1—added his two cents. First, he said that a coach had to have a voice that wasn't irritating; otherwise the players would just not want to listen after a while. Second, Herb said that a coach had to have a life outside basketball; otherwise the players would not relate to him. The players have families and interests outside the game. If their head coach didn't have other things outside basketball to make him seem human, they wouldn't have much to talk about besides work.

We couldn't have had that conversation with Brad if he had heard us having a more serious conversation. He wouldn't have walked over if he thought we were going to lecture him or try to teach him something. If all we ever talked about was work, he was going to find someone else to talk to.

Sports psychologists talk about how shared experiences like these enhance "cohesion" and "synchronicity" among people in a group. Those shared experiences in sports are typically games and practice but also the sideline session Brad had with us. When you bring together a group of people who may be from completely different family backgrounds or different countries, who may have very different ways of dealing with conflict, who make decisions in different ways, you need those shared experiences created by basketball to build bridges across the differences.

The differences don't disappear with shared experiences, but hopefully the comfort level goes up among everyone so that they can use those differences for the good of the group. A team is not about making everyone alike but about blending everyone's characteristics together. One of the coaches I worked with, Joseph Blair (or "JB" to everyone he liked), knew the importance of blending and resisted using the word "culture" because he believed that it implied something that stayed the same, whereas "community" was better because it represented bringing everyone's voices to the table.

All of this psychology may all sound very subjective and squishy for a book about basketball analytics. But chapter 11 was about measuring motivation, chapter 13 suggested that league changes in efficiency through the year are related to players getting familiar with each other, and chapter 16 had a mathematical model around teammate fit—all pretty squishy subjects in themselves. Psychology hasn't been the best-quantified field, and some have even called it a pseudoscience. But by allowing the numbers to help me understand the game, the numbers have guided me to parts of the game that can be labeled as psychological. They have also guided me to having conversations with sports psychologists and with coaches who believe that 50–100 percent of their job is psychology. If so much of the job is psychology, understanding it in whatever way is important.

But data to use psychology is not easy to get. At the end of chapter 11, on motivation, there was this statement: "On a day-by-day basis or minute-by-minute basis, [motivation/emotional] data doesn't exist."

That wasn't exactly true.

Good coaches have that data. They have "empathy," the ability to sense the emotions of players. They are accurately reading the data about motivational and emotional states that players give off. Coaches aren't writing it down or plugging it into a database, but they are measuring for themselves something psychological.

There is no data provider that gives that kind of data.[1] Even if there was one, knowing exactly how to use it would take additional time, time that Hall of Fame coach Gregg Popovich has already spent. He is known for his ability to relate to players and has said, "Relationships with people are what it's all about. You have to make players realize you care about them." He has been able to not only read what they're thinking but also learn how to keep them playing for him.

Not all coaches have that ability. Empathy is developed through more than the shared experiences of a team. A coach may create a shared experience by giving the team a common language on schemes and plays, for instance, but that coach has to be able to read whether the language makes sense to the players. Building a language is not the same as building conversations, and a coach needs to recognize when players are nodding not because they understand but because they're confused and just want to move on. Making players feel comfortable enough to actually raise those questions—whether that's labeled as empathy or just building an environment where people can speak freely—builds cohesion.

Building cohesion also means making all players feel involved. In a competitive sport where wins and job stability are clearly related, cohesion can be difficult. But there are two kinds of competition in this world. One kind is when there is defense, and the other kind is when there is not. A basketball game has defense, and a 100-meter sprint doesn't. But a basketball team has the competition among teammates for playing time and credit, where there shouldn't be any defense. Teammates shouldn't be undercutting each other or rooting against teammates, but it can happen if things aren't managed right. A coach has to manage the egos at the top of the pyramid and the anxiety at the bottom of it so that no one has the incentive to root against another team member.[2]

For all the analytical advancements that have been made in twenty years to understand basketball, very little has been done analytically to understand the coaching profession. David Berri, an economics professor who works a lot in sports, took an approach to evaluating coaches by carefully identifying whether players played better or worse under a specific head coach. Berri found that only a handful of head coaches could positively impact a team's winning percentage by about ten wins per season—Gregg Popovich and Phil Jackson among them. Most coaches had little influence on wins and losses.

Berri's method seemed like a good one.[3] A good coach should be maximizing the players' production through development and through putting them in the best position to succeed. But the study still said nothing about *how* they made the difference. Were they great at motivating players to work hard? Were they good at putting the right skills on the floor and getting guys to play together? Were they good at developing skills? Or were they great at the x's and o's of defensive schemes and drawing up plays?[4] Berri's study couldn't identify any of that. In addition, the study didn't firmly assign player performance changes to the head coaches because they could have been due to the assistant coaches around them. Those assistant coaches often get interviews for head coaching positions, but neither the coach nor the interviewers have a good way to separate their contribution from that of their head coach. It's not in Berri's method or anyone else's.

In *Basketball on Paper* twenty years ago, I tried myself to do a rough estimate of the value of coaches. After so long in the league and seeing how coaches work, I know now that that quest was misguided. I've seen the impact of motivation and the responsibility of coaching for that. I've seen how fitting players' skills together matters—you can't just add player values to get the total—and I've seen coaches think about this and overthink about this. I've seen how much player development can help build the skills of players and how to balance it with opponent scouting. I've been around the training staffs, the medical staffs, the scouts, and the psychologists whose input goes to coaches. I know a lot better the factors that go into coaching. That experience doesn't mean that I could build a good coaching metric, I assure you. But I think you can bring the principles above to better identify good coaches in a job interview and to evaluate the coaches that you already have.

Analytical Rules of Thumb

There are a few rules of thumb that I picked up while on a coaching staff that may not be common knowledge. Rules of thumb are generally true but not always true. I'll spell out here some that didn't make it into other chapters.

The first one relates to the psychological side that comprised the first section of this chapter. It's that every decision needs to be considered in light of three different time frames: are you managing the game, the season, or a player's career?

- If you're managing the game, you make decisions that go toward winning the game, usually ignoring any psychological impacts incurred by not playing guys or other means.
- If you're managing the season, you may start games with a veteran player over a younger one to show the veteran that his time spent matters and to keep the motivation high for the younger one. You also may take a technical foul to support your players who are not getting foul calls. You'd rather lose a point in the game than lose your player's buy-in.
- Managing a player's career is more to keep them healthy even beyond the current season. This is where some of the load management comes in, but it also shows that you care about the player's health, which goes beyond what they do for you on the court.

Second, on a more tactical note, a lot of coaches cringe at the shot they get at the start of a 2-for-1 possession. It's often an isolation play or a player looking up at the clock and thinking he needs to shoot the ball, making it a lower-percentage shot. But the value of getting the 2-for-1 is still higher than allowing the opponent to have the last shot because of that extra opportunity. In general, using the 2-for-1 means you win the rest of the quarter about half the time, play even a quarter of the time, and lose it a quarter of the time. Even with a low-quality first shot (under 40 percent), the chance of winning the rest of the quarter drops to 40–45 percent but the chance of losing it goes up to only about 30 percent, so it's still a good option. The advantage is maximized when taking the shot between 32 and 35 seconds on the game clock.

Third, the matchups that tend to hurt you are when you're badly cross-matched. If your point guard is guarding their shooting guard, that's generally fine. If your point guard is guarding their small forward or power forward, that costs you about 0.5–1 net point per game on its own, but probably more since it often means there is someone else also mismatched by a good amount. If your point guard is guarding an opposing center (or vice versa), that costs you closer to 1–2 net points per game. Obviously, these bad cross-matches don't persist for a whole game, so the effects of cross-matching, while not good, aren't devastating.

Fourth, the hot hand effect is real but small and usually is offset by players taking harder shots. Being "hot" tends to imply that a player is more likely than normal to make his next shot. NBA players can definitely act this way, but the increase in shooting percentage is only a couple percentage points, not 10–30 percent, which can be how it feels, having felt it myself. Offensively, this means that if a player looks hot, you may run more plays for them, set more screens for them, but you don't want them just launching from thirty-five feet. Defensively, you may be worried that the hot hand is going to make you look bad, but just playing him tougher usually offsets the little mental advantage he may have.[5] The hot hand is actually an interesting example of something apparently psychological that gets expressed in numbers pretty well—just through taking more shots in less time after making a few shots in a row.

Finally, as a bigger-picture rule of thumb, have real conversations not only with your players but with the analytics staff. There are at least a thousand decisions that coaches have to make in the course of a year—some of those decisions can be helped by analytical thought. Sometimes those decisions depend on a lot of factors that can't be measured. But rules of thumb have helped when not all details have been available—with taking layups and threes, with the 2-for-1 situation at the end of the game, with fouling up by three points late in the game. A conversation to ask for help on common decisions can be a shared experience to build cohesion across *all* the different people on the team. I was lucky to experience such conversations.

19

Player Files

An analytics person once told me, "The players are the best! They only want to be better."

It was true in my experience, too, and I would add that players also often asked good questions. They think about the game a lot, which is what I do, so I really enjoyed working with them. As the new generation of players has grown up with increasing knowledge of the messages of analytics, I anticipate that the relationship between analytics and players will only grow.

But another comment that I've gotten in the past has been that people are concerned about a possible tendency of analytics to treat players only "as numbers." I disagree with that for sure, because the phrase implies permanence, that players are their numbers and that the numbers don't change. I've tried to show in this book that numbers do change and those changes reflect changes in the players themselves, whether due to development, game plans, or emotion.

This chapter is about a few of the players over the years who have pushed themselves to change and thus changed my way of thinking.

LeBron, Steph, and Others: Of Greatness

More than anyone else, the greatest players change the way people think about the game. The fans think about those players, as do the media, the general managers, the coaches. We practically obsess over the unique skills of the greatest players, hailing them, trying to acquire them, or desperately trying to beat them.

There is so much written about these guys everywhere that what I want to add is just a couple things. First, I'll add table 37, showing how many wins they added above replacement through time in their careers,[1] just so people can see how the numbers viewed them. Presenting this table is my way of both praising these guys and giving readers a way to compare each of them with the others. The bottom line of the table shows the average number of wins in the players' best five years, which is something that Bill James did in evaluating historical baseball players because it captured both peak performance and longevity. Second, I'll talk about how each of these players made me change the way I think. To be clear, the players are listed chronologically by when they entered the league, not in any order of greatness.

LeBron

First of all, LeBron's numbers are ridiculous. He added more than twenty wins per season in his best five years—none of these other players did that. I don't know if Michael Jordan or Bill Russell or Wilt Chamberlain or Magic Johnson did that. The data isn't good enough to know. I'd love to go back to film and evaluate them all better, but that's a major project, even skipping Russell and Chamberlain because film of them is limited.

Basketball is perhaps the best sport for being able to see talent like LeBron's. You see his face, his build, his ability to jump, his ability to see the court, his ability to dominate a game on both ends. He made me realize that a player could enhance the fit of almost any group of players. He made me realize that there are some players—those with no weaknesses—that basic analytics really can't help to make better. His greatness exceeded any average and any control group, so there was no model for how to make him better. Maybe there was something that could be done on psychology, as Phil Jackson had done for Jordan, which is part of why I looked into that over the years.

D-Wade

Dwyane Wade's chronology of wins added has the ups and downs that illustrate to some degree that he put his body through a torture chamber. There was a legendary shoe commercial that showed him falling down seven times but getting up eight. That was how he played, and it took a toll on his body, which is why his win totals would drop during some seasons.

Wade had dominated the ball for the Heat for seven years before LeBron and Chris Bosh joined him in Miami for the 2011 season. LeBron was the clear alpha there, the player who could make plays for other people the best and still make plays for himself. Could Wade play with him? There was indeed an adjustment period. Before they joined up, Wade and LeBron both liked to have the ball at the left wing and attack from there. When they began to play together, one of them couldn't do that, so Wade drifted more to the corner with LeBron on the court, where he found his way to attack from the baseline. A lot of players shift to playing off the ball, and especially when they go to the corners, they become catch-and-shoot three-point shooters. That was not Wade's skill or his personality. He was able to still make plays from the baseline, driving the baseline or driving back up and through the middle. Being able to make that adjustment was a tribute to his greatness.

CP

Chris Paul's ability to control the game on offense and his ability to limit his matchup's ability on defense performance at the point guard position were essentially unprecedented, especially over the long career he had. When I was sitting on the sideline, he made sure to remind us how good he was. He would talk to our bench from the court, at least when he was winning, saying how he had seen every defense in the world. We couldn't force him left because he would just go there and come back right. He would say he'd do it, he would just go and do it, and then he would look at us. He definitely engaged the competitor in all of us.

For me on the intellectual side, CP was among a few players who mastered the midrange pull-up jump shot. He'd dribble around a screen, get his defender behind him, wait for the defense to help from somewhere, then pick it apart. But if they didn't help and they gave him that midrange shot, he'd take it, he'd make it, and he'd tell you about it.

In doing so, CP had several seasons where he shot 50 percent from midrange. "Was that good enough to be considered a 'good' shot?" I wondered. If three-point shots were going in at an effective 52–54 percent, was 50 percent enough for a long two-point shot? For a pull-up in the paint? What about if they could draw fouls like CP could? Or if they forced a defender to come off their man just a bit?

Table 37. Wins above replacement, using the composite metric, for some of the great players

Season	LeBron	Wade	CP	Steph
2004	3.8	3.0		
2005	15.2	10.1		
2006	18.7	15.9	10.1	
2007	18.4	9.5	8.3	
2008	18.6	5.6	16.0	
2009	25.9	19.7	19.6	
2010	24.5	17.5	7.6	4.7
2011	19.8	15.3	16.5	6.7
2012	16.3	8.4	13.7	2.7
2013	21.6	10.8	14.7	11.6
2014	17.4	5.0	16.5	17.9
2015	15.3	4.4	20.6	21.6
2016	19.6	3.7	16.4	24.8
2017	18.1	2.1	13.7	19.2
2018	16.3	1.3	11.6	10.9
2019	11.4	0.8	8.1	15.6
2020	15.9		11.6	0.5
2021	9.2		9.6	13.7
2022	11.2		10.9	13.8
2023	10.5		6.1	10.7
Avg best 5	22.3	15.8	17.9	19.8

Note: The bottom line is the average number of wins in players' best five seasons.

I figured out how to measure that, a technique that will come out in the section about Kevin Durant.

Steph

Steph Curry came along at the right time in basketball history. Analytically, teams were recognizing that shooting threes was better than shooting midrange. Optically, teams saw what Steph could do, and they didn't need numbers anymore to see the power of the deep shot.

Harden	Kawhi	Dame	Giannis	Jokić
4.6				
6.6				
8.2	3.8			
12.9	6.3	5.7		
15.4	9.6	8.4	1.3	
18.9	12.7	10.2	3.1	
16.3	16.9	8.9	6.0	9.3
17.1	15.8	11.7	13.7	11.5
18.0	1.0	14.1	13.7	12.6
21.6	10.6	14.7	16.0	14.5
18.6	12.6	13.1	15.6	12.6
8.1	10.5	12.0	12.4	17.0
9.8		3.4	15.7	21.9
10.6	9.8	12.7	11.9	18.9
18.8	13.7	13.3	14.9	17.0

Compared with all other players, Steph had a sniper rifle and they were just throwing rocks. As much as I loved Reggie Miller and Ray Allen as shooters, no one was as dominant as Curry with that one weapon.

As I watched others try to beat him, Steph made me think about how much movement or shooting off the catch mattered for jump shots because nothing seemed to affect him. Against greatness, you look for any kind of weakness. For him, there wasn't much.

He also made me think about how much a great shooter actually opened up offensive rebounding opportunities. He dragged a defender with him everywhere or forced switches, both actions opening up the offensive glass.

Harden

If Curry made everyone realize how valuable three-point shooting could be, then James Harden illustrated the broader skill set and team construction that came from analytical thinking: able to create for others, able to make tough finishes around the rim, able to shoot. In a less three-point-oriented world, he would still have been really good. But building a team of spacers around him and letting him go made him great.

At his peak, Harden seemed unstoppable, capable of dribbling into a three-point shot, dribbling to the rim to finish or find a teammate, making a decision at the very last second. It was that last part that really struck me—the ability to make a decision without affecting his shot. That is what is so hard for mortal players: the ability to see the rim so well and be simultaneously aware of where passing options are.

Several of the players in this section are like that—LeBron, Chris Paul, Dame, and Nikola Jokić. That is a skill, I decided at one point, that I would want to test players for.

Kawhi

Kawhi Leonard's name is probably the least known of the players I profile in this section. He missed significant parts of several seasons due to injury. He didn't crave the spotlight and quietly went about his business. But when he was on the court, he had a huge impact, leading two different franchises to titles, behind only LeBron, who led three.

Michael Jordan was known for, among many things, his huge hands, and Kawhi had them, too. But Jordan had so many other incredible skills that his hands didn't get the spotlight. With Kawhi, from the time he was a rookie, the size of his hands, in combination with his skill in using them, stood out. He could poke the ball away if you showed him the ball at all. I remember noting a play in his rookie year where he came from behind a ball handler well ahead of him in transition and just took the ball away.

Those hands helped Kawhi to have great steal numbers but also to have a low rate of turnovers. As much as he could take it away from others, it was hard to take the ball away from him. That was also a Jordan characteristic. Hand size is not as directly tied to eventual success as it is to the ability to make last-second decisions well, but it became part of my thinking.

Dame

As mentioned in chapter 14, about game planning, Damian Lillard made me think about pick-and-roll a lot. It wasn't just about whether a defense should go under or over the screen against him; it was also that he was just so good at running it. It is arguable that he was the best pick-and-roll ball handler of the pick-and-roll generation. Depending only a little on how you count things, he ran it more than anyone and was more efficient at it than anyone.

If pick-and-roll were out of fashion during his era, like it was throughout other eras of basketball, would Dame have become a superstar? Maybe a star, but probably not a superstar. A significant part of his value came from that one play type. He could run it with anyone, he could create shots for himself or anyone once he got that initial advantage, that initial head start. What a shame it would have been if he had been forced to play a different way!

Giannis

Giannis Antetokounmpo was 6 feet 11 and ran like a deer; it made sense that he played for the Bucks with the motto "Fear the Deer." Not only was he that big and that graceful, but he could be both big and graceful while handling the ball. And he did it so often, getting a rebound on the defensive side, then seemingly getting to the rim for a dunk on the opposite side in what seemed like four dribbles. If everyone could do that, they'd definitely need to make the court bigger.

Giannis made his living in transition, one of the best transition players ever seen, the best ever at his size. A significant fraction of his offensive production was that. The first goal in defending him was to get him to give the ball up in transition. The second rule was the same thing because it was that important.

In the half-court, Giannis was a good enough ball handler and decision-maker to have the ball go through him, but that wasn't what made him great. And that was strange. Half-court basketball has always been the biggest part of NBA basketball, just not for Giannis.

Jokić

No matter how slow a player is, no matter how much the game goes toward shooting three-pointers, there is an advantage to being tall and being a good passer. That's what Jokić made me remember. I always knew it, but so many of the guys above in this section were smaller and they could make anyone forget about the big guys. Jokić reminded everyone of just how good a big man with skills could be.

Like Harden, he could wait until the very last second to make a pass or decide to shoot. Like LeBron, he could make his teammates look so much better through his passes. He could get away with some of the no-look stuff he did because he was tall and kept the ball high. But he could also make passes that no one else would really see. Because of that, I couldn't create a convincing argument on whether to double-team him or even when to double-team him if we mixed it up. In his first five years in the league, he shot about 56 percent effectively from the field, and there was evidence that you'd rather he shoot it than pass it. But he hasn't shot under 60 percent since 2020, and over that time, we just hoped to get him in foul trouble. But I think the Denver coaching staff told him not to contest as many shots at the rim in order to counter that tactic of drawing fouls on him. They knew how valuable it was just to have him on the court, even if he had to manage his aggressiveness on the defensive side.

Kevin Durant: Of Aggression

Kevin Durant is a Hall of Famer, an MVP, a two-time NBA Finals MVP, and a top-75 player in NBA history; I very well could have put him in the first section of this chapter (he averaged 14.2 wins over his best five years, easily in the range of the others). But Durant's career had a couple unique things about it that had me thinking about him for years.

First, he is one of a handful of players who could be called a "four-level scorer." On TV they talk about "three-level scorers," but analytics tends to break things up into four "levels" of distances from the rim: layups or dunks at the rim, nonlayups but shots inside the painted area (often called "floaters"), long two-point jump shots outside the paint, and three-point shots. Across those four levels, a player whose individual points produced per hundred possessions on those shots is above the league average is labeled a "four-level scorer."[2] Being able to perform well at all four levels is hard to do, mainly because most players are not efficient with floaters and long two-point shots, the shots that most teams now don't want their players shooting.

Durant is not only one of those four-level scorers but also one who achieves it easily. Over the two most recent seasons, 2022 and 2023, Durant's offensive efficiency has been 165 on layups, 134 on floaters, 132 on long two-point shots, and 144 on three-pointers. The league's average efficiency over that period has been about 113, meaning that he exceeded that number by an average of 31 points per level, easily the highest of anyone in the league. He's been the most effective shooter in the league, even better than Steph Curry.[3] If you're coaching Durant, you let him take pretty much whatever shots he wants to take.

To be clear, what this metric captures is not only shooting ability but also the ability to create those shots, draw shooting fouls, and draw the defense, creating better opportunities for offensive rebounds if they do miss. This is how someone like James Harden, who shot only 45 percent on both floaters and long two-point shots, was better than league efficiency on those shots. He still generated ratings of 117 and 115, respectively, on those shots through his ability to draw fouls and draw defense.

With such an all-around ability to make shots from anywhere on the court, Durant has still had a history of not being as aggressive as people thought he could be, even occasionally getting labeled "passive." Durant takes a lot of shots—don't get me wrong—but why would someone with his ability not take even more shots? He has played with great players, for sure—guys like Harden, Kyrie Irving, Devin Booker, Curry, and Russell Westbrook—players who will take a lot of shots themselves. Those are definitely good players, but Durant's ability to make pretty much any shot should mean that he's taking more shots than those guys when on the floor together, right? That's not what happened.

In Durant's rookie year with Seattle in 2008, he used 26 percent of the team's possessions when he was on the floor. There was really no one else on that team who would shoot much, so Durant led the team in usage as a budding star should. The next year brought Westbrook into the mix, the number 3 pick in the draft, and he was aggressive. When on the floor together, Westbrook and Durant had the same usage, 25 percent, though Durant was clearly more effective, with +2.1 net points per 48 minutes to −0.7 for Westbrook. But Durant's usage of 25 percent with Westbrook on the floor was lower than what he had as a rookie. In Durant's third year, his usage with Westbrook on the floor went up to 28 percent, while Westbrook's went up to 27 percent. Westbrook wasn't totally deferring, but Durant was the leading possession user and he was good at it, with +3.9 net points per hundred possessions on offense (versus +0.8 for Westbrook). But in the playoffs that year—the first playoff series for both Durant and Westbrook—Durant had a couple awful shooting nights, going 5 of 23 from the field in the deciding Game 6, which they lost, and 7 of 24 in the first game. Over the series, with both of them on, they both used 29 percent of the possessions, and Westbrook was better than Durant.

After that point, every year that Westbrook and Durant played together, Westbrook's usage was 4–6 percent higher than Durant's even though Durant's efficiency was higher (see table 38). Westbrook established himself as the alpha player, even though he wasn't the better one. It always seemed strange from the outside, and it's hard to know exactly why it happened.[4] Was it that Westbrook saw Durant struggle in that first playoff series? Was it just that Westbrook was more naturally aggressive, and it took a few years to fully express itself? Was it that Durant, as good as he was, just didn't want to take on the responsibility of being the Man? From the outside, you can't know.

After the 2016 season, Durant left Oklahoma City to join Golden State, where Curry was the established dominant offensive weapon. In their first year together, Curry used 27 percent of possessions when the two were on the court together and Durant used 25 percent. They won the title that year, and Durant was named Finals MVP, easily outperforming Curry while continuing to use fewer possessions in those Finals (29 percent to 26 percent). The next year was similar, with Curry using

Table 38. Durant's usage and offensive productivity when on the floor with another star, along with the other star's usage and productivity

			Usage, on court together		Offensive net points per 48 min., together	
Season	Team	Other star	Durant	Other star	Durant	Other star
2008	Seattle	None				
2009	Oklahoma City	Westbrook	25.4%	25.4%	+2.1	−0.7
2010	Oklahoma City	Westbrook	28.2%	27.2%	+3.9	+0.8
2011	Oklahoma City	Westbrook	26.3%	32.7%	+2.7	+3.1
2012	Oklahoma City	Westbrook	28.4%	32.1%	+4.8	+3.3
2013	Oklahoma City	Westbrook	27.8%	31.5%	+5.3	+3.8
2014	Oklahoma City	Westbrook	27.7%	32.7%	+4.7	+3.7
2015	Oklahoma City	Westbrook	26.5%	33.0%	+5.5	+1.9
2016	Oklahoma City	Westbrook	27.9%	32.4%	+5.9	+4.1
2017	Golden State	Curry	24.5%	27.1%	+6.2	+5.0
2018	Golden State	Curry	25.2%	27.7%	+5.2	+6.2
2019	Golden State	Curry	24.7%	27.7%	+3.9	+5.8
2021	Brooklyn	Irving	29.1%	27.1%	+3.9	+4.9
2022	Brooklyn	Irving	28.9%	26.3%	+6.8	+2.4
2023	Brooklyn	Irving	28.1%	27.0%	+3.8	+2.4
2023	Phoenix	Booker	24.6%	26.7%	+8.4	+3.0

about 2 percent more possessions during the regular season. Then in the playoffs, Curry's usage stayed at 28 percent and Durant's increased to the same 28 percent while continuing to be really good, helping Durant win another Finals MVP award. Their last year together was 2019, and Curry again used more possessions than Durant in the regular season (28 percent to 25 percent), but that imbalance flipped in the playoffs, with Durant using 28 percent to Curry's 25 percent. The playoffs, unfortunately, were also when Durant hurt his Achilles tendon, missing the conference finals and then trying to play in the Finals but tearing it. But Durant was showing signs of being more aggressive every season with the Warriors, the opposite of what happened in Oklahoma City with Westbrook.

Durant would miss the entire 2020 season due to recovery from injury. The Brooklyn Nets signed him knowing that he would miss it, but they brought in Irving to pair with him when Durant got healthy. Upon returning to the floor in 2021, Durant was at his aggressive peak. This was *his* team. He was told that it was, and he acted accordingly, albeit only in thirty-five games in 2022, as injuries continued to limit his time. But he used 29 percent of the possessions even with Irving on the floor, who used just 27 percent. The Nets even traded for James Harden, one of the highest-usage players in the league, to join these two. When Durant was on the floor with Harden, his usage was 28 percent to Harden's 24 percent.[5] That was the first regular season since 2010 with another dominant scorer on the floor where he used more possessions, and he did it with both Irving and Harden. He did the same in 2022 with Irving and Harden, then again in 2023 with only Irving after Harden was traded away.

But the Nets' experiment with the super-team ended in 2023, as they traded away both Durant and Irving. Durant went to Phoenix to join Devin Booker, another dominant scorer. What happened with Durant and Booker on the floor together? Booker took 27 percent of possessions and Durant just 25 percent. Durant deferred again.

Historically, all of those dominant scorers who played with Durant—except for Irving—were more aggressive than he was when he was on the floor. But when Durant was on the floor by himself, he was much more aggressive. When he was on the floor with four other starters, his usage was a modest 26 percent. When he was on the floor with no other starters, his usage shot up to 35 percent and he was just as efficient, if not more so. It's as though the best defense against Durant was his own team having more good players next to him.

And that was the other strange pattern about Durant. When I looked into how to defend Durant, the results generally were that it didn't particularly matter. You could put a great defender on him or a bad one on him. You could double-team him or not double-team him. You could try to take away his threes or his layups or his midrange shots—none of it particularly mattered. It changed a bit admittedly when he was with Brooklyn, where he was the alpha scorer; then analysis pointed to a preference to double-team him but still not at the level of a lot of great players. What seems to matter most is whether Durant *decided* to be aggressive.

The main tactical thing that does matter is not to put a center on him, someone with rim protection responsibilities, which brings us to . . .

Rudy Gobert: Of Big Men Protecting the Paint

Rudy Gobert was the twenty-seventh pick in the 2013 draft, a 7-foot-1-inch center from France. Drafted that late, he wasn't supposed to become the three-time defensive player of the year even though his height was basically the first criterion for achieving such an honor, at least at that phase of the NBA, when eighteen of the previous twenty winners were big men. Being tall made it easy to plant oneself near the rim and deter or contest shots in the paint. Not every tall player did it as well as Gobert did, though. He not only contested shots in the paint as well as anyone else, but he also didn't give up a lot of backside offensive rebounds and putbacks, a great skill for big men. If someone did get the offensive rebound, Gobert's intimidation on the putback was as good as anyone's.

But what if those layups started going away? As three-point shots became so mainstream, that meant fewer layups.

But that's not what happened. Those shots in the paint that Gobert used to deter—they actually *increased* in number. It was midrange shots that declined. But what also declined was the ability to affect those shots in the paint. The NBA's count of contested shots in the paint declined from 67 percent of half-court shots in 2017 to just 52 percent in 2023.[6] Uncontested layups are easy (75–85 percent, depending on how you define them), and a lot more of those showed up in this period. They were happening so much more because the mere threat of three-point shots made it harder for defenders to stay near the rim.

And that affected Gobert.

Gobert contested roughly 40 percent of all shots in the paint when he was in the game from 2017 to 2021. The percentage dropped to 35 in 2022, and to 32 in 2023.[7] He and everyone in the league were struggling to get to shots in the paint like they used to, because they had to be more spaced out to protect the arc.

This flaw with Gobert was exposed most prominently in the 2021 playoffs by the Los Angeles Clippers. After he won his third Defensive Player of the Year award for his regular season defense, the Clippers made his presence in the paint irrelevant by playing five guys who could shoot from beyond the arc, which is called "5-out" offense. Gobert had no one that he could match up with and then drift away from to protect the paint. The Clippers had a 125 offensive rating against the Jazz when Gobert was in the game and they went with 5-out offense, a crazy high number.[8] And they did it almost 80 percent of the time when Gobert was in the game, so they saw a matchup advantage and they exploited it. Not only did it affect Gobert, but it also affected his backup, Derrick Favors, so it was the whole structure of the defense—one designated big protecting the rim when the guards were responsible for funneling the ball to him.

This advantage became obvious to the entire league, but there are a couple of strange things about it. One thing is that teams didn't particularly attack the Jazz with 5-out in the next regular season. This outcome is probably due to teams battling the eighty-two-game schedule, neither having time nor desire to adjust their rotation to one with more 5-out options.

A second strange thing about this, which may be related to the first strange thing, is that the Jazz with Gobert were actually pretty good against 5-out offenses in both the regular season of 2021 and in the regular season after the Clippers beat them.[9] They faced the 5-out offense a lot again in a 2022 playoff series against the Mavericks, and again, they

Table 39. Rudy Gobert's defensive career trajectory, along with the team defensive ratings with him on and off the court

			Defensive composite		Team defensive rating		
Season	Team	Min.	Per 48 min.	WAR	On court	Off court	Difference
2014	Utah	434	+2.3	1.1	100.6	113.1	12.5
2015	Utah	2,158	+3.3	7.1	102.6	109.6	7.1
2016	Utah	1,932	+3.2	6.1	104.2	105.4	1.2
2017	Utah	2,744	+4.6	11.7	104.0	111.6	7.6
2018	Utah	1,768	+3.6	6.1	103.2	111.3	8.1
2019	Utah	2,577	+3.6	9.0	109.5	112.4	2.8
2020	Utah	2,333	+4.1	9.0	110.2	118.3	8.1
2021	Utah	2,187	+5.7	11.0	104.7	116.6	11.9
2022	Utah	2,120	+4.5	8.8	110.2	114.0	3.9
2023	Minnesota	2,148	+3.1	6.7	113.4	116.8	3.4

couldn't stop it. Part of the reason is just that the Clippers and Mavs were both good shooting teams, not just any old teams that decided to go 5-out. The Jazz weren't bad against 5-out offense by average shooting teams, but good teams hurt them.

What does this finding say about Gobert as a defender? If his main skill is more effectively neutralized with the prevalence of shooters in the league, does he become a bad defender? Most of the metrics that I use in my composite have shown his defensive numbers to be worse in the 2022 and 2023 regular seasons than his average between 2017 and 2021, but not all. Some of those metrics show no decline in his defense. But there can be an issue with those metrics.

Those metrics have been frequently calibrated and constructed around a style in the NBA that has become less common: attacking the paint on offense and having a lot of help defenders to protect the paint. If that was the blueprint for defending in the past but not now, the value of stats that go into the metric—blocks, steals, defensive rebounds, uncontested layups, contested threes, overhelps—can all change. It could take several years from the time the NBA style changed to when the methods pick up the changes in the values of those stats. If the context is so important, too—like when 5-out is used versus when it's not—the methodology would also potentially have to adapt.

When those things fully get into defensive metrics, it seems likely that Gobert's prowess as a defender gets marked down a little bit.

Andre Iguodala: Of Adaptation

Andre Iguodala was a lottery pick of the Philadelphia 76ers out of Arizona, a versatile player with a great IQ, they said. The Philadelphia 76ers already had a star, Allen Iverson, when they drafted Iguodala, and Iverson was as ball-dominant a player as there has been. Usually, lottery picks like Iguodala are asked to be scorers pretty early on, but that task would be difficult alongside Iverson. Iguodala would adapt.

As a rookie, Iguodala could be described as what we now call "a ball mover," meaning that his first responsibility when he got the ball was to pass it but also taking opportunistic shots. His usage rate that first year was a Battier-esque 13 percent. He rebounded solidly (6 per game), passed it well (3 assists per game), was a good defender on and off the ball, and the team did well when he was on the court. Iguodala was on his way to being "the no-stats All-Star" even before Michael Lewis ever thought about writing such things. He had to be, because with Iverson on the team, there wasn't room for another normal star. In his rookie year, Iguodala had a composite metric of −0.2 on the offensive end, +0.5 on the defensive side, and +0.3 overall. By playing nearly 2,700 minutes, he added 4.7 wins above replacement.

In his second year, Iguodala was substantively better but stylistically the same—the same defending low-usage (15 percent) ball mover that he had been as a rookie. He shot better, turned it over less often, and got to the line a little more, all of which are normal evolutions for a young player. His value rose to +0.7 on offense, stayed essentially steady at +0.3 on defense, and went up to +1.0 overall. He added 7.0 wins over nearly thirty-one hundred minutes on the court.

But in Iguodala's third year, Iverson was traded early in the season and Iguodala was designated to pick up the offensive slack left by Iverson's departure. He had to adapt again. His usage jumped to 23 percent, and not surprising, his efficiency declined, shooting worse and turning it over more. The offense ran through him now, so he couldn't be just a ball mover.

Iguodala was doing what he could to adapt to the bigger role, and he got a lot better at it in his fourth year (see table 40), the second without Iverson. But he lost all rights to claiming no-stats All-Star credentials by taking on so much extra responsibility. He had good traditional stats—19.9 points per game, 5 rebounds, 5 assists, and 2 steals—but the team was actually worse with him on the floor in both his third and fourth years. Despite the good all-around stats, he wasn't an All-Star (so maybe he was an "all-stats nonstar").

Iguodala played another four years after this with Philadelphia, his usage declining steadily as the team brought in Elton Brand and as homegrown Lou Williams evolved into more of a scorer. But even as his usage fell, Iguodala's per-minute value didn't change much, partially because his defense got better, something that can happen as players no longer have to spend high energy on the offensive side.

Through those first eight years of Iguodala's career, he was on a lot of average 76ers teams, which won between twenty-seven and forty-three games. But he was good on those teams, contributing five wins as a rookie, then always between six and twelve wins, numbers that placed him consistently in the top fifty of all players every year and in the top twenty-five at his best. His value stayed fairly high even as his role changed (see table 40).

During the post-Iverson years, those Sixers offenses were among the most balanced in history in terms of players all using around 20 percent of possessions, not good (usually between fifteenth and twentieth in offense) but balanced. So when Iguodala was traded to Denver in the summer of 2012, which also had a well-balanced offense, he fit right in. No need to adapt. He was basically the third option in Denver, as he had become during the last couple years in Philadelphia. But in Denver, they won. They won fifty-seven games and were second in the Western Conference. He played essentially the same, adding nearly nine wins, close to what he did in Philly, but the team won fourteen more games.[10] That was the effect of better players around him.

Table 40. Andre Iguodala's career trajectory

				Composite metric per 48 min.			Wins above replacement		
Season	Team	Min.	Usage	Offense	Defense	Total	Offense	Defense	Total
2005	PHI	2,686	13%	−0.2	+0.5	+0.3	1.7	3.0	4.7
2006	PHI	3,086	15%	+0.7	+0.3	+1.0	3.9	3.1	7.0
2007	PHI	3,062	23%	+0.5	+0.1	+0.6	3.6	2.5	6.0
2008	PHI	3,242	24%	+1.2	+1.5	+2.6	5.3	6.0	11.3
2009	PHI	3,269	22%	+1.4	+1.4	+2.8	5.9	5.9	11.8
2010	PHI	3,193	22%	+0.9	+0.4	+1.3	4.6	3.3	7.9
2011	PHI	2,469	20%	+0.6	+1.9	+2.5	3.0	5.5	8.5
2012	PHI	2,209	18%	+0.5	+2.2	+2.7	2.6	5.3	7.9
2013	DEN	2,779	19%	+1.2	+1.0	+2.1	4.6	4.1	8.7
2014	GSW	2,040	14%	+0.8	+2.4	+3.2	2.8	5.2	8.0
2015	GSW	2,069	13%	−0.1	+1.3	+1.1	1.3	3.6	4.9
2016	GSW	1,732	13%	+0.1	+0.7	+0.9	1.5	2.2	3.8
2017	GSW	1,998	11%	+0.6	+1.1	+1.7	2.4	3.2	5.6
2018	GSW	1,622	13%	−1.0	+1.4	+0.4	−0.1	3.0	2.9
2019	GSW	1,578	12%	−0.5	+1.7	+1.2	0.6	3.2	3.8
2020	MIA	418	17%	−2.5	+1.1	−1.5	−0.5	0.7	0.2
2021	MIA	1,339	12%	−2.3	+0.6	−1.7	−1.3	1.6	0.3
2022	GSW	603	14%	−1.2	+2.2	+1.0	−0.1	1.5	1.4
2023	GSW	113	12%	−1.9	0.0	−1.9	−0.1	0.1	0.0
Overall		39,504	17%	+0.4	+1.1	+1.5	42	63	105

Note: PHI = Philadelphia; DEN = Denver; GSW = Golden State Warriors; MIA = Miami.

Iguodala changed addresses after one year in Denver, this time heading to Golden State, a place where he was going to be less than the third option. He had to go back to being the player he started off as—the no-stats guy. From this point on, he played ten more years, eight of them with the Warriors,[11] averaging a usage of about 13 percent, which means taking roughly one out of every eight shots. He was at least efficient with so few possessions, which meant that his overall offense was pretty much at league average. And his defense was critical as the

Warriors figured out early relative to the rest of the league that they could play versatile defenders like Iguodala and Draymond Green and Klay Thompson without a big man and be one of the best defenses doing so. So Iguodala adapted to guarding bigger guys and to being a small piece of the offense. He did it and won four NBA titles. He, along with Steph Curry, Thompson, and Green, won four titles in that dynasty.

Iguodala was unusual. As mentioned in chapter 17, he was a point forward for much of his career, which is already pretty rare, but he molded himself into a few different roles during the prime of his career, always being good, never bad, but also never at such a level that he was viewed as elite. The variation in his usage from 13 percent up to 24 percent then back down to around 13 percent based on who he played with is about as big a variation as I've really seen.

Fundamentally, he became a different player based on who he needed to be. He was a leader and a follower. He wasn't always a winner; he had to have help. He got unlucky in Philadelphia, and he got lucky elsewhere. He played well enough with the people he was with to stick around long enough to get lucky.

I didn't know Iguodala personally, but I did hear people's opinions about him from time to time. I knew people who loved him as a brother, and I knew people who called him a "politician." A good politician can be like a brother to many people, but there are some people who say that there is no such thing as a good politician. For me, it's interesting that I heard him labeled that way, because politicians do have to adapt to the people and the circumstances. And that is, for better or worse, what Iguodala did as a player.[12]

(As I neared finishing this book, the question of Iguodala's Hall of Fame status arose. In fact, he brought it up and said that he wasn't a Hall of Famer. Based on what he did in the first part of his career, I don't think anyone would suggest he is worthy of being a Hall of Famer. Based on what he did in the second part of his career when he was a role player on multiple championship teams, you would have to compare him to players like Robert Horry, Derek Fisher, Ron Harper, Steve Kerr, and Bruce Bowen. Are they Hall of Famers? Iguodala won a Finals MVP award, which those guys didn't win. But how much weight should that one award have? One player who won Finals MVP and likely will not make the Hall of Fame is Cedric Maxwell, who played that series with four other Hall of Famers in Larry Bird, Robert Parish, Tiny Archibald, and Kevin McHale. Kinda like Iguodala with Curry, Thompson, and Green.)

Jaylen Brown versus Jayson Tatum: Of an Illusion

Jaylen Brown and Jayson Tatum were the number 3 picks in successive drafts by the Boston Celtics, Brown in 2016 and Tatum in 2017. Both were considered high talent and high character picks that the Celtics could use to rebuild their franchise. Both were acquired (at least indirectly) through draft picks obtained by trading away core pieces of the Celtics' franchise a few years earlier (including Hall of Famers Kevin Garnett and Paul Pierce toward the end of their careers).

Both players lived up to being high draft picks. But a question came up more than once over their first six seasons together as to whether Brown or Tatum was the better player.

Seriously. (I believe that future readers of this chapter will be surprised by this.)

The answer is clearly Tatum—with essentially every offensive and every defensive statistic, from the basics to the advanced, being better for Tatum than for Brown. Even subjective awards are all in favor of Tatum. Brown was Second Team All-Rookie, Tatum was First Team. Brown made the All-NBA Second Team in 2023; Tatum made All-NBA *First* Team in 2022 and 2023. Counts of Player of the Week awards, Player of the Month awards, All-Star Games—all of these are, as of 2023, in favor of Tatum. So we're going to start with the answer that Tatum is better. And we're going to end with it, too. But why did this even come up?

Brown came out a year before Tatum did, so Brown had a little bit of a head start in his career. The composite player metric that is used here was pretty even for the two of them in their first year together—Brown contributing 5.9 wins above replacement, Tatum contributing 6.1, both being good numbers and good signs for the Celtics franchise.

But every year after that, Tatum's performance dwarfed that of Brown based on the same composite metric. Only one analytical metric that goes into the composite ever had Brown better than Tatum in a year after that first one (ESPN's RPM as late as their fourth year together, 2021).

The question about who was better lingered, though, into at least 2022. I heard it in locker rooms, on team buses, and from other staff members in the NBA who said that they liked Brown's toughness, defense, and leadership better than Tatum's. Toughness and leadership don't particularly have numbers associated with them. Defense does, and most of the metrics generally leaned toward Tatum.

Various media personalities that wanted to get clicks made the claim that Brown was better than Tatum, often after games where Brown played well or where Tatum didn't. That's not a big sample, that's not scientific, that's people playing with your mind to make you watch ads. I'd like to think that they don't have a stranglehold on people's brains, so I don't think that's why the question persisted.

TV ratings are three to four times higher for the playoffs than they are for the regular season. That's a lot more eyeballs and a lot more clicks, regardless of whether some pundit is aiming for clickbait. In particular, though, the extra eyeballs were on people who don't watch a lot of what happens the rest of the season. And what happened in the playoffs didn't favor Tatum.

In 2018, their first year together, Brown's playoff performance was worth +1.8 net points per 48 minutes versus Tatum's +0.9, both good but Brown was better. That was through three rounds of the playoffs, each round gathering more eyeballs.

In 2019, the Celtics played into the second round, where they got thoroughly disposed of by the Milwaukee Bucks. Tatum was bad almost throughout the series loss, shooting under 40 percent effectively from the field and having two games where he didn't score even ten points. Brown was clearly better, though still not good. It was a couple of young kids trying to carry their club before they were ready.

The year 2020 was the year of the COVID bubble, when teams were shuttled down to a compound in Orlando to finish the season without fans in the stands. Not only where there no fans in the stands, but TV ratings were very low, so relatively few people saw how good Tatum was in these playoffs. He was dominant in a four-game sweep of Philadelphia in the first round (+7.4 net points per 48 minutes, +3.7 for Brown), then the best player on the floor in a seven-game series win against Toronto (+3.7 for Tatum, +1.0 for Brown). In their series loss to Miami in the conference finals, though, the most watched of the Celtics' playoff matchups, Tatum was average, and Brown played well (+0.1 for Tatum, +2.0 for Brown).

The year 2021 was one with no fans almost throughout the regular season, and the Celtics made the playoffs as the number 7 seed. They went the last week of the season and the whole playoffs without Brown, who tore a ligament in his wrist. The Celtics faced the number 2 seed Brooklyn Nets and lost in five games. Tatum had a 50-point game where he completely carried the team to a victory, but he was overall just so-so compared with his standards (+1.6 net points per 48 min.), and the Celtics were done in five quick games where Tatum on his own wasn't enough.

In 2022 the Celtics went to the NBA Finals against the Warriors and lost in six games—that was a big stage. Even though Tatum outplayed Brown through the Eastern Conference playoffs, on that biggest stage when the Celtics lost, Brown was better than Tatum. The Celtics won two games, and Brown outscored Tatum in each of them, so he got the headlines. In Game 4, when Tatum had a double-double with 23 points and 11 rebounds, the main talking point postgame was how he only scored two points in the fourth quarter when the Warriors pulled away. In the series-deciding game that the Celtics lost, Brown scored 34 and Tatum just 13. Afterward, Brown said in the postgame press conference that he gave Tatum a hug to support him after a rough shooting night.

The human brain can spin these playoff lowlights a couple of ways. The first is to say that Tatum doesn't show up as well as Brown on the big stage. The second is that opponents knew that limiting Tatum was more important than limiting Brown in order to beat them.

Either way, though, all those extra eyeballs weren't seeing convincing evidence that Tatum was the better player. That includes the eyes of the media, the eyes of team personnel, and the eyes of the fans.[13] So it's not too surprising that the questions persisted about whether Brown was better . . .

. . . at least until 2023 when Brown turned the ball over eight times in a disastrous Game 7 loss to the Miami Heat in the Eastern Conference Finals. Tatum played far better throughout the Celtics' playoff run (+3.9 to Brown's −0.4). And then I really didn't hear the question much.

So, yes, Tatum is better than Brown, and I don't see that judgment changing.

Jeremy Lin: Of Great Expectations

Jeremy Lin was one of the top high school players in California in 2006. He led his team to the state championship and was named first-team All-State, yet he couldn't get a scholarship offer to play basketball in college. He fortunately had a backup plan, though not exactly one that everyone can do. He had studied hard enough in high school that Harvard admitted him, which gave him a spot on their team. He was driven to prove to the haters that he could play.

He did that, at least proving that he could play in college, making the first team All-Ivy League his junior and senior years. But that wasn't the NBA, and his chances were small when he got invited to the Portsmouth Invitational in 2010, where seniors can show off in front of NBA scouts. The scouts there didn't love him, both because they never love anyone there and because Lin didn't dominate. Still, Lin's hometown Golden State Warriors didn't hate him too much, and they gave him a chance with their minor league team as well as a total of 285 live NBA minutes in the 2011 season to see what they had.

Whether confirmation bias or not, the Warriors saw him as not good enough. So Lin was waived, picked up by Houston, then waived again, then picked up by the New York Knicks.

Fortunately for Lin, the Knicks' head coach was Mike D'Antoni, who had thrived by giving point guards room to play free. Also fortunately for Lin, D'Antoni's point guards at the time were bad, so bad that D'Antoni figured he didn't have much to lose by giving Lin a shot. On February

4, 2012, D'Antoni let Lin run the show for thirty-six minutes, and what a show it was. It's not as though Lin stepped on the court and instant magic happened. No, there was drama.

Lin didn't start the game, coming on late in the first quarter when the Knicks were down six points. In his first couple minutes, the Knicks fell down by twelve and Lin was part of the problem, being passive like a lot of backups can be as they try to avoid mistakes. Lin was part of the standard rotation that night, so he stayed in the game to start the second quarter, as slated. Whether someone said "be aggressive" or Lin just felt he had to be so for himself, he started off that second quarter making a floater, forcing a turnover, and getting a transition assist. Through the next timeout and the next substitution, D'Antoni let Lin stay in the game beyond his rotation minutes, not because Lin was dominating but because he wasn't hurting the team. At halftime, the Knicks had gone from down six when he entered to down two. He had six points and four assists, three of which were right at the rim.

In the third quarter, Lin came off the bench again, this time earlier, with around eight minutes left. He was aggressive again but this time missing three shots in his first minute on the court, another two shots in the next three minutes. Still D'Antoni gave him room to see how he played and, near the end of the third quarter, Lin had two three-point plays to help bring the Knicks within three points. D'Antoni left him out there for the fourth quarter, with the home fans enjoying the rise of the underdog. In that closing quarter, Lin scored twelve points by himself and fed the big men for two layups, igniting the fans with what he was doing and with the Knicks taking the lead. The Nets couldn't stop him, and the Knicks came away with an unlikely win. His teammates rallied around him, celebrating the underdog.

No one would stop the Linsanity for the next six games, all wins, a crazy U-turn on what started as a horrible season. He was riding the wave of positive emotions, especially considering that those wins all came without Carmelo Anthony and mostly without Amar'e Stoudemire, the Knicks' two designated stars.

The fairy tale didn't end so much as fade away. When the seven-game win streak came to an end, Anthony came back a game later and, whether it was him or the combination of him plus Lin and Stoudemire or just randomness, the Knicks would split a few games, then lose six straight, at which point D'Antoni resigned as coach. Under new coach Mike Woodson, they won six of their next seven, with Lin playing well until he started feeling the pain in his knee. It was supposed to just need a little bit of rest, so he sat out a couple of games. Then suddenly it was announced that he needed surgery that would keep him out for the rest of the year. And he would never wear a Knicks uniform again.

Lin quietly signed a free agent contract with the Houston Rockets in the subsequent offseason, then played seven more years.

How good was Lin? He was worthy of the hype in those first seven games, posting numbers that were easily All-Star level, +5.7 per 48 minutes overall. Over the rest of the season, he was solid but not at that level. Over the rest of what would be another seven years in the NBA, he was a rotation-level player. He was solid offensively and bad on defense—not terrible, just bad.

Table 41. Jeremy Lin's career trajectory

				Composite metric per 48 min.			Wins above replacement		
Season	Team	Min.	Usage	Offense	Defense	Total	Offense	Defense	Total
2011	GSW	285	17%	−1.4	+1.6	+0.2	−0.1	0.6	0.5
2012	NYK	940	30%	+2.2	0.0	+2.2	2.3	0.7	3.0
2013	HOU	2,640	22%	+0.7	−0.7	−0.1	3.3	0.5	3.8
2014	HOU	2,054	21%	0.0	−0.3	−0.3	1.5	1.1	2.7
2015	LAL	1,907	22%	+0.4	−0.8	−0.4	2.0	0.3	2.3
2016	CHA	2,048	22%	−0.8	+0.4	−0.4	0.3	2.2	2.4
2017	BRK	883	27%	+1.6	+0.3	+2.0	1.8	0.9	2.6
2018	BRK	47	30%	+1.0	−5.9	−4.8	0.0	−0.1	−0.1
2019	ATL-TOR	1,436	24%	−1.3	−0.5	−1.8	−0.3	0.5	0.2

Note: GSW = Golden State Warriors; NYK = New York Knicks; HOU = Houston; LAL = Los Angeles Lakers; CHA = Charlotte; BRK = Brooklyn; ATL = Atlanta; TOR =Toronto.

When he was waived by Toronto in 2019, he wanted to stay in the league but again couldn't get an invitation. He wasn't supposed to be able to stay in the league that long. He was like that other Harvard player from chapter 10, who according to my old boss, was going to "make a great doctor" someday. Lin had a Harvard degree, so he could have done something else besides basketball. But he is, as of this writing, still playing professionally over in Asia. Lin's degree was not in medicine but in economics, so maybe by playing for money at age thirty-five, he is actually using that degree.

Zach LaVine: Of Talent

Zach LaVine was drafted by the Minnesota Timberwolves out of UCLA in 2014 with the thirteenth pick. He was an eye-catching athlete, one who was quick horizontally and vertically. He didn't play a lot in his freshman year in college, but when he got onto the floor, the scouts noticed him, both for his physical ability and his tendency to launch jump shots that didn't go in. He had fifteen games in college where he made two shots or less, he scored under 10 points per game, he shot a lousy 47 percent effective against conference opponents. Those are the types of stats that would make a general manager leery of drafting him. He said in draft interviews that he thought he was a point guard, a position that he didn't play in college and that most people thought didn't fit his skills. Most players impress scouts with their basketball IQ or ability to make shots, but LaVine had neither of those. He impressed with pure athleticism.

And athletic he was. He won the NBA dunk contest in both his rookie and sophomore years in the league. He even added a double-pump to the free-throw-line dunk that Michael Jordan made legendary.

But whereas fans and players dreamed of "being like Mike," no one was dreaming of being like Zach at that point. At the time of his first dunk contest victory, his team was the second worst in the NBA and he was the worst player in the league, pretty easily.[14] At the time of his second dunk contest victory, his team was the fifth worst in the NBA and he was the fortieth worst player in the league.

In his third year, the 2017 season, LaVine tore his ACL in early February, at which point his Timberwolves were again the fifth worst team in the league and getting outscored by about 3 points per 48 minutes when LaVine was on the court. How good was LaVine? That was an interesting question.

At the time, ESPN had its original RPM metric, which a lot of people respected. I was tracking it weekly around then, and in the weeks after LaVine got hurt, I noticed that his value of RPM kept getting worse. As of twelve days after his last game, his RPM was +0.6 on offense, –2.5 on defense, and –1.9 overall, so he was bad. As of the end of the season, his offensive RPM declined to –0.6, a drop of 1.2. His defensive RPM went up slightly, so he declined overall about 1.1 per 48 minutes without playing a minute to –3.0, a terrible number. That happened because RPM (and a lot of the informed APM methods) try to estimate how good a player is using what happens even when that player is not playing. When the Timberwolves' offense improved from eleventh to fifth without LaVine in the lineup, the RPM method looked at who replaced him and gave them bumps in their offensive metric while subtracting from LaVine. The guys who principally took his time were Brandon Rush (an additional 22 minutes per game), Tyus Jones (+8 mpg), and Ricky Rubio (+6 mpg), but those guys didn't shoot any better than LaVine. Rush and Jones weren't good at all, but having Rubio at the point guard slot full-time (and not having LaVine there) made their two key scorers—Karl-Anthony Towns and Andrew Wiggins—a lot better.

Such was the nature of LaVine in Minnesota. He was flashy, but the team was bad with him on the floor. He was flashy enough that, in that offseason following his injury, the Chicago Bulls traded All-Star Jimmy Butler to get him (in a package with underwhelming rookie Kris Dunn plus a draft pick). From Minnesota's perspective, drafting LaVine got them three bad years but allowed them to pick up Butler, who would lead them to the franchise's best record since the Kevin Garnett days more than ten years prior.

But this is not about Minnesota.

This is about LaVine, who brought his postinjury athleticism to Chicago, which was still pretty good. In the 2018 season, he came back from the ACL injury in January and played two months before ending his season early with tendinitis. In that span, he was classically "inconsistent," as a lot of people like to say about bad players. He was indeed overall bad, but he was also *statistically* inconsistent, meaning that he had both really good and really bad offensive games.[15] Entering free agency that off-season, he showed the Bulls front office and the Bulls fans that he was still intriguing and frustrating. He had played four years and, in each of them, the team was bad with him on the court. In each of his second through fourth years, the team was actually a *net positive*—a winning team—with him *off the floor* but negative with him on.

That's who he *was*, but you typically aim to sign a player for what he is *going to be*.[16] Projecting what he was going to be could be done a variety of ways, but my methods all projected him to be better than he ever had been in the next year. The methods predicted him to be about an average player but one who played a lot of minutes in the next four years, like so many of the players he compared to. The high end was a good player, a borderline All-Star.

Table 42. Zach LaVine's career trajectory, with team net points, fit, and salary

					Team net points per 48 min.			
Season	Team	Min.	Net pts per 48 min.	WAR	On court	Off court	Smoothed fit	Salary ($M)
2015	MIN	1,902	−5.2	−4.5	−13.6	−4.3	−1.3	2.1
2016	MIN	2,293	−2.4	−0.6	−6.2	+0.1	−0.3	2.1
2017	MIN	1,749	−0.7	1.8	−3.2	+0.6	−0.8	2.2
2018	CHI	656	−1.8	0.1	−12.6	+5.3	−0.7	3.2
2019	CHI	2,171	−0.3	2.9	−6.7	−11.0	+0.2	19.5
2020	CHI	2,085	+0.4	3.8	−4.4	−0.1	+1.1	19.5
2021	CHI	2,034	+2.4	6.7	−0.2	+0.1	+0.8	19.5
2022	CHI	2,328	+1.3	5.9	−0.5	−0.7	−0.4	19.5
2023	CHI	2,768	+2.1	8.6	+0.3	+4.5	−0.3	37.1

In signing LaVine to a contract around the 90th percentile in the league, the Bulls banked on the high end of the projections and LaVine kinda met them. He actually did make two All-Star Games over the course of the contract. His metrics were good, actually at that high end of predictions, around +2.0 in 2021. But the Bulls were outscored with LaVine on the floor, making eight straight seasons where his team was outscored with him on the court.

The Bulls then gave him a max contract. And what happened the first year of that contract? Well, the Bulls did actually outscore their opponents with him on the floor for the first time in his career. But they outscored them by a lot more with him sitting on the bench.

LaVine is a paradoxical player, one of the more extreme in the sense that his teams pretty consistently were better without him despite him individually putting up pretty good stats, at least later in his career. In terms of fitting with his teammates, he hasn't done particularly well, unlike . . .

JJ Redick: Of Fitting In

JJ Redick was already mentioned in this book once, if you remember. He was at the start of chapter 11, "Emotion." Adam Morrison was the player who supposedly had the heart to make it in the NBA despite my draft prediction that he would fail; Morrison split various college Player of the Year awards with Redick. Morrison ended up playing four seasons in the NBA, and Redick had fifteen despite no one ever telling me he had great heart.[17]

Redick lasted fifteen years not because he was a great player. He never made an All-Star team. He led the NBA in three-point percentage one year. He started about half the games he played in and averaged twenty-five minutes per game for his career. He played most of his first seven seasons in the league with Orlando, then was traded to Milwaukee for twenty-eight games. Then he spent four seasons with the LA Clippers, then two with the Philadelphia 76ers, then faded his career to black with New Orleans and Dallas. Teams liked his ability to shoot, especially coming off screens, but didn't like that that's pretty much all he did well.

While Redick was a player, I noticed an interesting set of stats for him beginning around when he joined the Clippers, stats that were

Table 43. JJ Redick's career trajectory, with smoothed fit

			Composite production per 48 min.		
Season	Team	Min.	Offense	Defense	Total
2007	ORL	629	+0.1	−0.8	−0.6
2008	ORL	277	+0.8	−2.2	−1.3
2009	ORL	1,121	−0.4	−0.7	−1.1
2010	ORL	1,808	+1.7	−1.2	+0.5
2011	ORL	1,513	+0.7	−1.3	−0.6
2012	ORL	1,764	+1.3	−1.6	−0.3
2013	ORL-MIL	2,379	+2.2	−2.5	−0.3
2014	LAC	987	+2.7	−0.8	+1.9
2015	LAC	2,409	+2.6	−0.2	+2.4
2016	LAC	2,097	+2.9	+0.2	+3.1
2017	LAC	2,198	+2.1	−0.5	+1.6
2018	PHI	2,149	+2.6	−1.2	+1.4
2019	PHI	2,379	+1.8	−0.8	+1.1
2020	NOR	1,581	+2.1	−2.7	−0.6
2021	NOR-DAL	723	−0.2	−1.5	−1.7

Note: WAR = wins above replacement; ORL = Orlando; MIL = Milwaukee; LAC = Los Angeles Clippers; PHI = Philadelphia; NOR = New Orleans; DAL = Dallas.

rather extreme, but I didn't know what to do with them. More on that in a moment.

After his career was done, Redick became a podcaster and then broadcaster with ESPN. He got good interviews with players and coaches, not just high-quality opportunities to talk to people but high-quality conversations. It seemed that his guests were open with him. Former teammates genuinely seemed to like him.

I was listening to one of Redick's podcasts one day, this one with Celtics coach Joe Mazzulla, when Redick said this:

"I host a podcast and go on television. I'm certainly out there and I'm opinionated often. But I'm naturally very introverted. It took years and years of personal growth and evolution. Honestly, I think the biggest growth I had was when I played for the Clippers. High pressure, more

Composite WAR			Smoothed fit	
Offense	Defense	Total	Offense	Defense
0.5	0.1	0.6	0.0	−0.4
0.4	−0.2	0.1	+0.2	−0.7
0.5	0.2	0.7	+0.2	−0.4
3.6	−0.2	3.4	+0.1	−0.5
1.9	−0.3	1.6	−0.1	0.0
3.1	−0.8	2.3	+0.4	−0.1
5.8	−2.7	3.1	+1.1	−0.1
2.8	0.1	2.9	+0.9	−0.5
6.5	1.5	8.0	+2.8	+1.4
6.2	1.8	8.0	+1.7	+0.6
5.2	0.8	6.0	+1.6	+1.2
5.9	−0.3	5.6	+0.9	+0.4
5.1	0.4	5.5	+0.6	+1.4
3.7	−2.0	1.7	+0.5	−0.6
0.4	−0.3	0.2	0.0	−0.3

responsibility, big market, visible team, and it was a matter of survival. I had to evolve as a human, but it was not an easy process."[18]

That got me thinking back to the stats that jumped out at me when he was with the Clippers. They are the same statistics on fit that I mentioned in chapter 17 and above for Durant. From the time Redick joined the Clippers, the stats on his offensive fit with them were good, but they were extremely good in his second through fourth years. In his second year, his smoothed fit with the team was +2.8 points on offense and +1.4 points on defense. These numbers are usually between about −1 and +1 across the league, as they were for him in his first seven years in the league (see table 43); these numbers are tremendous outliers. In his third year with the Clippers, Redick's fit numbers were good at +1.7 and +0.6. In his fourth and final year there, they were +1.6 and +1.2, still really good. Redick's presence was adding more than his simple value—by a lot.

Fit is not just a one-person thing. The fit numbers for Redick came from looking at how well he paired with Chris Paul, Blake Griffin, DeAndre Jordan, and all of his teammates. And what was driving his overall number was how well he played with those starters: Paul, Griffin, and Jordan. In chapter 16, you'll recall, the top five-man lineup in 2023 in terms of fit was the starting lineup for the NBA champion Denver Nuggets, which had a +3.2 offensive fit and +0.8 defensive fit. The Clippers' starting five of 2015 (which was the above four players, plus Matt Barnes) had an offensive fit of +5.4 and a defensive fit of +1.2, which dwarf the numbers from the Nuggets. Those four Clippers played together for four years, from 2014 through 2017, all with really good fit (see table 44), but Paul, Griffin, and Jordan played together for two years prior to Redick's arrival. Those three alone didn't show this level of fit.

You see a reflection of this complementarity among the Clippers players in each of their performance metrics, too. If you look at how well each of them played in 2013 and 2018, the years before and after they were together, respectively, and then the years in between, every single one of them had better metrics when they were together than in the adjacent years (see table 45). That result is a reflection of them making each other better.

The Clippers' fit was unusually high. For example, the Bucks that won the title in 2021 didn't have particularly high fit numbers. The Lakers that won the title in 2020 didn't either. But those Warriors dynasty teams definitely had good fit, especially across Curry, Thompson, and Green (see table 44). Those Warriors teams were discussed some in chapter 16, and whole books have been written about them. The Clippers' unit has mostly been forgotten because they broke up the band after those four years, whereas the Warriors stuck with it.

So how much of the Clippers' good fit was just Redick's ability to shoot coming off screens? That ability was definitely part of it. At times, he talks in his podcast about specific play calls that created tough decisions for defenses because they took advantage of his skill as well as the skills of Paul, Griffin, and Jordan (specifically the play called "Delay," which is common now).

Table 44. Fit numbers for the Clippers' top four players and Warriors' top three players, with most-used five-man lineups

	Clippers smoothed fit			Warriors smoothed fit		
Season	Top 4	Top 5	5th player	Top 3	Top 5	4th, 5th players
2013				−0.2	+1.7	Jack, Lee
2014	+1.1	+1.7	Matt Barnes	+3.1	+4.1	Iguodala, O'Neal
2015	+6.2	+6.6	Matt Barnes	+3.7	+4.7	H. Barnes, Bogut
2016	+2.2	+1.3	Luc Mbah a Moute	+4.1	+3.2	H. Barnes, Bogut
2017	+4.8	+4.8	Luc Mbah a Moute	+2.8	+3.8	Durant, Pachulia
2018				+1.4	+1.7	Durant, Pachulia
2019				+2.7	+3.6	Durant, Looney
2023				+2.1	+3.2	Wiggins, Looney

Table 45. How well the Clippers' top four played before, after, and during their time together

	Composite values per 48 min.			
Season	Redick	Paul	Griffin	Jordan
2013 (before)	−0.3	+6.3	+2.4	+0.8
2018 (after)	+1.4	+6.4	+2.3	+0.1
2014–17 (together)	+2.2	+7.5	+2.8	+2.6
Difference	+1.6	+1.1	+0.4	+2.1

Note: The bottom line shows how much better the four were when together in 2014–17.

But was the fit good also because Redick was experiencing the "personal growth and evolution" to overcome being a complete introvert? Did he simply grow past being really introverted and into someone that his teammates liked, so they played better together? Hell, I don't know. Someone should ask him on his podcast.

The Triple-Double: Of Nikola Jokić and Russell Westbrook

Achieving 10+ points, rebounds, and assists in a game—a "triple-double"—is a badge of honor for players. It means that they'll get mentioned on Twitter (or X) or Instagram or ESPN, even if they had no highlight plays. There are players who will stay in a game when it's garbage time just so they can get that last assist or rebound. Sometimes this ambition leads to stupid things, like a player passing up good shots because they need an assist or taking bad shots to achieve the points goal or intentionally missing a shot to get a rebound.[19] But I looked at how players typically behave when they're one or two points, rebounds, or assists away from a triple-double, and that bad behavior really does not happen often. That was good to see.

Most triple-doubles are indeed good games. Out of over a thousand occurrences between 2014 and 2023, about 85 percent of them were positive overall games in terms of net points. The average net points statistic in those games was about +4.7, meaning they added close to five points to the team's scoring margin. That's All-Star level if maintained over a long time. In about 40 percent of those games, that single player's performance was enough to create the win, that is, their net points added was at least the margin of victory (called a "threshold win"). Because about 70 percent of the triple-doubles actually occur in wins, getting a triple-double and getting a win implies about a 60 percent chance that the player getting the triple-double had a threshold win—in other words, that they "won" the game for their team.

The best performance in a triple-double was Denver's Nikola Jokić in an early season game in 2018 when he scored 35 points and had 12 rebounds and 11 assists in just 31 minutes, all while not missing a single shot from the field and not committing a single turnover. He added +26 net points, and the Nuggets outscored the Suns by 28 with him on the floor. In NBA history, only Jokić and the legendary Wilt Chamberlain had triple-doubles without missing a shot. And I'd guess that Chamberlain had a few turnovers, but that stat didn't exist back then.

That was Jokić's best triple-double, but he had another 122 of them, behind only Russell Westbrook's 203. That's a lot of good games, and if the average value of a triple-double was +4.7 for all players, the average value of a Jokić triple-double was +7.1, another couple of points better. The only player with more valuable triple-doubles was Steph Curry, with +7.7.

That's the positive stuff. The negative stuff is that about 15 percent of triple-doubles were in bad games, where a player's net points figure actually was below zero. Of the 180 bad triple-doubles, Westbrook had 51 of them. The worst two triple-doubles in this period were Westbrook's. One was a game where he shot 7 of 30 from the field, with five turnovers in a 2-point loss for Houston. The other one came with nine turnovers and 1 of 6 from the free throw line in a 29-point loss for Washington. Overall, 25 percent of Westbrook's triple-doubles have been bad, which is not as high as Ja Morant (42 percent) or Dejounte Murray (26 percent) but higher than everyone else.

But think about this: getting on Westbrook's case about bad triple-doubles is merely saying that he has a little lower level of greatness. He got his face not on the twenty-dollar bill but on the two-dollar bill. If you throw out all 51 of Westbrook's bad triple-doubles, he still had 152 that were good, more than anyone else. His average net points across all his triple-doubles—good and bad—is +3.4, which is still All-Star quality.

On a side note, a case may be made that Westbrook is the most interesting man in basketball, and not just because of this triple-double trivia. Consider:

He was the dominant personality with the ultratalented Kevin Durant, as documented above.

Westbrook was traded to the Los Angeles Lakers in 2021 because LeBron wanted him there. Then, to almost no one's surprise, the fit of Russ with LeBron and the rest of that team was absolutely terrible, and the team really struggled. He handled the ball and tried to defer to the stars, but when they had periods of playing poorly, he would take over because of his nature and that would sometimes make it worse.

Despite questions of how well he fit with various players, it's reasonable to say that Durant, Bradley Beal and Paul George, as well as role players like Serge Ibaka, Daniel Gafford, André Roberson, and Steven Adams, had great, if not their best, seasons while playing with Westbrook.

His skill set has no outside shooting ability, just fierce aggression that is expressed in his willingness to run, his eagerness to get rebounds, and his need to have the ball in his hands. There is nothing delicate or elegant about his game. I would have a hard time believing that Westbrook plays golf. At the same time, he is actually a fashion icon.

How many guys enter this league as athletes with no jump shot who never get a jump shot and still end up great? Most athletes like this end up as wing players trying to develop their three-point shot.

There is no one who shot over 80 percent from the foul line pretty much each of his first nine years and then had a hard time making even 70 percent. No one, that is, but Westbrook.

Over the first six years of his career, Westbrook averaged 7 rebounds per 48 minutes. Over the remainder of it, he averaged 12. When someone told him that transition is easier to get into when the point guard gets the defensive rebound, he literally ran with it.

Back to triple-doubles.

In general, a triple-double is a shortcut for trying to identify good players. It's a pretty good indicator because 85 percent of triple-doubles are positive. But here are a couple things to help narrow down whether a specific instance is actually valuable.

In good triple-doubles, players usually score 24 ppg versus just 18 ppg in bad ones.

In good triple-doubles, players usually shoot an effective 55 percent from the field versus just 39 percent in bad ones.

In good triple-doubles, the player's team usually outscores the opponents by about 10 points when on the floor versus being outscored in bad ones. The player's team wins close to 80 percent of the time with a good triple-double but about 45 percent of the time with a bad one.

As an endnote, I bring this up because fans and staff are often looking for simple indicators of player value. Usually simple comes with inaccuracy, though. In this case, a triple-double is a good indicator, but it can be better if you consider the context.

Kobe Bryant: Of Inspiration

I was sitting on the team bus, waiting to leave for the Atlanta Hawks' arena, when the news came that Kobe Bryant had died in a helicopter crash. There were doubts about whether the news was true because details were sparse. Because no one really knew anything, I was trying to think about the game plan and goals for our game, but the rumors distracted me. Me and everyone else.

Upon arriving at the arena, we saw that all of the televisions in the locker room were tuned to the news. Though there wasn't 100 percent confirmation of his death, it was clearly close to 100 percent, as there were pictures of the ruins and reports from air traffic control. As we sat and watched the news in the locker room, it really hit our team that Kobe had died. We had players who knew him personally, coaches who knew him personally, and everyone who knew him as a great basketball player.

Our pregame routine went out the window that day, and we didn't even talk about the game plan with the players. Instead, the players talked to us about Kobe. Players who knew him cried. Several didn't want to play that night, but they had to. For some, Kobe's death motivated them that night, but that was not generally true for our team.

Kobe was simply an icon, worshipped by even other NBA stars. He was symbolic of hard work and excellence but also hard-headed hard work, sticking to who he was. Players played harder in their careers because Kobe played hard. They dedicated themselves to being their best because Kobe aimed to be his best. They knew and admitted Kobe's flaws, not whitewashing them, but they admired the parts of Kobe that athletes generally aim to be—competitive, fearless, and ultimately successful.

In being himself, Kobe didn't succeed because he was a good guy like Redick. He didn't let his outstanding athleticism cause him to struggle with team success like LaVine either. Kobe was good enough to take bad shots but not nearly as good as Durant at them. Durant, in fact, was better than Kobe in pretty much everything, but Kobe was more of an icon than Durant was. I don't know exactly why. I can look through the numbers, and they don't really capture it. I listened to the players on the night he died and then to all the speakers at his memorial a month later—and that didn't fully explain it.

Icons don't necessarily win all of the awards, they don't necessarily have the best metrics, but they change the world. Kobe changed a lot of people's worlds.

Back in chapter 7, I said that a player metric could not fully reflect the different dimensions of a player, the context they played in, or their role. And I said that those were actually reasons for *having* player metrics, but I didn't explain why. This chapter is why. This chapter uses player metrics to show changes in various players' careers. The metrics show changes pretty quickly, and that ability allows you to dig in to find some of the stories here.

20

The Journey, Part 4

You the competitor started as a child by winning all the time. You played the game, and it was fun because winning was easy. Your talents, your size, your knowledge dominated everyone else. You could always go to your right with your dribble because you were just so much better than everyone at the game. They could know your weakness, but they couldn't stop it.

You knew your own weakness, too, but because they couldn't stop you, you didn't fix it. Then they got better. They caught up to you in size, speed, or strength, either because you stopped growing or they kept growing. You may still have won, but it was harder.

At some point when you were a competitive athlete, you couldn't dominate anymore. You started losing and had to start learning. You went from wanting to be bigger, faster, stronger to *needing* to be leaner, steadier, and smarter. You were already as big, as fast, and as strong as you could be. Then you had to cut the fat, cut the downside, and learn as much as you can. You had to fix your weaknesses.

Maybe the greats didn't have to lose to go there. LeBron was so big, so fast, so strong, and so talented that he could figure out the leaner, steadier, smarter parts while he kept winning at a high level. But even LeBron lost. He didn't win an NBA ring until his ninth season. He still needed something.

You needed something a lot earlier. You lost earlier and you lost more. You fought it, though. You couldn't just give in—imposing your will had worked so well in the past. But then you had to lose some more to figure out how to help a team without being the star. You had to figure out that you were better than the star at rebounding or protecting the rim or shooting off the catch or something, then focus your fire on that. You weren't adjusting to losing, you were then adjusting to winning when you weren't the hero. That dream—winning as a team but being the hero of that team—had to change.

You're not alone, as most of the NBA's five hundred players had to change that dream, too. Winning a championship was still there for them, but being the hero? My god, being the elite of the elite needs not only working harder, not only pushing through pain, not only going without sleep—it needs talent. A special kind of talent.

You've got a talent, but maybe it's not one that makes you the hero. Your specific talent can still get you the win but by rebounding or defending or by being a trainer or a coach or a decision-maker. You're just off the big stage. There are a lot of people who win as a team by being just offstage. You can win without being the hero.

When you walk out of the locker room at the end of a normal season, which is one where you don't win a title, it's a moment of loneliness. After months of being surrounded by your team, the group of people who were your family in the fight for the last many months—they go away. The routine of travel and constant work is suddenly gone. It's not like finishing a year in school or graduating from college, where you feel like you accomplished something. The end of a season typically feels like a failure, whether you missed the playoffs or lost in the Finals, no matter how young your team was or how much you overachieved.

I always needed at least a week of mourning after a season to let it sink in and to think about things that could have been done better.

An NBA season, with its pace and its highs and lows, never gave me time and brain space to put into perspective all of the analytics I practiced. I used analytics daily to prepare for the next opponent and know more than just about anyone about Damian Lillard. I used it to study Kristaps Porziņģis in the year he was entering the draft. I used it to help Porziņģis be a better player when I coached him in Washington.

This year, I finally made time to think about what this all meant, beyond the next game, the next draft pick, or the next set of players on our roster. After some time, I realized what it meant for me. It meant that measuring performance better and better still left room for understanding what isn't measured. What isn't measured won't turn a bad player into a great one, but it can make an average player good. What isn't measured won't magically make 1+1 = 10, but it can make the whole a bit greater than the sum of the parts.

This is not the book I originally set out to write. That one was more of the techniques underlying the framework. The methodology behind the player metric would have been spelled out in more detail. The mathematics to predict a player's future and how to change it—I would have given more of that away. The statistical methods that can go into a game plan or a draft model would have been here. I worked in the NBA in a lot of capacities, so the toolkit is big.

But that information would have been better placed in a textbook or in weekly columns, not this book. It would have also given away some of the tools that I use to remain competitive, even in my role offstage. And it would have buried the conclusions that keep coming to mind when I watch or work in the game.

Player performance changes, due to a lot of factors. I used to think that players were fairly constant, changing mostly because of age. But I know now that they can change with role, with fit, with familiarity with each other, with varying defense, with development, with media coverage, with mental or physical fatigue, with motivation, and with demotivation. Some of these effects are fairly big.

You can coach players to be better, but we don't measure the process very well to *know* how to do it. Given how much time is spent in practice, in shootarounds, and overall working with coaches, more of that data is needed to understand what makes players better. At a basic level, is it more reps or more representative reps?

It takes time for a group of players to come together, especially regarding decision-making. Decision-making is not an easy skill to master when situations change so much. The Heat of 2017 were an extreme case of figuring out how to play together, almost flipping the switch at some point to really understanding each other. But they were an exception only in magnitude, not in frequency. The league-wide improvement in jump shooting and turnovers as the season plays out suggest that teammates need time to get used to each other.

Nonscorers are rarely good offensive players. They can be solid, but they have to be efficient—making shots, getting offensive boards, committing few turnovers—in order to reach that level.

Prepare for opponents primarily by being the best version of who you are. Overemphasis on adjusting to opponents, especially early, can lead to not building your own identity and establishing what you do well.

Thinking about data before you have it gives you a head start in using it the right way. Saying just that you need more data can mean less efficient use of the data you already have and the next data set that you get.

A defense is so much about how much it helps and recovers and the ways that it does so. Looking at who is helping, when they're helping, and how much they help suggests their role and the level of responsibility they should have for what happened.

The hot hand is real, but its effect is small and is usually offset by players taking harder shots.

Player metrics should add up to something real because if they don't, you're not managing something real. They should be reasonably predictable so that you can make forecasts. They should be explainable so that you can make adjustments to improve those forecasts. They should be granular to apply across all the circumstances that matter. And they should be flexible to incorporate new information. People will still evaluate player metrics based on whether they "seem" right. You can't stop it. You can just be prepared to dig into why things may "seem" wrong.

A coach can manage the game, the season, or players' careers. These factors sometimes conflict, but be clear about which one you're choosing at the time they conflict.

There are two kinds of competition in this world, one where there's defense and one where there's not. The game of basketball is set up to have defense, obviously, but competition *among teammates* becomes unhealthy if they play defense on each other. Teammates do compete among each other for individual credit for the success of a team, but hopefully they don't push each other down to do so.

Basketball is a people business. Analytics shouldn't be segregated; it should be integrated as a way of thinking across the people business. Building relationships to integrate analytics knowledge into that business is critical.

Several of these concepts are not basketball-specific. Things like motivation, teamwork, competition, and how people change with different roles—all have analogies beyond basketball and perhaps beyond sports. I haven't emphasized that because I don't want to give the impression that Basketball Is Life, the rest being details. Basketball is not life. It is a game with aspects that can look like life. But that is because basketball is my passion and my expertise. By being so passionate about this game, I've learned things that are relevant when I have been passionate about other things in life, whether that's investing or parenting or staying in shape or writing a book.

To the coaches out there so passionate about your craft—I hope these concepts help you persevere through the many hurdles you face. It's a tough profession.

To the basketball fans, the scientists, the teachers, the parents, the competitors, and the athletes who are passionate about what you do—I hope that you found this work thought-provoking enough to inspire you in your craft.

Twenty years ago, I quit my six-figure job to chase a dream . . .

Appendix 1

Player Metrics

Player metrics are just models of how much players contribute to winning. Like any models, there are some factors involved in evaluating them. This appendix has some of the details behind the evaluation of various overall player metrics in chapter 7, "Cutting the Cake." It also has a bit more detail on the Net Points algorithm.

This appendix uses NBA metrics values as they existed at the end of the 2023 season. These are the principal varieties of metrics that were looked at (in alphabetical order):

DARKO, from Kostya Medvedovsky. This was named the favorite public metric by anonymous executives within the NBA in 2021. It was meant to be predictive, not explanatory. I had access to this data going back to the 1998 season.

EPM, from dunksandthrees.com. This was the runner-up among favorites of anonymous executives and is meant to be a blend of predictive and explanatory. This data was available since 2014.

LEBRON, from bball-index.com. This was the third-place metric in terms of favorites among anonymous executives and is also meant to be predictive, not explanatory. LEBRON data was available since 2010.

Net Points, which I created and is explained more below. It is purely explanatory, though methods exist for predicting its future values (not explained in this book). This metric was not evaluated by anonymous executives because it was always private. I had this data going back into the 1980s.

RAPTOR, from FiveThirtyEight.com. This metric placed number 4 in the survey of anonymous executives. It was meant to be explanatory and not predictive. It had an additional step, called CARMELO, to create predictive numbers. Available since 2014, it was discontinued in 2023, with FiveThirtyEight dismissing its sports coverage. I have some suspicion that it will be back.

RPM, from ESPN.com. A version created by Jeremias Engelmann was discontinued and replaced. I have used the replacement, though I have had concerns in doing so, since some of its results seem extreme, as documented somewhat below. This metric has been available since 2002, but I believe it was taken offline by the end of 2023.

These are also the metrics that were used in the composite metric at various points in the book. Each of those available for a season were equally weighted and averaged. In general, I used only regular season data. Some had playoff data, but I generally did not use it. At times I wasn't sure whether the numbers I had were from combined regular season and playoffs.

I also looked into a variety of other metrics over the years but spent less time with them for this book.

Four Factors RAPM, from nbashotcharts.com. This was number 5 in the survey of NBA executives. It goes back to 2010 and continued to 2023. I considered using it, but pure RAPM methods concerned me, in general, for some of their lack of explainability along with results that could use explanation.

Boxscore Plus-Minus (BPM), from Daniel Myers and Basketball-Reference.com. This is a very handy metric.

Wins Produced, from boxscoregeeks.com and David Berri's work in *Wages of Wins*. There was no distinction between offense and defense in the results I found, only a combined metric.

RAPM, from basketball-analytics.gitlab.io. They discontinued their results in 2019.

PIPM, from Jacob Goldstein before his services were hired away by a team.

RAPM, from Joe Sill before his services were hired away by a team.

Win Shares, on Basketball-Reference.com. This was an extension of methods that were in *Basketball on Paper*. In part because it used the box-score level stats and in part because I think the Win Shares algorithm isn't capturing the right things, I don't think these numbers are particularly useful.

PER, from John Hollinger. It's a linear weights metric that doesn't add to anything, so I couldn't really do much with it.

TENDEX, from Dave Heeren. It's a linear weights metric that doesn't add to anything, so I couldn't really do much with it.

Points Created, from Bob Bellotti. It's a linear weights metric that doesn't add to anything, so I couldn't really do much with it.

I considered five general criteria for evaluating the metrics.

Add up. Do they add up to something real, like a team point differential or win total? If they don't add up somewhat close, then they really don't have much use. This criterion can exclude methods from further evaluation.

Predictable. Are they relatively predictable from one year to the next? A year time frame is relevant because players often get evaluated over a year, don't normally get traded more than once per year, and there is one trade deadline per year. Pragmatically, the values available for the metrics are commonly available on an entire-season basis, so I couldn't do things more granular than that.

Explainable. Do they tell you why a player is good or bad? Can the metric be broken down so that it says what a player does well?

Granularity. How granular are the metrics? Do they add up on a game level? On a play level?

Expandable. Can they be extended with new data? With increasing amounts of data, can that be used to better infer player value? Does it continue to tell you why a player is good or bad?

I've gone through the general evaluations of the methods for these characteristics in the main text. I'll dig into the first two criteria a little more in this appendix.

Do They Add Up to Something?

This is the first criterion because, without it, there isn't much to constrain metrics. If a metric doesn't add up to anything real on the team level (point differential or wins), then there is no further point to evaluating the metric. This is true for some of the linear weights methods.

If a metric doesn't add up perfectly, it is automatically introducing some sort of error, what I'll call "aggregation error." Maybe that error is because the metric is trying to predict the future rather than explain the past, but we use metrics to look both forward and backward. For instance, if you want to know why your team has been struggling on offense, you want to be able to look backward and not have a bias for looking forward.

The Net Points method has this constraint built into it. Net Points automatically adds up perfectly over the season and over a game and over a play because that is its algorithm. If, however, you add opponent adjustment to Net Points, this is no longer true. Two good teams playing against each other, for instance, with one team winning by 6 would mean that the total net points for the winning team is +6 and then −6 for the losing team. But if you opponent-adjust Net Points, then the winning team would have a total Net Points value of +8, for example, and the losing team would have a total Net Points value of −4. Because NBA schedules are pretty well balanced, even including opponent adjustment doesn't dramatically alter whether Net Points adds up.

Across the other metrics, I looked at the time frame between 2014 and 2023 when all of these metrics were available and evaluated their error in adding up to a team total point differential. So each player's value for the season was multiplied by their minutes to get their total productivity, then added up. Some metrics don't calculate a number for players with low minutes, so a value of −2 per 48 minutes was used for them. What this yields is something like table 46 for each of the metrics.

The column for 2014, for instance, shows that the actual point differential for Atlanta was only 4 points off from what RPM would estimate based on its player values. That is quite accurate. On the other hand, for Chicago, it was too low by 168 points, over 2 points per game, which is a lot.

Table 46. Differences between estimated point differential and actual point differential by team

Team	2014	2015	2016	2017	2018	2019	2020	2021	2022	2023
ATL	4	−116	81	−79	67	111	−7	−83	204	29
BOS	−7	68	130	−23	−35	21	−136	−121	211	180
BRK	44	−187	11	138	109	9	33	25	−237	37
CHA	−78	−178	−191	−195	−75	−114	94	163	373	341
CHI	−168	−181	−153	−76	205	−21	−61	−186	−171	−16
CLE	−7	−45	−66	−22	−73	−46	−20	191	31	−80
DAL	−108	59	−81	71	68	−22	−47	−229	91	152

Note: ATL = Atlanta, BOS = Boston, BRK = Brooklyn, CHA = Charlotte, CHI = Chicago, CLE = Cleveland, DAL = Dallas.

Table 47. Average point differential error across all teams by season for each method

Method	2014	2015	2016	2017	2018	2019	2020	2021	2022	2023	Average
DARKO	42	36	72	66	40	63	31	36	43	13	44
EPM	62	−6	−4	−5	−8	−5	−8	−16	−18	−15	−2
LEBRON	36	38	33	39	20	19	16	9	30	14	25
Net Points	0	0	0	0	0	0	0	0	0	0	0
RAPTOR	8	0	−3	6	4	4	15	4	3	6	5
RPM	−5	−3	−6	−5	−3	−6	−2	36	89	101	20

Note: Ideally, all errors would be zero.

With tables like this for several metrics, table 47 shows the average difference per team for the different metrics, basically reflecting whether they are biased high or low. These should ideally all be zero, but most metrics tend to be biased a little high. DARKO ends up high by about 44 points per team per year, for example, which is about half a point per game (or about 0.1 point per player on the floor).[1]

I believe that the general bias high for LEBRON, DARKO, and RPM exists because of the metrics' predictive goal,[2] which causes them to regress younger players with fairly small sample sizes closer to an average value from their early struggles. I see that the errors by team are negatively correlated with average team age, in general, which is consistent with mistakes on the younger players. That explanation doesn't fit for EPM, though, which produces only small errors and aims to be at least partially predictive. RAPTOR is not predictive but explanatory, so it's good that its absolute error is close to zero. When I look at the correlation between RAPTOR team errors and the team errors for the others, they are pretty strongly negatively correlated. RAPTOR errors seem to be more correlated with truer forms of adjusted plus-minus. That implies more implicit weight on how the team did than on the individual.

Table 48 highlights the standard deviation across teams in each year, reflecting the amount of typical absolute error that each metric had over a season. Ideally, this is again zero, which Net Points gets by construction. The others are 100–135 or so. This is not a perfect translation, but it is suggesting that metrics are off about 1.5 points per game (or about 0.3 points per player on the floor). DARKO and RPM added up the least well.

Overall, the actual errors and average absolute errors are not huge for these metrics but are definitely relevant.

Table 48. Standard deviation of team errors by method

Method	2014	2015	2016	2017	2018	2019	2020	2021	2022	2023	Average
DARKO	115	141	127	126	133	111	117	128	166	166	133
EPM	56	68	54	49	50	35	40	56	70	55	53
LEBRON	82	82	111	91	94	100	98	159	124	123	106
Net Points	0	0	0	0	0	0	0	0	0	0	0
RAPTOR	140	131	96	101	95	101	95	83	97	73	101
RPM	109	134	134	102	118	131	90	163	180	139	130

How Predictable Are They?

Remember that DARKO, LEBRON, RPM, and EPM to some degree were designed to be predictive on their own. That means that these metrics are trying less to explain the past than to have a value that represents what will happen in the next game. As a default, these should be more predictive than Net Points or RAPTOR, which look backward.

There are a lot of ways to test predictability. I stuck to the following for now.

1. Season over season stability for individual players from one year to the next (value and rank)
2. Stability in the experience range of three to eight years, which is after the early break-in and before definite declines
3. Season over season stability just for players who change teams

Even though I stuck to those, there are a lot of other ways to look at predictability. I brainstormed just a few. Prediction is a broad business.

1. Evaluating game results with given minutes and a season-long metric.
2. Predicting both individual productivity and player minutes on a game-by-game basis.
3. Explicitly looking for simple mathematical models that use each of the metrics to predict the next year.
4. Doing any of those first tests over not one year but two years, three years, or four years.

Sticking just with the first three prediction tests, I eliminated players who played fewer than eight hundred minutes; then I evaluated the metrics. The results are summarized in table 49. What it generally says is that DARKO has the most self-consistent predictable results from year to year, regardless of whether you're looking at all players and all years, just players in their third through eighth years, or just players who changed teams.

Table 49. The average absolute error difference from one year to the next by method, over three classes of players

Test type	DARKO	EPM	LEBRON	Net Points	RAPTOR	RPM
All players, all years	0.82	1.45	1.08	1.25	1.83	1.62
Years 3–8	0.81	1.62	0.97	1.08	1.56	1.38
Change teams	0.93	1.48	1.15	1.30	1.84	1.70
Average	0.85	1.52	1.07	1.21	1.74	1.57

Note: Smaller numbers are better.

I should emphasize the "self-consistent" part here. These are how well they predict *themselves* from one year to the next. You can do that reasonably if they add up to team values reasonably well, which they all do.

I also looked at how often players changed ranks since decision-makers often use ranks more than the actual numbers themselves. Table 50 breaks down how often players changed their percentile ranking by at least 10 percent, 20 percent, 40 percent, or 50 percent. As with the other approaches of evaluating the different metrics, this one also paints DARKO as the most self-consistent.

Table 50. How often players changed ranking within a method from one season to the next

Method	10%	20%	40%	50%	Average
DARKO	50%	25%	4%	2%	20.3%
EPM	60%	36%	10%	4%	27.4%
LEBRON	60%	35%	9%	4%	27.1%
Net Points	62%	39%	10%	5%	28.9%
RAPTOR	65%	41%	14%	6%	31.7%
RPM	64%	42%	15%	7%	31.9%

Note: Smaller numbers are better.

A Couple Other Stats

Overall correlations across informed APM, APM, and Net Points methods are reasonably high at a season level, at about 0.8+ for offensive values, 0.6+ for defensive values, and 0.7+ across overall values for players with at least eight hundred minutes in a season. LEBRON and DARKO correlate the most strongly between any two, at 0.85–0.9 for offense, defense, and overall.

If you look at the top thirty-five players ranked by each method in each year since they've been around, there is a solid amount of agreement, having usually twenty-three to twenty-four common players on average. LEBRON and RAPTOR tend to have the most players that all agree upon, but Net Points and DARKO are close.

Those are both statements of how similar the methods are to each other, though, not of predictability and usefulness.

The Basics of Net Points

The Net Points methodology works in a way that is completely different from the other methods used to value players. It is based on dividing the credit and the blame among teammates on every event in the play-by-play. The method is a granularization of what was laid out in *Basketball on Paper*, though, capturing the individual scoring possessions, individual total possessions, and individual points produced so that they all add up to the team totals. The original method worked on estimates that had to be made from the box score statistics. With play-by-play, I could make it more granular. With tracking data, I could make that granular part better. I could potentially make the method more granular, but each step requires a good amount of work.

Each of the four primary events in a play-by-play—shots, turnovers, rebounds, and free throws—have a possession value.[3] A made shot or turnover ends a possession, a missed shot has a partial possession associated with it. A made second free throw of two ends a possession, a missed one has a partial possession associated with it. An offensive rebound has a negative possession associated with it, whereas a defensive rebound turns the partial possession into a completed one. And we have a ton of information from play-by-play and player tracking on how to assign how much of a possession is partial.

Dividing the credit or blame on each of those possessions or partial possessions is the nitty-gritty, the weeds, and the thing that can keep the machine learning crowd busy. There are equations behind dividing credit optimally so that players feel properly rewarded, but they can be difficult to parameterize. For example, on a pick-and-roll, when the guard goes over the screen and tries to pass to the screener, but the pass is a little high, still catchable, but high, so it gets turned over—what was the chance of that pass being completed at the time he threw it? What was the chance that the screener could have caught the pass? Those are numbers that go into division of blame, in this case. Neither of those answers is easy to evaluate, but doing so is better than doing what the stat keepers are forced to do—decide if the turnover was on the passer or on the pass catcher. Dividing credit and blame poorly is better than not dividing it at all.

But that is why a machine learning, or even a human learning, process has made some sense. Evaluating a lot of situations where credit and blame can be divided, then determining the factors that affect the division—that gives you a lot to work with.

Once you've divided the credit or blame on a possession, then you can turn the divided possessions into net points using the Pue equation, which is in the next appendix.

Appendix 2

The Pue Equation

The Pue equation, whose name comes from "*p*roductivity-*u*sage-*e*fficiency," relates all three of these things together for individual players. The equation for offense is slightly different from the one for defense.

All three of these things must be related, and I knew it when *Basketball on Paper* came out, but I hadn't quite figured out the relationship. The important part here is that the equation addresses the question of the balance between volume and efficiency. So if a player shoots a lot more but their efficiency declines, are they actually a better or worse player? This equation answers that question.

It is most interesting on the offensive end, which has this formula:

$$\text{Productivity} = \text{Usage} \times (\text{Efficiency} - R \times \text{LgRtg}) - \frac{(1 - R)}{N} \times \text{LgRtg}$$

Here:

Productivity is offensive net points per 100 possessions, whether that's from Net Points itself or from LEBRON's offensive metric or something else. It's a number like −1.7 or +3.2.

Usage is individual offensive possessions used per 100 team possessions used, a number like 0.24. This strictly should come from the Net Points methodology of appendix 1 or the framework from *Basketball on Paper*. The public usage numbers tend to be quite close to them, though so it's fair to use that as a substitute.

Efficiency is an individual's offensive rating, individual points produced (divided credit version) per 100 individual possessions used. This is a number like 125 for someone like Steph Curry and a number around 97 for bad offensive players. The formula was laid out in detail in *Basketball on Paper*, then recapped to some degree in appendix 1, adding that it can be done on a play level. This is *not* what NBA.com shows on its website as ORTG and DRTG for players. What NBA.com shows are the team's offensive and defensive efficiencies with that player on the floor. That is not this efficiency. This is the divided credit version of points produced per hundred divided credit possessions, which is what you'll see on Basketball-Reference.com for individuals.

LgRtg is the average offensive efficiency across the league, which has been between about 105 and 115 over the past twenty years.

N is the number of players on the team, which is usually five, of course. But this equation works for other size teams.

R is the percentage of the league offensive rating that defines replacement level, often evaluated by looking at some of the worst offensive teams in the league relative to average. I've always used a value of 0.92 here.

On the defensive side, its form is only slightly different:

$$\text{Productivity} = \text{Usage} \times [(2 - R) \times \text{LgRtg} - \text{Efficiency}] - \frac{(1 - R)}{N} \times \text{LgRtg}$$

Here:

Productivity is now the defensive net points per 100 possessions. Or, as mentioned, defensive informed APM of whatever brand you like. It's a number typically between about −2.0 and +3.0.

Usage is individual defensive possessions used per 100 team possessions used. The average is always 0.2. On defense, this tends to range between about 0.17 and 0.25. There is no public version of defensive usage, as far as I know.

Efficiency is an individual's defensive rating, individual points allowed (divided credit version) per 100 individual possessions used. This number is about 125 for someone like Steph Curry and around 97 for bad offensive players. This rating is available on Basketball-Reference.com using the framework in

Basketball on Paper, though I've updated it to work at a granular level since then.

LgRtg, *N*, and *R* are the same as those in the offensive version.

These equations must be satisfied for any player metric. Most player metrics skip over this calculation to just get to productivity, not having a step of calculating usage or individual efficiency. Without those things, the numbers can't really be checked.

If you're getting geeky about it, this equation basically says that a player's productivity is not only the product of their usage and efficiency. It's the product of their usage and efficiency *above replacement level*, then subtracting a charge for being on the court. The charge for being on the court is bigger when playing three-on-three than when playing five-on-five. That charge is also larger when playing in less competitive leagues, like high school, which then makes it a little more valuable to use possessions at those levels.

Appendix 3

Fit Calculations

The estimate of fit used in this book is independent of player metrics. It just uses information about how the team played with players on the floor versus those same players off the floor. It has its limitations in that it gives only relative fit to other players or lineups on the team. Hence, a unit that has a +6 fit doesn't explicitly compare to a –1 fit for a unit on another team. But if you think most teams are reasonably constructed, you can compare them to some degree.

The calculation method is summarized pretty easily if you know how to read math. For instance, b_{ij} is the "basic" offensive fit between player i and player j and it is given by

$$b_{ij} = \left[O_{ij} - \frac{M_{i,No\,j}O_{i,No\,j} + M_{No\,i,j}O_{No\,i,j}}{M_{i,No\,j} + M_{No\,i,j}} \right] \frac{\sqrt{M_{ij}/48}}{12}$$

where O_{ij} is the offensive rating with both players i and j on the floor, M_{ij} is the minutes with both players on the floor together, $M_{i,No\,j}$ is the minutes of player i on without player j, $O_{i,\,No\,j}$ is the offensive rating with player i on without player j. If you want defensive fit, it's the same equation, replacing the offensive ratings with defensive ratings. This is really just the team offensive rating when the players are together minus a weighted average of the team offensive rating when they're apart, scaled by a factor involving how much they played together.[1]

If you want the "overall" offensive fit across two players, ij, it works this way:

$$F_{ij} = b_{ij} \times \frac{2}{5}$$

If you want it across three players, *ijk*, it looks like this:

$$F_{ijk} = \frac{M_{ij}b_{ij} + M_{ik}b_{ik} + M_{jk}b_{jk}}{M_{ij} + M_{ik} + M_{jk}} \times \frac{3}{5}$$

If you want it for four players, it's the weighted average of basic fit across each of the pairs of players, multiplied by ⁴⁄₅. You can see the pattern for five players.

Without the kind of detailed model that exists for frescobol, it's not easy to explicitly calculate fit for a lineup of basketball players. You'd like to just look at the difference between the whole (the lineup's overall performance) and subtract the sum of the parts (the individual player's average player metrics), but that doesn't work. It doesn't work because

1. metrics of individual value implicitly incorporate fit into them, so there is a chicken-and-egg problem, and
2. sample size for these lineups can be quite small and, hence, noisy. As a result, estimates of fit are also pretty variable.

The second problem can be addressed somewhat by looking at two-man lineups instead of five-man lineups. There are a lot more reps for two guys in combination than five. Instead of just 31 five-man units across the league reaching five hundred possessions together, there were 1,500 two-man lineups reaching that level in 2023, or roughly 50 per team. If you try to construct a five-man lineup, looking at two players at a time to do so gives more reliable results.

The smoothed fit values shown in chapter 16 and chapter 19 are based on using two-man pairings, as shown above. It calculates fit without using a player metric, avoiding the chicken-and-egg problem. It just looks systematically at how the team did with a pair of players, then at how it did with each player without the other. I built this metric to approximately represent what I have seen in gains and losses in productivity, using a little bit of theory. But as with a lot of things, it was done quickly to address a problem that needed something reasonable, not slowly and steadily to be absolutely correct.

Appendix 4

Player Classification

I have seen a number of attempts to classify players, most of which I haven't liked because they stray too far from the classic positions, which still get used a lot. The method used in chapter 17, about Draymond Green, keeps the basis of the classical positions but adds a bit of nuance to try to fit with how the language is evolving. It was built with the idea that it could be used without advanced statistics, making it somewhat challenging but more broadly useful, even if it is at times a little less accurate.

In particular, the method looks at the following series of statistics:

Height
Defensive rebounding rate per 40 minutes
Offensive rebounds per 40 minutes
Blocks per 40 minutes
FGA per 40 minutes
Assists per 40 minutes
PPR, John Hollinger's Pure Point Ratio, which just uses assists, turnovers, and minutes
Three-point field goal attempts per 40 minutes
Points per 40 minutes

The classification takes place in two phases, one for the defense and one for the offense.

The defensive classification is simple. If height (in inches) plus defensive rebounds per 40 minutes plus blocks per 40 minutes is more than 89, the classification is as a 5. Alternatively, if height plus blocks per 40 minutes is more than 82, the classification is also a 5. If height plus defensive rebounds per 40 minutes is less than 81, the classification is a 1; otherwise it's a 3.

The idea is that a defensive classification of 1 means they primarily guard on the perimeter. A defensive classification of 5 means they primarily guard the paint and bigger players; protecting the paint is the key part here. A defensive classification of 3 means they are more versatile and can have mixed responsibilities around protecting the paint and guarding on the perimeter. With the existence of matchup data and data around where a player spends most of their time defensively, you could use that to replace the heuristic formulas so that the method is capturing who they're guarding and whether they're protecting the paint.

The offensive classification is a little bit more involved, reflecting five different roles:

A classification of 1 means a distributor, someone who passes a lot.

A classification of 2 means a player who is a threat from the three-point arc.

A classification of 3 means a more versatile scorer, one who can generally score inside and outside with enough ability to be asked to do so.

A classification of 4 means mostly an inside scorer, one you have less to worry about on the perimeter.

A classification of 5 means having a very limited offensive role or, as I like to call them, a "get-outta-the-way" kind of offensive player.

In order to put players into these categories, these are the rules to follow in sequence:

1. If PPR plus AST/40 min. minus FGA/40 min. is greater than 1, then classify as 1
2. If PPR minus OREB/40 min. is greater than 3, then classify as 1
3. If FG3A/40 min. is less than 6 and if FG2A/40 min. is greater than 9 and if OREB/40 min. is greater than 2, then classify as 4
4. If PTS/40 min. is less than 10, then classify as 5
5. If FG3A/40 min. is greater than 4 and FG2A/40 min. is greater than 9, then classify as 3

6. If FG3A/40 min. is greater than 6, then classify as 2
7. If PTS/40 min. minus 3 times PPR is less than 10 and PPR is greater than 3, then classify as 1
8. If (AST/40 min. minus 3.5)/2.3 is greater than 0 and (AST/40 min. minus 3.5)/2.3 is greater than (FGA/40 min. minus 13.5)/4.5, then classify as 1
9. If (FGA/40 min. minus 13.5)/4.5 is greater than –1 and the player's percentage of total shots as three-point shots is greater than 35 percent, then classify as 2
10. If (FGA/40 min. minus 13.5)/4.5 is greater than –1 and DREB/40 min. is less than 6 and FGA/40 min. is greater than 16, then classify as 3
11. If (FTA/40 min. minus 13.5)/4.5 is greater than –1 and the player's percentage of total shots as three-point shots is less than 35 percent, then classify as 4
12. Otherwise, classify as 5

This classification scheme was developed quickly and ended up useful enough that I never went back to build it in a more refined way. It could be done using machine learning along with basic historical statistics and people's instinctive classification to train the machine. That, frankly, would be fine, as I've found that people don't mind using a black box to do labeling.

There is no absolutely "correct" way to do this. It's a matter of categorization, and there can be many reasons to change categories. There is some value in having a uniform system, however, which is one benefit of giving away this simple scheme.

Notes

1. Beyond Paper

1. Sadly, Mark Warkentien passed away in 2022. His memorial gathering brought together a lot of people from the world of basketball who valued his knowledge and enthusiasm.

2. The Journey, Part 1

1. A movie, *Quantum Hoops*, was about the program.
2. Technically, it was called the NBA Pre-Draft Camp at the time but is now called the NBA Combine.

3. Who Blamed J.R.?

1. Different media outlets report somewhat different odds, but these represent a common pattern.
2. Events now are recorded even more frequently than that. The data that was available for a long time was at that rate, and it was already a handful to work with.
3. More on division of credit and blame appears in appendix 1.
4. There were also decisions to push NASA harder to have more launches, as well as a number of other factors. Going through all of them has been done elsewhere.

4. Data, Data Everywhere

1. I've read that nearly one hundred different factors go into shot quality metrics, but those I've listed are apparently the most important. I'm a bit skeptical about how there could be one hundred *useful* factors.
2. Second Spectrum said that QSP stood for *q*uantified *s*hot *p*robability, but that name never stuck with me.
3. Quantified shot quality numbers capture the effective field goal percentage that would be expected. So 60 percent on shots worth three points means that they would only go in 40 percent of the time. On the more typical two-point

shots, a shot quality of 60 percent means that they would be expected to go in 60 percent of the time.

4. They were in the top thirty in both the 2022 and 2023 seasons.
5. This finding occurs while using the Second Spectrum matchups data. The NBA assigns matchups differently and does assign a matchup in transition. Reconciling these assignments is challenging and comes with the landscape of having new data and different sources to interpret it.
6. "Analytics" the word is a marriage between "analysis" and "metrics," I believe, and metrics are derived from data. Analytics fundamentally tells more of a story than a piece of data does on its surface.

5. Beyond the Four Factors

1. This factor captures both how often teams get to the foul line and how well they make those shots. The former is a little more important.
2. I've tried to use stats from the NBA most of the time, but there are small discrepancies between those and stats from different sources. The discrepancies don't change the nature of this analysis.
3. That confidence and free throw percentage would hold for this year plus another year in Miami. But for whatever reason that I could not find, Whiteside's free throw percentage would take a dive the year after that. If it was his confidence, why did it decline? It's a good question that goes beyond this chapter.

6. Everyone Hates Defense

1. There are more sophisticated details to both the Warriors' and the Bucks' defenses than I want to present here. The characteristics I do present are more easily recognized, and they serve the purpose of this chapter. To go into all the details would definitely get tedious.
2. Points off steals, not points off turnovers, should be what is in a box score, by the way. Points off turnovers include all those dead ball turnovers, which have no real advantage. If you gavc up a lot of points off dead ball turnovers, that's not the fault of the guy who turned it over. Put points allowed off your own live ball turnovers in the box score. That would say something useful.

7. Cutting the Cake

1. The metrics used for this chapter were the versions available at the end of the 2023 season. Some metrics do get modified with time, but this chapter is taking a snapshot from when their methodologies have mostly stabilized.
2. There has been good work, originally by Joe Sill, to break down this type of method into explaining things more in terms of the Four Factors, but it's difficult to expand beyond that.

3. The shot quality used here, QSP, includes the shooter's ability along with elements of shot distance, shot value (2 or 3), defender distance, and so forth. There are times to talk about shot quality without regard to who the shooter is, but this example uses it.
4. This is true when the data is available, which it mostly has been since the 2014 NBA season.
5. The labels of play types are not mine, by the way, but those provided by the tracking company or the NBA, which are not perfect themselves.
6. This leaves out his 2019 season, when an injury forced him to miss all but about three hundred minutes.
7. Smart actually replaced Brooks in Memphis the year that Brooks got his big contract in Houston.
8. P.J. Tucker never made an All-Defense team, which particularly surprised me.
9. As a late note, Memphis did trade Tyus the older to acquire Marcus Smart from Boston in 2023. Smart was mentioned earlier in the chapter as an excellent defender. Tyus Jones's biggest weakness in the RPM metric was his defense, perhaps coincidentally, perhaps not.

8. The Journey, Part 2

1. I had compiled all of the preseason prognostications I could get across about fifteen seasons heading into that one (thanks to Ray Lebov, who had a treasure trove). For that season, I found twenty-one different projections, the average of which was a 31-51 record, ahead of only the Clippers in the West and Charlotte, Atlanta, and Chicago in the East.
2. Confidence is a hell of a drug . . . or an aphrodisiac . . . or both.
3. Having a report emphasizing that Parker should be kept out of the paint is the easy thing; knowing *how* to do it is the hard part that I wasn't involved in.
4. Wilkins would miss the playoffs the next year, the year after that, and another three years after that. He finally made it again in 2011, then never again. I felt bad about it for a while.
5. We took someone who would be quickly forgotten by history, Saer Sene, a foreign player having few stats for me to work with, but he was thought to be a good rim protector, which we needed. Rondo would get drafted at number 21 and go on to be a four-time All-Star.

9. Defending a Three-Point Lead

1. To be clear, this was all of the three-point shots that weren't in the corner, sometimes called "above-the-break" threes.

10. Playing Draft

1. The chance of a rookie playing even 1,500 minutes with a positive plus-or-minus is about 1 in 30. It's about 1 in 15 for first-round picks.

2. A player who missed a lot of games was someone we wanted to rule out in this case, which is why we used available games, not just half of all games that they played. "The most important ability is availability" is a common phrase in the NBA.
3. In the 2000 draft, the two starters were considered Kenyon Martin and Morris Peterson with this method, but Mike Miller, Jamal Crawford, and Hedo Türkoğlu all started in the prime of their careers. Translation between the word "starter" and the mathematical definition could take a lot of forms.
4. It's debatable whether the draft has become more efficient—making fewer mistakes with picks—as analytics have grown. It's debatable also whether it *should* have gotten more efficient, due to more young players entering the draft with limited information available about them.
5. Alexander was drafted eighth but lasted only just over seven hundred minutes in the NBA, which is among the fewest minutes for any top ten pick.
6. There were, of course, occasional players who moved up in March and April and became good players in the NBA. Mike Conley and Gordon Hayward are two examples.
7. Scouting reports vary a lot among the organizations I've seen. Standardization has been attempted by vendors who want to work with teams, but even those standards are only partially used because of different emphases between organizations.
8. Essentially half of all picks stay with their original team for four years.
9. Smoothed to avoid historic noise and based on a composite of metrics from chapter 7.
10. See, for example, http://nbasense.com/draft-pick-trade-value/4/jacob-goldstein-4 and the three other versions shown there.
11. In other words, he wasn't a mistake. That year, the pick before him was Jrue Holiday, not a mistake, and the pick after Lawson was Jeff Teague, also not a mistake. It's rare for three consecutive first-round selections to all be effectively the best player available, despite so many teams saying that's their goal.

11. Emotion

1. Spelling out when garbage time and "normal time" begin and end would make for some rather boring reading. In my experience with coaches and players, they wait until very late before they relax, roughly when there's a 99.7 percent chance of one team winning. The problem is a little more complex than that, but starting there is a pretty good proxy for what is used in this analysis.
2. The hot hand, which is when it appears that a player is going to make his next shot because he has made his last few, has been both hard to define and hard to study. A group that looked simply at sequences of shots originally didn't find

the presence of a hot hand, but a separate group of researchers later pointed out a subtle flaw in the original study that suggests it does exist. Another group controlled for difficulty of shot and a player's tendency to believe in their own hot hand. They found evidence of a small amount of streakiness. My point in *Basketball on Paper* was that even if it the hot hand effect was small, it affected the way the game was played.

12. The Problem with Nonscorers

1. There really are three classifications of low-usage and useful players. There is three-and-D like Bowen or Battier. There is big-and-D like Biyombo or Collison. And then there is distributor-and-D like Nate McMillan or Eric Snow. But the "and-D" part is pretty critical when you don't shoot much.
2. DARKO, Net Points, and RPM have histories going back to 1998. Also used here are LEBRON, RAPTOR, and EPM when available. The composite is just an average of what is available.
3. Even though Battier was fourth among these players, if you adjust for the average shooting percentage of the era, Battier was a very close second to Collison because he played in a league with a lower overall shooting percentage.
4. When headline writers and game summaries highlight a player who led the team in scoring, they have about a 50 percent chance of identifying the best offensive player for that team.
5. This "individual efficiency" is the individual offensive rating from *Basketball on Paper*, not the NBA's ORTG, which is the team offensive rating with that player on the floor. Other factors in the Pue equation are the league overall efficiency, where replacement level is, and how many players there are on a team.
6. Table 26 uses the composite productivity values, usage numbers from Basketball-Reference.com, the league average ratings, and a replacement level of 92 percent of the average. This analysis isn't perfect because other player metrics don't have the Pue relationship built in and because it's best to do things on a season basis, but this is close enough for the point being made.
7. Technically, I am employing possession usage here, which is not the same as the usage values seen on Basketball-Reference.com, though they are similar.
8. By Net Points alone instead of the composite metric, Bridges's midseason change from Phoenix to Brooklyn not only increased his usage but also his productivity—from +1.3 to +3.9. The other metrics here were available only over the course of a full season.

13. Make 'Em Better

1. Lefties will go right to shoot a three off the dribble as much as they stay still. They go right six times as much as they go left. Righties go left about a third of

the time off the dribble, half the time with no direction, and 10–15 percent to the right. So lefties are more extreme than righties.

2. At one point, I estimated that each free throw is worth about $8,000 in the NBA. For max players like Shaq, it wouldn't matter, but for other guys, it's a lot more money than the $100 at the end of practice for whoever makes a half-court shot first.
3. Tim Daniels, "Ben Simmons' HS Coach Believes 76ers Star's Shooting Struggles Are 'Mental,'" *B/R* (*Bleacher Report*), blog, June 2, 2021, https://bleacherreport.com/articles/10006550-ben-simmons-hs-coach-believes-76ers-stars-shooting-struggles-are-mental.
4. This is roughly the percentage at which a player's net points on the shot go from negative to positive, which accounts for offensive rebounding and defensive dynamics. In college, it's probably 2 percent lower. In high school, the variable levels of competition make it tougher, but probably 45 percent is still needed.
5. My rule of thumb, which should be checked at different levels and for different players, is that shooting 50 percent in practice is equivalent to about 30 percent in a game. The rule is crude because it doesn't control for what is happening in practice, but it's still useful.
6. Some teams do seem to try to distract free throw shooters, but that's a whole other story and the effect appears to be small.
7. Transition threes don't actually seem to get better, nor do buzzer beating threes; it's just those half-court threes where thinking can get in the way.
8. The details of the method aren't completely clear, but this is the basic idea.

14. Game Planning 'Em

1. NBA players and staff eat PB&J more than kids do, I now believe. I ate more PB&J in the NBA than I did since I was . . . well, maybe I don't want to admit the age that I first cut down on that habit. Never mind.
2. Even if you include free throws from shots in the paint, this stat doesn't really change.
3. You can replace "players" with "fans," and I think the statement would also be accurate. We underestimate people's ability to understand things, I believe.
4. These percentages incorporate the quality of the player taking the shot. If you don't include that part, the numbers drop to about 52 percent and 56 percent, respectively.
5. My publisher would hate me, too, because it would mean a lot more tables to print.
6. You can be more sophisticated than using points and assists by using shot attempts and assist opportunities, for example, but the general recommendation wouldn't change.

7. Academic research suggests that mental fatigue takes away from players' abilities to make shots. Basic film study was somewhat fatiguing, but it didn't seem to have the negative effect on shooting. Bryce D. Daub, Blake D. McLean, Aaron D. Heishman, Keldon M. Peak, and Aaron J. Coutts, "Impacts of Mental Fatigue and Sport Specific Film Sessions on Basketball Shooting Tasks," *European Journal of Sport Science* 23, no. 8 (2023): 1500–1508.
8. The "contest" statistic from the NBA is probably a bit biased, awarded too much on missed shots and not enough on made shots. Despite the bias, I believe it is an important stat to emphasize. The range of numbers reflects some of the uncertainty.
9. I arrived at that number without a lot of rigor. I'm not sure exactly how to do so, but I'm guessing someone will figure it out.

15. The Journey, Part 3

1. Gregg Popovich coached Pomona-Pitzer, a team in the same conference as my own college basketball team, so I played against Pop when he was still a Division III coach.

16. What Does Frescobol Have to Do with It?

1. Malone was known to like country music. He was the first but not only NBA player I heard talk about liking country music.
2. The scientific article behind the calculations is "Importance of Teammate Fit: Frescoball Example," by Dean Oliver and Mike N. Fienen, in the *Journal of Quantitative Analysis in Sports* 5, no. 1 (2009), https://doi.org/10.2202/1559-0410.1098.
3. Fortunately, our chemistry was really good.
4. Correlation between an NBA team's win-loss record in one year and the stability of the following year's roster is about +0.4 historically. In the frescobol article, the correlation was in the same range, at about +0.45.
5. I think it would be fun to have a barnstorming league with very frequent rotation of teammates. Players would have to adapt to the players they're with, taking on different roles.
6. And extremely bad results imply bad fit.
7. There was huge statistical significance in the difference in player quality between the top half and the bottom half of frescobol teams.
8. *Basketball on Paper* has a chapter about how the media covering the bad Golden State Warriors would get so excited when the team won just three games in a row. Amazing how things changed for this book.

17. Draymond with a *D*

1. Jonathan Givony qtd. in Walker Beeken, Jonathan Givony, Matt Williams, Kyle Nelson, and Joseph Treutlein, "Top NBA Draft Prospects in the Big Ten, Part

Four," DraftExpress, September 10, 2010, http://www.draftexpress.com/article/Top-NBA-Draft-Prospects-in-the-Big-Ten-Part-Four-16-20---3558/.

18. Coach 'Em Up

1. As mentioned in chapter 4, Disney has technology that reads the facial expressions of audiences who watch their movies, so maybe quantifying emotions is possible. Some people have suggested that passing data in a game—how often players pass to each other—reflects on emotion, but whether a player passes to another is so much more driven by whether the pass helps improve the chance of scoring that it drowns out any reflection on emotion.
2. Notably, the Net Points algorithm for evaluating players is built on the principle that when the team succeeds on a play, each player succeeds, and when the team fails, each player fails. These are coaching concepts. How much credit or blame goes to each individual depends on the situation. I don't think this aspect makes the algorithm a psychological tool, but it doesn't hurt.
3. Many people suggested that Berri's method of measuring player productivity was flawed, but they weren't questioning the approach of looking for *differences* in productivity associated with the coach.
4. These, if you recall from chapter 1, were actually factors that my old boss Mark Warkentien stated were critical to the success of a team.
5. The topic of hot hand effect came up in practice once, and while I was telling the analytical story, former player James Posey was telling his version on the other side of the court, but both had the same conclusion. Posey knew that guys believed the hot hand more than they could live it, so he prepared as a defender for those guys to launch some bad ones.

19. Player Files

1. Data in table 37 was calculated by using the composite metric and a replacement level of −2.0 net points per 48 minutes. A player's wins above replacement was calculated as the difference between their composite metric and that replacement level, then multiplied by their minutes played, divided by the forty-eight minutes in a game, which gives points above replacement. Wins above replacement was found by dividing that by 27.5.
2. See appendix 1 for more on the methodology, which is what feeds into Net Points.
3. The nine other players who came out as four-level scorers in this period, from best to worst in terms of exceeding average, are Austin Reaves, Kawhi Leonard, Nikola Jokić, Tyrese Haliburton, DeMar DeRozan, Damian Lillard, Trae Young, Devin Booker, and James Harden. A lot of overall great players are in that list. Reaves barely qualified because he didn't take a lot of long twos. Other players who have often been four-level scorers are Chris Paul, Kyrie Irving, Dirk

Nowitzki, and Luka Dončić. Some who got close are Carmelo Anthony, Mike Conley, Khris Middleton, Gordon Hayward, Spencer Dinwiddie, Paul George, Jrue Holiday, and Seth Curry.

4. The smoothed-fit metric from chapter 16 shows that Durant and Westbrook had positive offensive fit their first two years together, then negative for three years, then marginally positive the remaining three years. Their defensive fit was negative all years but one, when offensive fit was slightly positive.
5. Harden played with Westbrook and Durant for three years in Oklahoma City early on, Harden being the youngest of them. He deferred to both Westbrook and Durant back then even though he was good quickly. He deferred again to Durant with the Nets, but he and Irving split possessions essentially equally.
6. The year 2017 was the first that the NBA manually tracked contested shots. The statistic has its flaws, but those shouldn't matter here.
7. These are half-court layups, not transition and not putback situations.
8. I defined 5-out offense as when teams had five players who all took at least 20 percent of their shots from beyond the arc. These stats also throw out garbage time minutes.
9. There was a third strange thing about it in that the Clippers scored just as well when not using a 5-out lineup in that 2021 playoff series. But this finding seemed to be due to a lot of nonshooting fouls called, which are more random. Strange, but probably random.
10. The Sixers of 2012 were 35-31 in a shortened season, which works out to roughly forty-three wins in an eighty-two-game season, thus a difference of about fourteen wins.
11. The other two years were with the Miami Heat, who had in their front office—perhaps not coincidentally—Shane Battier, Mr. No-Stats All-Star himself. There probably should be a study into when management brings in players who played like them and how well that worked. *Moneyball* hinted that it didn't work, but no one has studied it, probably because it's hard.
12. Throughout his playing career, Iguodala was also heavily involved in the NBA Players Association in political offices, perhaps coincidentally, perhaps not.
13. Yes, the eyes of team personnel can be fooled, too. For instance, there was a study showing that teams tend to trade for players who played better than their normal level against them, then tend to be disappointed when the player reverts to their normal self. See "'Overattention' to First-Hand Experience in Hiring Decisions: Evidence from Professional Basketball," by Michael Dalton and Peter Landry, in the *Journal of Economic Behavior and Organization* 175 (July 2020): 98–113, https://doi.org/10.1016/j.jebo.2020.04.015.
14. LaVine was considered the worst on the basis of net points per 48 minutes, which is what was available at the time of the All-Star Game.

15. He had the third highest standard deviation of offensive net points per 48 minutes across games in that period, among players with 600+ minutes.
16. This rule is not as true as it once was. Legendary players can get paid for what they did in the past. Nonlegendary players can get signed for values that can be helpful in trades. In this case, Chicago was mostly trying to capture LaVine's future value. Sacramento helped them by signing him to an offer sheet.
17. Redick was actually hated in college, but by opposing players, not teammates.
18. "The Joe Mazzulla Interview," *The Old Man and the Three, with JJ Redick and Tommy Alter*, episode 176, podcast, posted October 4, 2023, YouTube, 1 hr., 13 min., https://youtu.be/fShVcFTK6RM?si=D4EWxPUedZZySFVJ.
19. One player, Ricky Davis, even intentionally took a shot at the wrong basket to try to get the one rebound he needed for a triple-double. The NBA denied him that credit.

Appendix 1

1. Note also that ESPN's RPM metric was fairly unbiased until the 2021 season, when it became biased high and continued to get worse. This bias may be a sign of not keeping track of league average efficiency, which did generally go up in this time.
2. The fact that RPM had a negative error until the most recent three years, then grew very large, implies that the method was calibrated to something before and may need to be recalibrated. This is one of a few oddities in various metrics that I couldn't fully dig into.
3. The algorithm doesn't divide credit on *every* event in the play-by-play, just these. Not jump balls or timeouts or substitutions. Jump balls is the one that could be done, but I haven't.

Appendix 3

1. Basically it's the standard deviation of a typical game's offensive rating, 12, along with something to capture how many effective games they played together.

Index